The Business of Human Rights
an evolving agenda for corporate responsibility

edited by Aurora Voiculescu and
Helen Yanacopulos

Zed Books
LONDON | NEW YORK

The Business of Human Rights: an evolving agenda for corporate responsibility was first published in 2011 by Zed Books Ltd, 7 Cynthia Street, London N1 9JF, UK and Room 400, 175 Fifth Avenue, New York, NY 10010, USA in association with The Open University, Walton Hall, Milton Keynes, MK7 6AA, Buckinghamshire, UK.

www.zedbooks.co.uk
www.open.ac.uk

All reasonable efforts have been made by the publishers to contact the copyright holders of the work reproduced in this volume.

Set in OurType Arnhem and Futura Bold by Ewan Smith, London
Index: ed.emery@thefreeuniversity.net
Cover designed by Rogue Four Design
Printed and bound in Great Britain by CPI Antony Rowe, Chippenham and Eastbourne

Distributed in the USA exclusively by Palgrave Macmillan, a division of St Martin's Press, LLC, 175 Fifth Avenue, New York, NY 10010, USA

A catalogue record for this book is available from the British Library
Library of Congress Cataloging in Publication Data available

ISBN 978 1 84813 863 6 hb
ISBN 978 1 84813 862 9 pb
ISBN 978 1 84813 864 3 eb

About this book

In a time when multinational corporations have become truly globalised, demands for global standards on their behaviour are increasingly difficult to dismiss. Work conditions in sweatshops, widespread destruction of the environment, and pharmaceutical trials in third world countries are only the tip of the iceberg. This timely collection of essays addresses the interface between the calls for corporate social responsibility (CSR) and the demands for an extension of international human rights standards.

Scholars from a vast variety of backgrounds provide expert yet accessible accounts of questions of law, politics, economics and international relations and how they relate to one another, while also encouraging non-legal perspectives on how businesses operate within and around human rights. The result is an essential incursion for a wide range of scholars, practitioners and students in law, development, business studies and international studies, in this emerging area of human rights.

This reader forms part of The Open University module 'Business, Human Rights Law and Corporate Social Responsibility' (W822), a module that features in a variety of postgraduate programmes, including the Postgraduate Certificate in Human Rights and Development Management and the Master in Business Administration.

Details of this and other Open University modules can be obtained from:

Student Registration and Enquiry Service
The Open University
PO Box 197
Milton Keynes
MK7 6BJ
United Kingdom

Telephone: +44 (0) 845 300 6090
email: general-enquiries@open.ac.uk

Alternatively, you may wish to visit The Open University website at www.open.ac.uk. There you can learn more about the wide range of modules and packs offered at all levels by The Open University.

About the editors

Aurora Voiculescu is Senior Lecturer in Socio-Legal Studies and Human Rights in the Department of Advanced Legal Studies, School of Law, the University of Westminster (London). After her PhD in Law at the London School of Economics and Political Sciences, she held a British Academy Post-doctoral Fellowship, at Lincoln College, Oxford University. Her research focuses on issues of human rights and global governance, with particular interest in the interplay between the human rights discourse and the global market agencies such as the transnational corporations and the intergovernmental economic and financial institutions. She is the author of various articles and book chapters on human rights and corporate social responsibility and co-editor (with D. McBarnet and T. Campbell) of *The New Corporate Accountability: Corporate Social Responsibility and the Law* (2007).

Helen Yanacopulos is Senior Lecturer in International Politics and Development at The Open University. She worked in finance in the corporate and the not-for-profit sectors before her PhD in social and political sciences at the University of Cambridge. Her research focuses on how political institutions and processes involve and affect people in the South, specifically in Africa and Asia. She is author of the forthcoming book *NGO Activism, Engagement and Advocacy: Spaces of Change* and is co-editor of *Civil War, Civil Peace* (2005). She has acted as a consultant to various international agencies in matters of civil society, labour and human rights.

Contents

Figures and tables

Abbreviations and acronyms

AMA	American Marketing Association
BPI	Bribe Payers Index
CCA	Centre for Corporate Accountability
CESCR	Committee on Economic, Social and Cultural Rights
COSP	Conference of the State Parties
CSR	corporate social responsibility
DAC	Development Assistance Committee
EITI	Extractive Industries Transparency Initiative
ESRC	Economic and Social Research Council
FCPA	Foreign Corrupt Practices Act
GDP	gross domestic product
GSK	GlaxoSmith Kline
ICESCR	International Covenant on Economic, Social and Cultural Rights
ICT	information and communications technology
ILO	International Labour Organization
ILRF	International Labor Rights Fund/Forum
ILS	international labour standards
IPR	intellectual property rights
IT	information technology
LHWP	Lesotho Highlands Water Project
MNC	multinational corporation
MNE	multinational enterprise
NGO	non-governmental organisation
NNPC	Nigerian National Petroleum Corporation
OECD	Organisation for Economic Co-operation and Development
PPP	public–private partnership
SFO	Serious Fraud Office
SGBP	Shell General Business Principles
SRSG	Special Representative of the UN Secretary-General
TI	Transparency International
TNC	transnational corporation
TRIPS	Trade-Related Aspects of Intellectual Property Rights
UDHR	Universal Declaration of Human Rights

UNCAC	UN Convention against Corruption
UNCTAD	UN Conference on Trade and Development
UNICEF	UN Children's Fund
WGB	Working Group on Bribery in International Business Transactions
WHO	World Health Organization
WTO	World Trade Organization

1 | Human rights in business contexts: an overview

AURORA VOICULESCU AND
HELEN YANACOPULOS

The business and human rights nexus

The role and responsibility of business in issues of labour, environment and society has been a key point of discussion over the past few decades, and has led to such terms as 'corporate social responsibility' entering common parlance. Corporations have rushed to incorporate voluntary instruments into their business practices – frequently as a response to public criticism, but also frequently as a means of 'doing good'. Businesses have been encouraged to do this by international frameworks and declarations, and by pressure to ensure that they achieve some international standards. The framework of human rights has become an international social norm, to which many international businesses now subscribe.

Why has this been seen as necessary? First of all, large corporations have become increasingly international (some would say 'global') and, in terms of their supply chains, even more interconnected than before with medium-sized and smaller producers across the globe. In their primary aim of reducing costs (and consequently increasing their profit margins), corporations have fuelled what has been called the 'race to the bottom' – finding the cheapest labour to produce their products. Furthermore, in trying to maximise profits, some corporations have frequently cut corners, resulting in damage to the environment where products are produced or disposed of (typically not the same locations as where the products are consumed). This has inevitably generated harsh public criticism. The internationalisation and globalisation of business has also meant that, whereas in the past businesses have been linked to local communities via production and consumption, this link is now (with few exceptions) severed.

Second, frequently there is a disjuncture between the needs of individuals and societies, and the agencies – largely governmental – that can (or have the duty to) provide/protect/promote/fulfil these needs. This broken link may be detected with regard to instances of individual harm and the perpetrator agency (for instance a transnational corporation), as well as instances of harm and the compensatory agency (generally, national governments). However, aside from this severed link between needs and the duty-bearing agencies, there is also a perceived conceptual and legal dislocation of duties and responsibilities.

Corporate social responsibility

Businesses today are expected to conduct their operations responsibly and with accountability to wider society. The responsibility and accountability derived from these expectations have found their platform in the corporate social responsibility debate. The concept of corporate social responsibility itself is multifaceted. Zenisek (1979), for instance, spoke of corporate social responsibility as meaning 'something', but not always the same 'something' to everyone. To some it conveys the idea of legal responsibility or liability; to others it means socially responsible behaviour in an ethical sense; to still others the meaning transmitted is that of 'responsible for' in a causal mode; many simply equate it with 'charitable contributions'; many of those who embrace it see it as a mere synonym for 'legitimacy'; a few see it as a sort of fiduciary duty.

In a similar vein, Carroll (1979) suggested that the definition of corporate social responsibility (CSR) should encompass the range of social expectations placed on companies, including economic, legal, ethical and philanthropic responsibilities. From this perspective, he spoke of at least four types of corporate responsibility. First of all, of course, there is economic responsibility, which corresponds readily with a business's self-perception of its scope and role in society. This would imply the primary responsibility of a business organisation to produce goods and services in a way that is profitable for its owners.

Second, while assuming their fundamental economic role, companies are expected to comply with the laws and regulations that reflect society's values and norms. Legal expectations apply to companies as legal entities that can act as persons; but they also affect individuals in their role as employees. This represents the legal dimension of a business organisation's social responsibilities.

Third, business organisations are expected to abide by the ethical norms of society. Carroll argues that, because these norms are not written down in law, they are more ambiguous than legal requirements and therefore more difficult for companies to anticipate and follow. Nevertheless, as we shall see throughout this volume, there is an inherent link between legal and ethical responsibilities, because ethical expectations can be seen to underpin and predict the emergence of new laws and regulations. For example, social movements – including those that promote labour rights, women's rights and environmental protection – have advocated values that have later been codified into law. Moreover, the law has its own insidious ways of cross-pollinating what was initially regarded as the domain of voluntarism and philanthropy.

Philanthropy is the fourth dimension of the business responsibilities identified by Carroll. Businesses may, for instance, engage in activities that go beyond the expectations of society – through such activities as volunteer work, sponsorship of philanthropic projects and donations to public and non-profit organisations (such as sports clubs). Even though lack of engagement in discretionary activities is not perceived as irresponsible, it is quite common for companies to carry out such roles in society. Carroll's four-part model is useful in distinguishing and clarifying the motives and contradictions behind corporate behaviour (Griseri and Seppala 2010).

Stemming from the CSR debate, as well as from a host of complex factors related to globalisation processes, is the growing acknowledgement of international human rights as potential rules of a globally operating, ethical market economy. An increase in the speed and efficiency of communications has brought the way in which we view events across the world into sharper focus, including the suffering and exploitation that goes hand in hand with the complex modes of production associated with the global market economy. An increased realisation of the potential link between democracy, rule of law and development – passing via accountability and good governance in both politics and trade and business – has again brought human rights into focus as potentially offering a conceptual framework within which to build a fairer world.

Why human rights?

This book is in tune with the growing acknowledgement of international human rights standards as rules for a globally operating ethical market economy. Historically, human rights and the marketplace have occupied very different places in the normative landscape, exemplifying the classic distinction between the public and the private sphere.

A classic definition of a legal right is that of the Stanford and Yale law professor and theorist Wesley Hohfeld (cited in Kinley 1998: 15) as 'one's affirmative claim against another'. According to Hohfeld, the correlative of a right was a duty and all rights are *human* rights. Human rights are 'international norms that help to protect all people everywhere from severe political, legal, and social abuses' (Nickel 2006). Nickel

3

distinguishes between different senses of human rights: political, moral and legal. In political terms, 'human rights are political norms dealing with how people should be treated by their governments and institutions'. In the moral sense, 'a human right can exist as a shared norm of actual human moralities, as a justified moral norm supported by strong reasons'. Legal human rights are those recognised under national or international law.

While in philosophy, the existence, content, nature, universality, justification and legal status of human rights are subject to continuing debate (ibid.), a generally accepted understanding of human rights is encapsulated in the 1948 Universal Declaration of Human Rights. Although the Declaration emerged long before the idea of corporate social responsibility took any real shape, it is regarded as the first international document to go beyond the classic governmental responsibility for the realisation of human rights, this responsibility being assigned to both governments and 'other organs of society'. In this sense, the preamble of the Declaration recognises the state's primary responsibility to protect and promote human rights, while at the same time allowing for other organs of society – such as business organisations – to be conceived as bearers of human rights responsibilities.

These processes bringing human rights into focus have their potential dangers. The predominantly Western concept of human rights brings inevitable allegations of conceptual and cultural imperialism that is intended to support the now more refined forms of economic imperialism. Economic globalisation and the globalisation of the human rights discourse appear on multiple agendas from multiple sources that nuance the relationship between business and human rights.

The United Nations agencies, for instance, have often been at the centre of various initiatives aimed at formulating universally acceptable standards or norms for the activities of business organisation in general and the activities of transnational corporations (TNCs) in particular. Its long-debated and failed draft UN Code of Conduct for TNCs contained a wide range of responsibilities – from respect for tax and competition rules to respect for the sovereignty and the political system of the host country, as well as respect for human rights norms and abstention from corrupt practices. Similarly, the Organisation for Economic Co-operation and Development (OECD) has made the link between business practices and human rights through various inter-governmentally endorsed documents. Among other things, the OECD Guidelines for Multinational Enterprises (MNE), revised in 2000, addressed the MNEs' duty to contribute to sustainable development in their host countries, to respect

4

human rights and to refrain from seeking or accepting exceptions from the host country's regulatory framework in the areas of environment, health and safety, labour rights and other protective measures.

The UN Global Compact – another UN initiative that attempts to build a bridge between business, human rights, labour, environment and anti-corruption – can be seen as particularly relevant in addressing the question: 'Why human rights?' Enjoying, as it does, quite a wide acceptance among business organisations (largely because of its rather vague formulation of responsibilities), the Global Compact is in fact based on three international documents that have human rights and human development at their heart. At least two of these benefit from fairly broad domestic legal endorsement, and all three can be seen as actual or credible sources of potential new legislation. The first document is the Universal Declaration of Human Rights, with its enhanced assignation of responsibility for human rights to individuals as well as to 'other organs of society'. The second provides the basis for the UN approach to this issue – the International Labour Organization's Declaration on Fundamental Principles and Rights at Work. The Declaration requires respect for freedom of association, recognition of collective bargaining, elimination of all forced and compulsory labour, the effective abolition of child labour and the elimination of discrimination with respect to employment. While it remains a 'declaration', the document was the result of debate within the International Labour Organization (ILO) as a tripartite organisation, which brings together government, employers and trade union representatives. Finally, the Rio Declaration of the UN Conference on Environment and Development represents the third pillar of the UN strategy, which, while focusing on the environment, has at its heart the aim of human development and implicit human rights values (Bradlow 2001).

Structure and chapters

This edited collection sets out to bring together different perspectives on human rights in a business context. There are ethical conceptions and perspectives of human rights (that respect by all rational actors for human rights is, at the least, an ethical requirement). There are political perceptions and conceptions of human rights (that human rights are political agreements and are part of a social contract, for individuals as well as for organisations). And there are legal conceptions of human rights (that human rights are social demands conveyed via legal mechanisms). This book aims to equip the reader to take a systematic critical approach to identifying business responsibilities within human rights frameworks. It introduces and builds on questions of law, politics, economics and international relations, and maps out the extent to which human rights law can be instrumental in the business ethics debate. Thus, it sits at the nexus of three areas: human rights, business and ethics. And, with varying emphasis, all chapters address the intersection of these three areas.

The international legal landscape is shifting in the field of human rights and business. In Chapter 2, Voiculescu explores a key issue in the debate on business responsibility for human rights: that of corporate self-regulation versus international enforceable rules. Should adherence to ethical guidelines be achieved predominantly through social dialogue and self-regulatory mechanisms? Or should the international community come together to design a set of clear, enforceable rules that are applicable to all business enterprises? By focusing her analysis on these questions and on the international initiatives of the ILO, the OECD and the UN in particular, Voiculescu illustrates the various points of tension between the imperative nature of human rights discourse (requiring a strong normative commitment) and the predominantly conversational nature of the voluntary approach.

As international initiatives strive to reach agreement on corporations' legal and normative responsibilities with regard to human rights, corporations' behaviour is also shaped by marketing and branding considerations. A number of major brands have had their reputations damaged when human rights abuses have been associated with their (or their subcontractors') activities. Corporate social responsibility has therefore become a key element in many leading brands' identities. In Chapter 3, Harris considers tensions between marketing and corporate social responsibility, with specific reference to branding and reputation management.

The global recession that started in 2008 has meant that there is now even more pressure on companies to keep labour costs of production low, in order to maintain low prices for consumers. What has been called the 'race to the bottom' – corporations' quest to find the cheapest labour to produce their products – has been the cause of labour abuses across the globe. As a result, an increasing share of the human population has been drawn into waged labour. In Chapter 4, Pangsapa and Smith argue that labour rights must be central to business ethics and, while independent monitoring and verification of factories might be quite effective, in order to address these injustices we need to shift from a system of labour standards to one of labour rights.

The dynamic relationship – potentially supportive – between an ethical and a legal dimension of business responsibility for human rights is illustrated in Slapper's Chapter 5 on violent corporate crime, corporate social responsibility and human rights. Saving us from being blinded by innocuous expressions such as 'industrial accident', Slapper argues that at least some of these 'accidents' can easily be construed as murder, manslaughter or criminal negligence. Focusing on the way law can be used to enhance corporate social responsibility and to encourage compliance with human rights, Slapper argues in favour of the recognition in law – and even in 'global law' – of the business responsibility for such human rights principles as the right to life.

Bringing together 'hard law' and compelling ethics, in Chapter 6 Bright and Muraguri consider the responsibility of pharmaceutical companies to share scientific advances and the various initiatives undertaken by the public and private sectors to promote the right to health. By using the pharmaceutical industry as a case study, the authors argue that human rights concepts have shaped the use of intellectual property rights and the development of health-related legal and social infrastructure mechanisms in poorer countries. Looking at legal institutional traditions and the international human rights debate, Bright and Muraguri highlight how a combination of shaming, generic competition, increased dialogue and creative thinking can result in an enhanced right to health – and ultimately to life.

In Chapter 7, Yanacopulos examines a sector whose relationship to business, ethics and human rights has been underexplored – that of the large foundations. Large foundations (such as Gates, Ford and Rockefeller) give more than $6 billion annually, and have changed over the past two decades, as we have seen the rise of what have been called the 'new' foundations, 'philanthrocapitalists' or 'billanthropists'. These 'new' foundations have emerged out of IT and finance company profits and have been operating in a different manner from their older foundation predecessors, which frequently reveal a clash between philanthropy, business ethics and human rights.

In Chapter 8, Hatchard highlights the issues related to the business impact on human rights by examining the link between business practices and corruption and by arguing for corrupt practices to be regarded as a significant impediment in the realisation of human rights. Exploring the issues of transnational corruption from the 'supply side', Hatchard analyses the key international and domestic efforts to use criminal law in an attempt to combat the bribery of foreign public officials. Hatchard questions whether this is the most effective approach to tackling bribery, and goes on to outline alternative and complementary approaches. These approaches could enhance the chances of success in combating corporate corruption of public officials, and therefore could positively affect development, good governance and human rights.

How should corporations operate in zones of conflict? Deitelhoff and Wolf, in Chapter 9, assess direct and indirect corporate governance contributions to peace and security in zones of conflict. They examine the types of governance contributions that can realistically be expected from TNCs where the state fails to provide fundamental collective goods or to protect human rights and basic normative standards. By assessing a range of corporate governance contributions, they explore the idea that there could be a nascent new understanding of responsible engagement in the business sector in conflict zones.

Chapter 10 brings Shell and Nigeria under scrutiny and gives Amao the opportunity to explore the business, human rights and ethics nexus at its rawest. Using Nigeria as a case study enables him to examine corporate social responsibility practices from a developing country perspective, as well as the relationship between these practices, the ethical imperatives and the human rights principles and law. Amao makes suggestions as to how business should respond to ethics and human rights challenges by weighing up profit considerations against the social and environmental impacts of corporate decisions. He also further considers emerging issues in the social responsibility discourse, including corporate strategies, the widening scope of business stakeholders, the increasing role of pressure groups and the potential exposure to international human rights litigation for violations of human rights.

Finally, the conditions that lead to human rights violations are often the same as those that generate environmental degradation and result in infringements of labour standards. Yet these issues are typically examined and addressed separately, and it is common for researchers, governments, lawyers, non-governmental organisations (NGOs) and businesses to focus exclusively either on human rights, labour issues or environmental sustainability. As well as clearly defined NGO and government reports, there is an extensive research literature that reflects this tendency. Relatively little has been said or reported on how these areas coincide and how, in many cases, their combined presence intensifies the negative effects of each. In Chapter 11, Smith and Pangsapa holistically weave together these 'clusters of injustices' that involve environmental degradation, labour standard violations and human rights.

References

Bradlow, D. (2001) 'The World Commission on Dams' contribution to the broader debate on development decision-making', *American University International Law Review*, 16(1531).

Carroll, A. B. (1979) 'A three-dimensional model of corporate performance', *Academy of Management Review*, 4(4).

Griseri, P. and N. Seppala (2010) *Business Ethics and Corporate Social Responsibility*, Singapore: Cengage Learning Business Press.

Kinley, D. (1998) *Human Rights in Australian Law*, Sydney: Federation Press.

Nickel, J. (2006) *Making Sense of Human Rights*, second edn, Oxford: Blackwell Publishing.

Zenisek, T. J. (1979) 'Corporate social responsibility: A conceptualisation based on organisational literature', *Academy of Management Review*, 4(3): 359–68.

2 | Human rights and the normative ordering of global capitalism

AURORA VOICULESCU

Human rights have come to represent the moral dimension of globalisation: the affirmation of universal standards to which we can look for guidance for the humanisation of capitalism, the revitalisation of democratic control and the protection of the values that give meaning and importance to human life. More particularly, in their affirmation of the equal worth and supreme value of every human being, human rights set the parameters and goals for any legitimate human organisations. It therefore seems appropriate to see human rights as a source of ideas for determining the normative ordering of global capitalism and its governmental structures. Campbell (2004: 11)

Introduction

This chapter provides a conceptual approach to the link between human rights and business as developed in the international arena. Exploring the various international initiatives related to human rights and corporate social responsibility, it examines the theoretical, conceptual and ideological changes in perspective that have taken place in the past decades. In particular, it considers the impact these changes have brought to the 'balance of normativities' – i.e. the balance between legal, regulatory normativity and ethical, voluntary normativity. In this context, the chapter explores the way in which international human rights law, as a system involving an internationally recognised set of values, can influence what is seen as the global neighbourhood and offer a firmer normative fabric for the global governance of an incipient global village. The chapter focuses in particular on the role played by UN agencies in seeking to address the human rights and business nexus. The succession of initiatives taken by various UN agencies illustrates one of the most debated issues of corporate social responsibility in general, and human rights in business in particular: the issue of the voluntary versus the legal normative nature of a business organisation's responsibilities in relation to human rights.

This analysis will focus primarily on two initiatives that allow a contrastive approach and analysis of the concepts involved: the UN Economic and Social Council initiative that produced the UN Draft Norms on the Responsibilities of Transnational Corporations and other Business Enterprises with Regard to Human Rights; and the UN Human Rights Commission's initiative, which produced a set of reports in 2008/09 that focused on the human rights responsibilities of business organisations. The UN norms' 'failure' and the reports' 'success' in promoting consensus on the issues will serve as a vehicle to illustrate two contrasting ways of approaching business and human rights in the global market environment, and will highlight the complexity of the social, economic and political issues that are at stake.

The once widely accepted dichotomy between state and non-state agencies is now increasingly blurring (Schachter 1998), and the debate around the human rights responsibilities of business is contributing to this haziness and to the emergence of new paradigms of normativity and responsibility. The human rights obligations spelt out in the Universal Declaration of Human Rights address not only governments but also business enterprises as 'organs of society'. However, traditional views on human rights obligations still distinguish between public and private actors. The state is seen as the main entity responsible for implementing programmes to reduce poverty, to promote human development and generally to protect and promote human rights. Private actors, whose rights are established and enforced by state action, may now be deemed liable for violations of economic, social and cultural rights, and may also often be seen as responsible, in conjunction with the state, for the implementation of policies that would enhance the realisation of these rights. Of all the private actors taken into the partnership to address the complex issues of human rights, transnational corporations (TNCs) are some of the most controversial. The activities of TNCs in less developed countries have multiplied considerably over the past three decades. Capital mobility has increased substantially, and TNCs have become 'footloose', acquiring an increased flexibility in choosing their bases. This has given TNCs enormous bargaining power in relation to the state and trade unions. At the same time, some immediate drawbacks of the TNCs' activities have started to emerge: environmental devastation, poor labour standards, discrimination and child labour (to name but a few) (Klein 2000). Alongside these, there has been increasing pressure from various stakeholders for the activities of TNCs to be better regulated (Greider 1997; Robé 1999: 15).

The pressure from the different stakeholders for some kind of framework of human rights responsibility for corporations has turned predominantly towards various intergovernmental settings. This is due, to a large extent, to a reluctance on the part of the less developed countries to regulate TNCs and forfeit their chances of direct investment, as well as to the unwillingness of the 'TNC-exporting' (predominantly developed) countries to impose social responsibility on the corporations they send abroad (Robé 1997). The first initiatives in this direction occurred in the 1970s, mainly via the UN, the ILO and the OECD.

Early UN negotiation attempts

The initiative of the UN Centre for Transnational Corporations (UNCTC) to achieve a code of conduct for TNCs (called the 'Draft Code') was one of the first of the UN's systematic attempts to regulate transnational corporations (UNCTC 1977). The discussions surrounding the Draft Code began in 1977 and were abandoned in 1992 without any enforceable treaty having been agreed. This initiative was an attempt to get corporations to assume responsibility for the complexity of their impact on the host countries, rather than just for their bottom-line results. The UNCTC had the task of identifying the rights and responsibilities of both TNCs and the countries in which they operated. The proposed code had a number of positive aspects. It confirmed the TNCs' role as important social actors, collaborating in global governance policies; it also created a basis for more clearly defined social responsibilities of TNCs in their host countries, particularly in those countries where the law would not offer the minimum desired social protection. The proposed system was, therefore, meant to empower TNCs. If successfully adopted and implemented, the code would have had a significant impact on the way in which TNCs operated in their host countries.

During the negotiations on the Draft Code, it was acknowledged that the TNCs were part both of the problem and of the solution regarding the negative impacts of the process of market globalisation (UNCTC 1986: 2, 7–9). However, the prospects for the Draft Code were fairly poor. Some of the major stumbling blocks included the North–South tensions that polarised the issues, the proposed issue of economic sanctions against repressive regimes, the Eastern European (at the time the communist bloc's) attempts to exempt public enterprises from the scope of the code, and finally the issue of the code's position within the international law system and the UN's role in administering it. Another very contentious issue was the possibility of an enforceable dimension to the code and of a credible monitoring system. The broad scope of the Draft Code and the obscure and imprecise language had the effect of making consensus even more difficult to attain and served to hamper achievement of the articulated goals. In spite of some progress, deep disagreements stalled the negotiations, and in 1992 the UNCTC abandoned the code (Friends of the Earth 1998).

A tripartite approach from the ILO

The Tripartite Declaration of Principles Concerning Multinational Enterprises and Social Policy (the Tripartite Declaration), proposed and promoted by the ILO (at the same time as the UN was trying to negotiate the Draft Code), was adopted in November 1977 (ILO 1977). In designing the Declaration, the ILO brought together governments and employer and worker organisations with the stated aim of encouraging 'the positive contribution which multinational enterprises [i.e. TNCs] can make to economic and social progress and to minimise and resolve the difficulties to which their various operations may give rise'.

In spite of the tripartite consultation, the Declaration is not legally binding and its triennial monitoring review has shown little impact. The document does not offer an easily available mechanism that can be used to redress misuse of power by the multinational enterprises (MNEs), even when such a misuse breaches the Declaration itself. While there has been some progress on the supervision of compliance from the 1977 ILO Tripartite Declaration to the present (Alston 2005), the mechanisms instituted by the ILO remain a rather 'soft' tool, limited in scope and unlikely to capture the complexity of the MNEs' activities, behaviour and social impact (Maupain 2005). The strength of the Tripartite Declaration lies in the fact that it encourages dialogue between MNEs and the home and host countries. It also attempts to affect and change the behaviour of governments – who are the signatories of the Declaration – as well as of multinationals.

Intergovernmental approach from the OECD

Externally generated attempts to 'teach' corporate citizens civic virtues and to involve them as partners in the civic duty of global governance have been made by other organisations. As with the ILO attempts, these codes have taken the form of recommendations. They include the OECD Guidelines for Multinational Enterprises, the Kimberley Process of diamond certification, the Sweatshop and Clean Clothes campaigns and the 'football codes' (the FIFA code[1] and the Sialkot code). Of all these CSR initiatives, the OECD Guidelines are probably the best known, given their intergovernmental origin and broader applicability (as opposed to those codes designed for a particular industry).

The Guidelines (OECD 1976) are not legally binding and only

recommend that MNEs and OECD member states should observe certain rules of conduct in the course of their economic activities in a host country. The observance of the Guidelines is, once again, voluntary. Although the OECD Guidelines have been agreed by a number of sovereign governments, the stage has never been reached for their status to change from recommendations into an international legal norm. One significant feature of the OECD document is that it provides a system of national contact points (NCPs), where complaints can be brought in relation to compliance with the Guidelines. However, the performance of the NCPs has been rather inconsistent and has been widely criticised. Moreover, the Guidelines only include the most vague human rights provisions, and it is difficult to offer any enforcement guidance (De Schutter 2006: 9; Kinley and Chambers 2005). Up until the 2000 revision, the Guidelines gave absolute priority to national laws. Such priority of jurisdiction, often encountered in CSR documents, means that the obligations established can only supplement – but never contradict – obligations stemming from the national laws of the host states.

In spite of some progress in defining CSR, initiatives such as the ILO Declaration or the OECD Guidelines could do nothing to address the root causes of the corporate scandals related to human rights in the extractive industries or in the apparel and sports industries. However, the documents did offer fertile ground for the proliferation in the following two decades of both reactive and proactive voluntary codes of conduct and other self-regulatory instruments (Murray 1998).

Moving away from voluntarism

Designating authoritative international human rights documents that corporations should comply with has been one way of diluting the voluntary approach to human rights embedded in the initial intergovernmental initiatives. The ILO took such a step in 1998 with the adoption of the ILO Declaration on Fundamental Principles and Rights at Work (the Declaration) (ILO 1998). Adopted two decades after the ILO Tripartite Declaration, the Declaration emphasises the particular importance of a set of ILO conventions, namely: the conventions of freedom of association and the effective recognition of the rights to collective bargaining; the elimination of all forms of forced or compulsory labour; the effective abolition of child labour; and the elimination of discrimination in respect of employment and occupation.

Addressing the need for socially responsible action on the part of corporations, this document represents an important symbolic step towards a more consistent approach to corporate social responsibility by setting itself up as the foundation upon which individual corporate social policies must be built. The Declaration makes a symbolic move towards the regulatory consolidation of CSR by stating that all ILO members, even if they have not ratified the conventions in question, have an obligation that arises from their very membership of the ILO to respect, promote and realise, in good faith and in accordance with the Constitution, the principles concerning the fundamental rights that are the subject of those conventions (ibid.). While the absence of a proper enforcement mechanism makes of the 1998 Declaration a rather 'soft' regulatory tool, it still represents a step towards a tighter definition of the rights to be included in the corporate social policies and corporate codes of conduct.[2]

The OECD Guidelines have also been taken through various stages. The original (1976) Guidelines focused on the MNEs' compliance with the national law and practice of the host country. The revised Guidelines (OECD 2000) now place the emphasis on MNEs' obligations to meet a range of international standards. The profile of international law is now placed much higher than in the original Guidelines, with explicit references to a number of international instruments, such as the 1948 Universal Declaration of Human Rights and the 1998 ILO Declaration. Moreover, the revised Guidelines now use the regulatory technique of directly specifying a number of standards to be met, requesting of MNEs that they engage in conduct consistent with all the core labour standards of the ILO 1998 Declaration. While the OECD revised Guidelines remain largely a non-regulatory instrument, they do go one step further from the realm of voluntary CSR standards by establishing a firmer link with international human rights norms (Muchlinski 2001).

The use of international documents as a point of reference has also been endorsed by the Global Compact, a 1999 initiative by UN Secretary-General Kofi Annan. The values and principles proposed in the Global Compact are not necessarily new: human rights, labour standards, environmental protection and anti-corruption, each of them with its specific impact on human development (UN 1999). The Global Compact requires corporations to support and respect the protection of the recognised international human rights within their own sphere of influence and to make sure that they are not complicit in human rights abuses. The Global Compact, however, took a different attitude towards voluntarism than did the other transnational CSR initiatives and, rather than proposing ways to address the weaknesses of the corporate voluntarism identified earlier, it chose to encourage it, thereby legitimising voluntarism and self-regulation as major tools for addressing the human rights and global market issues (Amnesty International 2000).

UN norms: an attempt at comprehensiveness and normativity

The problematic relationship between human rights and corporate voluntarism has not remained unaddressed at the UN level. After years of consultations and negotiations, in August 2003 the Sub-Commission on the Protection and Promotion of Human Rights within the UN Commission on Human Rights adopted the Norms on the Responsibilities of Transnational Corporations and other Business Enterprises with Regard to Human Rights (the Norms). Unlike the Global Compact, which promoted an approach based exclusively on the idea of voluntarism (Jerbi 2009), the UN Norms directly addressed all the tension points characterising such self-regulatory CSR instruments as the voluntary corporate codes of conduct: the substance of the human rights to be included in a CSR document; the enforcement and monitoring mechanisms; and the issue of stakeholder involvement (Deva 2004). Acknowledging the state's primary responsibility for human rights, the Norms also set out the responsibility of business enterprises 'within their sphere of activity and influence'.

By referring to a comprehensive list of international documents, the UN Norms linked the notion of CSR to a very comprehensive list of rights: civil and political human rights; socio-economic and cultural rights; 'third generation' rights, referring to human development and community rights; and also specific issues formally outside the human rights agenda, yet with a deep impact on communities in the context of global market economy, such as marketing and advertising practices, as well as safety and quality of goods and services (UNHCR 2003).

The human rights obligations of business organisations are expressed in the Norms in terms of 'shall', giving the signal of a moral, if not yet legal, imperative. Moreover, international human rights law appears to be given authoritative precedence over the domestic law of a TNC's host country (ibid.: paragraphs 10 and 4). The Norms ultimately anticipated a dynamic relation with the CSR concept: while resting upon international human rights law, it was also suggested that the Norms 'will contribute to *the making and development of international law*' which will address the corporate responsibilities and obligations (ibid.: preamble, emphasis added). Since ethical expectations can often be seen to underpin and predict the emergence of new laws and regulations, the prospect of the Norms inducing the development of new international law was taken very seriously by the business lobby.

Placing human rights on the corporate agenda via the UN Norms was predicted to affect and influence the corporate self-regulatory instruments by offering them a firm point of reference that would fill in some of the normative gaps and offer more substance to those corporate documents addressing corporate social responsibilities. The expectation that the UN Norms would end up being used for grafting the corporate social policies – i.e. their codes of conduct – was confirmed by the 2002 discussions of the UN Working Group on the UN Draft Norms and the Commentary on the Norms that took place prior to their adoption. Moreover, the Norms required that each corporation 'shall adopt, disseminate and implement *internal rules of operation* in compliance with the Norms' (ibid.: Part H: General Provisions of Implementation, emphasis added). Because the Norms referred expressly to authoritative sets of standards established via recognised international documents, the codes of conduct informed by such norms could potentially lose that dimension of pure voluntarism.

The weaknesses of voluntarism in the context of corporate human rights action were acknowledged in the UN Norms through the recognition of the role of the state and the importance of regulation. In this sense, moving on from the past two decades of corporate voluntary actions in the human rights sphere, the Norms affirm that states 'should establish and reinforce the necessary *legal and administrative framework*' for ensuring that the Norms and other relevant national and international laws are implemented by transnational corporations and other business enterprises (ibid., emphasis added). In other words, the UN Norms broke the taboo-like attitude to CSR regulation and looked beyond voluntarism, asserting the need for a firmer legal basis for the protection and promotion of human rights (Hillemanns 2003).

Apart from bringing specificity to the human rights standards – specificity that could potentially be integrated into the corporate codes and policies – the UN Norms also addressed the very important issue of implementation of the prescribed human rights by corporations. Not only do the Norms stipulate the imperative of adopting, disseminating and implementing corporate internal rules of operation in compliance with the Norms, but they also require business entities to apply and incorporate them in their contracts or other arrangements with contractors, subcontractors and suppliers (ibid.). Therefore, according to the Norms, a TNC's social responsibility for human rights protection and implementation would cover its whole chain of production and distribution, regardless of the number of links in the chain. Adopting codes of conduct and implementing them within the narrow circle of production would no longer be sufficient to demonstrate an effective and comprehensive human rights policy. Moreover, in order to stimulate implementation, the UN Norms demanded that, through their CSR documents and policies, corporations *shall* provide prompt, effective and adequate reparation to those persons, entities and communities that are adversely affected by failure to comply with the Norms (ibid.).

Of course, the Norms could not offer an immediate, perfect approach to CSR and human rights. The document, for instance, has rightly been criticised on account of various (some might say remediable) shortcomings, such as its inclusion of a long list of rights that are insufficiently defined for the business context, its lack of provision for a monitoring and compliance system, or its reliance on vague terminology, such as 'sphere of influence' and 'complicity', that has little basis in law. It was, however, argued that, given half a chance, the Norms – still in draft form – could have been refined and built upon (Weissbrodt and Kruger 2005: 332; Kinley and Chambers 2005: 491; De Schutter 2006: 21). The Norms, for instance, did provide for an implementation mechanism with a transparent and independent monitoring system. Within this system, TNCs and other business organisations were required to conduct periodic evaluations of the impact of their own activities on human rights. According to the Norms, the business enterprises would be subject to periodic monitoring and verification of their compliance with the Norms, both by the United Nations and by 'other international and national mechanisms already in existence *or yet to be created*' (UN-HCR 2003: Part H, emphasis added). Judging by the development of the CSR policies so far, and in spite of the UN Norms being superseded rather brutally by another UN initiative, it is conceivable that this type of complex and expansive monitoring system will, in time, acquire a significant presence in the monitoring of the (increasingly less voluntary) CSR instruments (McBarnet et al. 2007). The Norms have given consistent signals of departure from the principle of voluntarism so forcefully promoted by the business lobby, as well as by certain governments. In this sense, they have been described as 'the first non-voluntary initiative accepted at the international level' (Weissbrodt and Kruger 2005: 318).

The UN framework: from mapping to operationalisation

The wide-ranging normative character and the promise of enforceability of the Norms did not secure success (Voiculescu 2007). The draft document was adopted unanimously by the Sub-Commission in August 2003 and was considered for the first time by the UN Human Rights Commission in April 2004. During the period of consultation and preparation of the UN Norms, and throughout their discussion in 2004, the Commission was the target of intense lobbying against the UN Norms by certain business groups, such as the International Chamber of Commerce and the International Organisation of Employers, as well as by certain national governments (Backer 2005; Jerbi 2009; Kinley et al. 2007). In an attempt to prevent the premature discarding of a process just started, an oral statement sponsored by almost 200 NGOs and human rights advocates was made during the 60th Session of the Commission, asking it not to take any action that would prematurely undermine the Norms before all stakeholders had had more time to analyse the document. In spite of this, at its 60th Session, the Commission declared that the draft proposal of the UN Norms had no legal standing and that the Sub-Commission should not perform any monitoring function under paragraph 16 of the Norms. By the same decision, the commission asked the Office of the High Commissioner for Human Rights to compile a report that, after consultation with all stakeholders, would map the scope and legal status of all existing initiatives and standards, including the UN Norms, on business responsibilities with regard to human rights (UNHCHR 2004). It is in this mapping mandate that the UN framework for business responsibility for human rights originated. Under this mandate, entrusted to John Ruggie as Special Representative of the UN Secretary-General (SRSG), a series of documents was produced, with the first and second reports largely expounding the preparatory work, the third encapsulating the framework itself, and two further reports and documentation seeking to operationalise the framework.

The mandate for the framework and the associated reports was established in order to overcome the disagreements that had prevented the adoption – the discussion even – of the UN Norms. The Norms had, undoubtedly, met with controversy. Some commentators described the whole UN standard-setting exercise as 'engulfed by its own doctrinal excesses' (Ruggie 2006: 59), while others praised it for 'marking out the boundaries of debate' and for achieving 'an important step in what inevitably will be a long journey' (Kinley et al. 2007: 470; Weissbrodt and Kruger 2003: 903). Thus, while the UN Norms have, from the very beginning, been riddled with controversy, the framework offered by the SRSG's third report appears to have been met with greater consensus.

Established by the Human Rights Council, the SRSG's mandate was both wide and narrow. To a certain extent this explains its consensus-building potential: it was wide in the sense that it represented an attempt at comprehensiveness; but it was narrow with respect to the ambit of what it should achieve. The mandate required the SRSG to identify and clarify the standards of corporate responsibility and accountability; to elaborate on the role of states in effectively regulating and adjudicating the role of TNCs and other business enterprises with regard to human rights, including through international cooperation; to research and clarify concepts such as 'complicity' and 'sphere of influence' (introduced by the UN Global Compact and taken forward in the UN Norms); and to compile a compendium of best practice among states and businesses. In other words, the mandate required the production of a comprehensive 'map' of current international standards and practices relating to business and human rights (Cernic 2008: 6). This relatively narrow mandate, focusing as it did on mapping the CSR and human rights environment, was bound to be less controversial than the UN Norms' proposed link to international human rights documents (Ruggie 2008a: 9).

The three-pillar framework for corporate accountability in human rights proposed by the Third Report is structured by the three key terms of its title: 'Protect, Respect and Remedy' and reflects 'differentiated but complementary responsibilities' that include a state's duty to protect people against human rights violations by (or involving) corporations; the corporate responsibility to respect human rights; and the responsibility (mainly, but not exclusively, on the part of the state) to provide effective access to remedies. In this sense, the Third Report emphasised the 'bedrock role of the State' in protecting and promoting human rights, largely by creating a framework of incentives for business enterprises to respect human rights. In the context of this framework, states are encouraged to strengthen their domestic regulatory systems governing human rights and business, and corporations are advised to respect human rights and to exercise due diligence in their activities. A combination of judicial and non-judicial mechanisms that could potentially strengthen the enforcement of corporate responsibilities was proposed as the third pillar of the framework.

The report articulates the link between corporate responsibility for human rights and the concept of legal responsibility rather timidly though, with the focus being maintained on a fairly vague notion of 'policy alignment' at both domestic and international level (ibid.: 11). Moreover, the part of the document dedicated to the responsibility of corporations to respect human rights is built predominantly around dimensions of insufficiently specified legal or ethical content. As for the section dealing with access to remedy, state and non-state non-judicial mechanisms and company-level mechanisms practically dominate the analysis. This, of course, is not surprising, given the SRSG's 'mapping' mandate.

The Third Report, therefore, stops short of proposing legal concepts and instruments that would make operational the link between business and human rights law. A stage of operationalisation of the Third Report was, however, promised by the SRSG in a subsequent (2008) statement to the UN Human Rights Commission (Ruggie 2008b), and, more recently, this promise was revisited – though not yet fulfilled – in the SRSG's Fourth and Fifth Reports (Ruggie 2009, 2010). In these two reports – aimed, respectively, 'towards operationalising' and at providing 'further steps toward the operationalisation' of the Third Report – the SRSG refines its mapping exercise, addressing the various elements that define the three pillars of the established framework, all in preparation for a forthcoming 'Guiding Principles' document promised for 2011. In relation to the state duty to protect, for instance, the SRSG highlighted in the Fourth Report the importance played by corporate law, by the investment and trade agreements signed by states, and by the international cooperation agreements in which corporations play an increasing role. As for access to remedies, the SRSG rehearsed the various judicial and non-judicial mechanisms, emphasising the importance of their interplay in supporting the first two pillars: the state duty to protect and the corporate responsibility to respect human rights.

The SRSG's Fifth Report (at the time of this book's publication, the most recent) reiterated the initial thesis stated in the Third Report regarding the state's primary duty to protect human rights, the corporate responsibility – rather than legal duty – to respect human rights, and the use of predominantly soft remedial tools for human rights harms. Though this Fifth Report was written under the banner of 'further steps toward the operationalisation' of the Third Report and as a preamble to the forthcoming 2011 'Guiding Principles' report, the SRSG's mandate has yet to articulate comprehensive answers to the many questions it has raised. In a written submission, the International Federation for Human Rights and the Human Rights in China associations raised questions about the inconsistencies in the SRSG's latest statement regarding the duty to protect, as outlined by the report – in particular in the Chinese context (International Federation for Human Rights/Human Rights in China 2010). The same intervention pointed out the need for further work on the issue of extraterritorial jurisdiction with respect to human rights violations, and further clarification of the (as yet insufficiently specified) concepts of complicity, due diligence and company's duty of care. All these have been concepts to which the SRSG has returned in all five of its reports so far, and yet one could say that the human rights community finds itself none the wiser.

On a more conceptual basis, other human rights advocates have expressed apprehension over the SRSG's propensity to root the business responsibility to respect human rights in the realm of general social norms and market expectations. Human Rights Watch, for instance (as well as other NGOs), has taken issue with the SRSG's statement that the corporate responsibility to respect human rights is not an obligation that current international human rights law generally imposes directly on companies, but rather constitutes 'a standard of expected social conduct' (Ruggie 2010: 12). Questioning this position, NGOs have urged the Human Rights Council 'to consider the actual and potential role of international law in further defining the corporate responsibility for human rights' (Human Rights Watch/ESCR-Net 2010).

The conceptual tools that could become instrumental in the future process of operationalisation of the link between corporate activities and the legal responsibility for human rights have yet to be refined. However, given that the Third, the Fourth and now the Fifth Reports have explicitly contained the promise that the mapping exercise will be followed by a stage of operationalisation, the presumption is that an important part of the Sixth (and presumably final) Report will be dedicated to it. The SRSG's initial use of the notion of 'shared responsibility' needs to live up to its potential (Young 2004). This concept implies an acknowledgement that the challenges arising from globalisation are structural in character, involving governance gaps and governance failures. Accordingly, they cannot be resolved by an individual liability model and state responsibility alone, and need to be dealt with in their own right. This suggests the need for a model of strategically coherent systemic action, focused on 'realigning the relationships among actors', including states, corporations, and civil society (UNHCHR 2006). It is also acknowledged, throughout the process, that rule making in this domain must factor in the likely reactions of all the social actors that would be affected by the adoption of new rules. In other words, there is a need for both a systemic and a dynamic framework, in order to respond effectively to the human rights challenges posed by corporate globalisation (ibid.).

The SRSG's Third Report situated the business and human rights nexus on the 'bedrock' of state responsibility. This saves the Third Report from the sort of dangerous cleavages (such as that between the business lobbies and human rights activists) that brought the UN Norms to an abrupt halt (Kinley et al. 2007). However, when assessing the long-term potential for the success of such initiatives as the UN Norms or the framework of the Third Report, one should also bear in mind that, while controversy may be hard to live with, its absence may prove even more difficult. This will become apparent sooner rather than later in relation to the Third Report, once the reflection time is up and the SRSG has to offer 'greater operational detail' (Ruggie 2008b) and 'concrete guidance for all relevant actors' (Ruggie 2009: 116).

The limitations placed on the Third Report by its mandate have therefore, one could say, contributed to its success in consensus building, while the UN Norms – which attempted to go half a step further and to articulate the legal conceptualisation of human rights for business – appear to have been too controversial, too soon, and were exposed to powerful lobbying forces. In its Interim Report (Ruggie 2006), the SRSG dealt with the 'shadow' that the UN Norms appeared to have cast over the new mapping process (ibid.: 55) by discarding the UN Norms altogether and by proposing to start afresh and build on 'promising areas of consensus and cooperation' (ibid.: 69). The wisdom of discarding the Norms and starting anew has been questioned (Kinley and Chambers 2005: 460) on the grounds that they should be seen as a project that aims to investigate the legal dimensions – international and (implicitly) domestic – of the human rights responsibilities of corporations, and could enrich the SRSG's endeavour. Simply because the debate stirred up by the Norms revealed divisions and conflicts of interest is not a good enough reason to cast aside all the good elements they could offer. Ultimately, the framework proposed by the SRSG itself will want to reach a similar stage of operationalisation and will be hard pushed to avoid some of the questions (and even some of the conclusions) articulated by the UN Norms. The great challenge that the SRSG faces now is to maintain the consensus built around the Third Report, while at the same time being taken through stages of more operational detail in a way that would correspond to the social expectations. For the time being – one step (or one report) away from the final operationalising document promised for 2011 – the international community, and the human rights agencies in particular, are waiting anxiously for 'clearer guidance', 'greater clarity' and 'clear legal standards', as essential elements for the operationalisation of the human rights framework for business (Amnesty International 2010).

Conclusions

From analysis of the documents generated at three important levels of the transnational discourse on corporate responsibility (the ILO, the OECD and the UN), we see that significant progress has been made over the past decade in acknowledging (if not dealing with) the points of tension that exist between the imperative nature of the human rights discourse and corporate voluntarism. A striving for tighter definitions and authoritative specificity, for comprehensiveness and effectiveness, reveals an aspiration for structures and processes where corporate voluntarism is carefully managed through externally induced human rights standards and substance. In other words, where self-regulation is gradually converted into interactive regulation.

At the same time, all these instruments remain relatively weak from a normative point of view and comparatively ineffective from a practical standpoint. The issue of voluntary versus regulatory therefore remains largely unresolved. While the UN Draft Code, the ILO Declaration and the OECD Guidelines are all voluntary, it is recognised that such non-binding agreements are generally less effective than are potential mandatory ones, and that (in many cases) the former delay and hamper the introduction of better-articulated mandatory instruments. The corporate 'surrender' to voluntarily assumed codes of conduct is often seen in fact as a digression used by corporate actors in order to avoid domestic or international regulatory intervention. In spite of this criticism, it is also acknowledged that voluntary agreements are more easily negotiated and are sometimes seen as a way of influencing the corporate culture through dialogue, cooperation and constructive compromise – part maybe of a pre- or interactive regulatory phase.

The extent to which the latest UN initiative will prove successful in combining voluntary and mandatory tools and mechanisms of human rights responsibility for business depends largely on the international context and the evolution of the debate itself, rather than on the virtues of the mapping process undertaken so far. For the time being, it can be said that the failure of the UN Norms and the success of the SRSG Third Report in conjuring consensus reveal much about the two contrasting ways of approaching business and human rights in the global market environment (Joseph 2000: 75; Amnesty International 1998; Frynas and Pegg 2003). While both the UN Norms and the Third Report undertook a process of mapping the existing approaches to business and human rights in the global market environment, the final outcome was very different in the two instances. The UN Norms were aimed and presented – prematurely, perhaps – already at the level of operationalisation, in this case normative operationalisation. They proposed an almost 'ready-to-apply' system of legal rules (based principally on international human rights documents) after a fairly comprehensive mapping process and gestation period. The Third Report, however, stopped – frustrated by its mandate – at the mapping stage, with the promise of operationalisation in the near future (Ruggie 2008b, 2009). As for the subsequent Fourth and Fifth Reports from the SRSG's office, although based on comprehensive research and consultation, these documents continue to leave vague certain important points of the SRSG's operationalisation plan. However, in spite of these persistently obscure areas, there are hopes for a normative momentum that would tie in with the forthcoming Guiding Principles and that would answer, at least partially, the social expectations for justice.

Notes

1 Code of Labour Practice for Production of Goods Licensed by the Fédération Internationale de Football Association (FIFA), 1996.

2 The 1998 ILO Declaration led to the formation of a Committee of Experts on the Application of Conventions and Recommendations (ILO 1998: Annex paragraph 2).

References

Alston, P. (2005) 'Labour rights as human rights: The not so happy state of the art', in P. Alston (ed.), *Labour Rights as Human Rights*, Oxford: Oxford University Press.

Amnesty International (1998) *Human Rights Guidelines for Companies*, London: Amnesty International.

— (2000) 'Amnesty International and the United Nations Global Compact', available at: http://web.amnesty.org/pages/ec-globalcompact-eng

— (2010) 'Submission to the UN Human Rights Council', 14th Session, June 2010.

Backer, L. C. (2005) 'Multinational corporations, transnational law: The United Nations' norms on the responsibilities of transnational corporations as harbinger of corporate responsibility in international law', *Columbia Human Rights Law Review*, 37.

Campbell, T. (2004) 'Moral dimension of human rights', in T. Campbell and S. Miller (eds), *Human Rights and the Moral Responsibilities of Corporate and Public Sector Organisations*, The Hague: Kluwer Academic Publishers.

— (2007) 'Moral and analytical issues in corporate social responsibility and the law', in D. McBarnet, A. Voiculescu and T. Campbell (eds), *The New Corporate Accountability: Corporate social responsibility and the law*, Cambridge: Cambridge University Press.

Cernic, L. C. (2008) *Corporate Responsibility for Human Rights*, Libertas Working Paper No. 1/2008, available at: www.ssrn.com/abstract=1152354

De Schutter, O. (2006) 'The challenge of imposing human rights norms on corporate actors', in O. De Schutter (ed.), *Transnational Corporations and Human Rights*, Oxford: Hart Publishing.

Deva, S. (2004) 'UN human rights norms for transnational corporations and other business enterprises: A wrong foot in the right direction?', *ILSA Journal of International and Comparative Law*, 10.

Friends of the Earth (1998) 'A history of attempts to regulate the activities of transnational corporations: What lessons can be learned?' Discussion Paper for

Working Group II, 'Toward a Progressive International Economy: A Working Conference', Washington, DC, November.

Frynas, J. G. and S. Pegg (eds) (2003) *Transnational Corporations and Human Rights*, Basingstoke: Palgrave Macmillan.

Greider, W. (1997) *One World, Ready or Not: The manic logic of global capitalism*, New York: Simon and Schuster.

Hillemanns, C. (2003) 'UN norms on the responsibilities of transnational corporations and other business enterprises with regard to human rights', *German Law Journal*, 4.

Human Rights Watch/ESCR-Net (2010) 'Joint statement – 14th Session of the Human Rights Council', Geneva, 4 June.

ILO (1977) *Tripartite Declaration of Principles Concerning Multinational Enterprises and Social Policy (1977)*, 17 ILM 422, Geneva: ILO.

— (1998) *Declaration on Fundamental Principles and Rights at Work*, available at www.ilo.org/punlic/english/standards/decl/declaration/tindex.htm

International Federation for Human Rights/Human Rights in China (2010) 'Joint Statement by FIDH and HRIC on the occasion of the interactive dialogue with the Special Representative on the issue of business and human rights', Human Rights Council 14th session, June.

Jerbi, S. (2009) 'Business and human rights at the UN: What might happen next?' *Human Rights Quarterly*, 31.

Joseph, S. (2000) 'An overview of the human rights accountability of multinational enterprises' in M. Kamminga and S. Zia-Zarifi (eds), *Liability of Multinational Corporations under International Law*, The Hague: Kluwer Law International.

Kinley, D. and R. Chambers (2005) 'The UN human rights norms for corporations: The private implications of public international law', *Human Rights Law Review*, 6(3).

Kinley, D., J. Nolan and N. Zerial (2007) '"The norms are dead! Long live the norms!" The politics behind the UN human rights norms for corporations', in D. McBarnet, A. Voiculescu and T. Campbell (eds), *The New Corporate Accountability: Corporate social responsibility and the law*, Cambridge: Cambridge University Press.

Klein, N. (2000) *No Logo*, London: Flamingo.

Maupain, F. (2005) 'Is the ILO effective in upholding labour rights?: Reflections on the Myanmar experience', in P. Alston (ed.), *Labour Rights as Human Rights*, Oxford: Oxford University Press.

McBarnet, D., A. Voiculescu and T. Campbell (eds) (2007) *The New Corporate Accountability: Corporate social responsibility and the law*, Cambridge: Cambridge University Press.

Muchlinski, P. (2001) 'Human rights and multinationals: Is there a problem?', *International Affairs*, 77.

Murray, J. (1998) 'Corporate codes of conduct and labour standards', in R. Kyloh (ed.), *Mastering the Challenges of Globalization: Towards a Trade Union Agenda*, Geneva: ILO.

OECD (1976) 'OECD guidelines for multinational enterprises', 15 ILM 967-79.

— (2000) 'Guidelines for multinational enterprises: Decision of the Council', June.

Robé, J.-Ph. (1997) 'Multinational enterprises: The constitution of a pluralistic legal order', in G. Teubner (ed.), *Global Law without a State*, Brookfield: Dartmouth Publishing Group.

— (1999) *'L'entreprise et le droit'*, *Que sais-je?* No. 3442, Paris: P.U.F.

Ruggie, J. (2006) *Interim Report of the Special Representative of the Secretary-General on the Issue of Human Rights and Transnational Corporations and Other Business Enterprises*, UN Doc. E/CN/4/2006/97 (22 February).

— (2008a) *Protect, Respect and Remedy: A Framework for Business and Human Rights*, Report of the Special Representative of the Secretary-General on the Issue of Human Rights and Transnational Corporations and Other Business Enterprises (Third Report), UN Doc. A/HRC/8/5 (7 April).

— (2008b) 'Statement to United Nations Human Rights Council: Mandate Review', Geneva, 5 June, available at: www.business-humanrights.org/Links/Repository/210872/jump

— (2009) *Business and Human Rights: Towards Operationalizing the 'Protect, Respect and Remedy' Framework*, Report of the Special Representative of the Secretary-General on the Issue of Human Rights and Transnational Corporations and Other Business Enterprises (Fourth Report), UN Doc. A/HRC/11/13 (22 April).

— (2010) *Business and Human Rights: Further Steps Toward the Operationalization of the 'Protect, Respect and Remedy' Framework*, Report of the Special Representative of the Secretary-General on the Issue of Human Rights and Transnational Corporations and

Other Business Enterprises (Fifth Report), UN Doc. A/HRC/14/27 (9 April).

Schachter, O. (1998) 'The erosion of state authority and its implications for equitable development', in F. Weiss, E. Denters and P. De Waart (eds), *International Economic Law with a Human Face*, The Hague: Kluwer Law International.

UN (1999) 'Secretary-General proposes global compact on human rights, labour, environment, in address to World Economic Forum in Davos', UN press release, 1 February [SG/SM/6881], available at: www.unglobalcompact.org

UN Commission on Transnational Corporations (UNCTC) (1977) *Report of the Inter-governmental Working Group on the Code of Conduct (First and Second Sessions)*, UN Doc. E/C/10/31 (Pt. I, II).

UNCTC (1986) *Reporter*, 22 (Autumn).

UNHCHR (2003) *Norms on the Responsibilities of Transnational Corporations and Other Business Enterprises with Regard to Human Rights* (UN Norms), UN Doc. E/CN/4/Sub.2/2003/12/Rev.2, 26 August.

— (2004) 'Report to the Economic and Social Council on the Sixtieth Session of the Commission', UN Doc. E/CN.4/2004/L.11/Add.7, available at: www.unhchr.ch/huridocda/huridoca.nsf/e06a5300f90fa0238025668700518ca4/169143c3c1009015c1256e830058c441/$FILE/G0413976.pdf

— (2006) 'Workshop on attributing corporate responsibility for human rights under international law co-convened by New York University Center for Human Rights & Global Justice and

Realizing Rights: The Ethical Globalization Initiative', NYU School of Law, 17 November.

Voiculescu, A. (2007) 'Spheres of influence/spheres of responsibility: Multinational corporations and human rights', Nottingham University International Centre for Corporate Responsibility Symposium, November.

Weissbrodt, D. and M. Kruger (2003) 'Norms on the responsibilities of transnational corporations and other business enterprises with regard to human rights', *American Journal of International Law*, 97.

— (2005) 'Human rights responsibility of businesses as non-state actors' in P. Alston (ed.), *Non-State Actors and Human Rights*, Oxford: Oxford University Press.

Young, I. M. (2004) 'Responsibility and global labor justice', *Journal of Political Philosophy*, 12(4).

3 | Brands, corporate social responsibility and reputation management

FIONA HARRIS

Introduction

Businesses increasingly need to concern themselves with human rights issues, as global trade brings them into contact with countries in which workers' or communities' human rights may be compromised by the operations of corporations or of their subcontractors. There is growing awareness of corporations' activities and of the demands on them to practise social responsibility. While international initiatives strive to reach agreement about corporations' legal and normative responsibilities with regard to human rights, the behaviour of corporations is also shaped by marketing and branding considerations. A number of major brands have had their reputations damaged when human rights abuses have been associated with their or their subcontractors' activities. Corporate social responsibility has therefore become a key element in the identity of many leading brands. However, debates continue over the justification for, and the extent of, corporations' social responsibilities and how these might best be managed.

This chapter examines the tensions between law, business and society in relation to human rights and corporate social responsibility. These tensions are considered from a marketing perspective, with specific reference to branding and reputation management. Marketing is one of the interfaces between an organisation and society, and, while it attempts to satisfy the needs of consumers, the current definitions of marketing recognise its interaction with society more generally. For example, the American Marketing Association (AMA) defines marketing as 'the activity, set of institutions, and processes for creating, communicating, delivering, and exchanging offerings that have value for customers, clients, partners, and society at large' (AMA 2007).

We start by introducing a marketing perspective and explaining the nature and role of brands, brand identity and reputation, and the importance of brand equity. Discussion then focuses on the following three debates: (i) justifications for corporations' social responsibilities; (ii) the nature of corporations' social responsibilities; and (iii) how

29

corporations' social responsibilities should be managed. These are explored in the context of human rights and with respect to branding and reputation management.

A marketing perspective

A focus on consumers and their needs has been at the centre of modern approaches to marketing and forms the bedrock for many definitions of marketing. However, account increasingly needs to be taken of a much wider range of stakeholders and concerns. The activities of organisations have come under greater scrutiny, as has their behaviour towards employees, associations with suppliers and contractors, and their impact on communities and the environment. The increased emphasis on corporate branding (Mitchell 1994; King 1991; Berthon et al. 1999; Macrae 1999), whereby an organisation's name is used as the brand name, means that products are more closely identified with the organisations[1] responsible for them. The activities of an organisation therefore reflect on the way in which any human rights violations by the organisation or its producers will impact on the brand's reputation. The growing use of outsourcing by organisations can make them vulnerable to negative publicity if the companies to which they outsource are found to engage in practices that conflict with the human rights standards prevailing in the home market.

Intermediaries, such as market analysts, reporters or campaigners, can refract information among an organisation's stakeholders, who use it to supplement their incomplete information about the organisation (Fombrun and van Riel 1997). For example, consumers who have limited familiarity with a particular brand may be influenced by media reports about it when they make a purchasing decision. A brand's reputation is defined as 'a collective representation of a brand's past actions and results that describes the brand's ability to deliver valued outcomes to multiple stakeholders' (Harris 2001). This highlights the importance of considering the impact of an organisation's activities on its various stakeholders and recognising what matters to them. Damage to the brand's reputation from bad publicity can be long-lasting, as has been demonstrated by the case of Nestlé, which has long been the target of boycotts, originally because of its mismarketing of formula milk to mothers in Africa (and since then over a range of issues). Corporate social responsibility, as will be discussed later in the chapter, is about corporations taking responsibility for the conduct and impact of their business.

The nature and role of brands

An internationally accepted legal definition of a brand is 'a sign or set of signs certifying the origin of a product or service and differentiating it from the competition' (Kapferer 2008: 10). Although a brand started off as an identifying device that allowed offerings to be differentiated from each other and their authenticity to be established, marketing's own definition of a brand has evolved. Over time, the concept of a brand has been applied to an expanded variety of entities (for example, individual people, places and political parties) and the ways in which brands are differentiated have become more sophisticated. This is reflected in the expansion in professional definitions of a brand from visual and symbolic differentiation to include cognitive differentiation. The AMA's 1960 definition of a brand was:

> a name, term, sign, symbol, or design, or a combination of them intended to identify the goods and services of one seller or group of sellers and to differentiate them from those of competitors.

In contrast, a classic modern definition of a brand is 'a set of mental associations, held by the consumer, which add to the perceived value of a product or service' (Keller 1998). However, emotion is now also an essential component of strong brands (Kapferer 2008).

People's reactions to individual brands may vary, but bad stories about brands, particularly high-profile ones, tend to linger, particularly online. Especially when faced with conflicting information, it can be difficult to assess the veracity of negative stories about brands – or to know whether the competitors are any better. Indeed, the majority of consumers are unlikely to have the time or the expertise to investigate stories more closely. Nevertheless, such stories and reports may contribute to the set of mental associations held by consumers. These matter because brands have a greater role to play than merely that of a legal trademark.

A brand may be viewed as a company's most important asset, summed up in the concept of 'brand equity'. Kapferer (1997: 24) defines brand equity (or accounting goodwill) as:

> the monetary value of the psychological goodwill which the brand has created over time through communication investment and consistent focus on products, both of which help build the reputation of the name.

He claims: 'the value of a brand comes from its ability to gain an exclusive, positive and prominent meaning in the minds of a large number of consumers' (ibid.: 25). For example, Shop Direct Home Shopping reportedly paid between £5 million and £10 million for the Woolworths brand name to use for an online business (BBC News 2009).

In addition to representing guarantees of future income (Doyle 1989), successful brands allow premium pricing, deter potential competitors from entering a market, act as springboards into new markets (Kapferer 1997) and confer bargaining power when it comes to distribution channels (Aaker 1991). A brand encapsulates an organisation's promise to consumers (Goodyear 1996) and helps consumers to recognise products (Berthon et al. 1999), which gives the organisation an advantage, since familiar brands tend to be preferred to unknown ones (Aaker 1991).

From the consumer point of view, by assisting in identification (Kapferer 1997), brands reduce search costs (Berthon et al. 1999): they act as a shorthand device (de Chernatony and Dall'Olmo Riley 1998), helping consumers to interpret, process and store large quantities of product information (Aaker 1991). Brands can also facilitate consumer decision-making by offering added value – functional and emotional benefits – that differentiates them from their competitors (de Chernatony et al. 2000). For example, the car brand BMW offers functional added value (such as 'the ultimate driving machine') and emotional added value (such as 'joy'). On its website, BMW proclaims:

> JOY.
> On the back of this three-letter word, we built a company. We don't just build cars. We are the creators of emotion. We are the guardians of ecstasy, the thrills and chills, the laughs and smiles, and all the words that can't be found in a dictionary. We are the Joy of Driving. No car company can rival our history, replicate our passion, our vision. Innovation is our backbone but joy is our heart. We will not stray from our three-letter purpose. This is the story of BMW. This is the story of joy. (BMW 2009)

The emotional added value of a brand is more sustainable, because it is harder for competitors to copy (de Chernatony et al. 2000), suggesting that the corporate social responsibility of organisations could be an important differentiator between brands. Brands may also provide consumers with increased confidence in their purchase selections (Aaker 1991), reduce the perceived risk (social as well as quality) of purchases (Berthon et al. 1999) and give consumers a means of expressing their identities (Goodyear 1996; Kapferer 1997; Lury 1998). An increasing number of consumers also base their consumption decisions on ethical considerations (see Harrison et al. 2005).

Olins (1989) described three levels of branding: (i) 'monolithic' (corporate branding), in which the brand name is the organisation's name (for example, British Airways); (ii) 'endorsed', where the brand name includes both the organisation's name and a line or product name (for example, Microsoft Office); and (iii) 'branded' (line brands), in which the brand name is different from that of the organisation (for example, the Lexus luxury car brand produced by Toyota). The growth of corporate branding, while offering advantages with regard to globalisation and economies of scale, has made the organisation behind a brand more visible and has exposed the brand to the risk that any misdemeanours by the organisation will damage the brand through synonymous association.

Many organisations have shifted or outsourced production to developing countries in order to take advantage of lower costs. However, such strategies have reflected badly on such high-profile brands as Nike, Gap and Disney. The layoffs resulting from factory closures and the organisations' attempts to dissociate themselves from the poor labour practices in so-called 'sweatshops' operated by contractors abroad were powerfully condemned in Naomi Klein's bestselling book *No Logo*. She was particularly critical of the way organisations offloaded their production responsibilities and instead just focused their efforts on their profit-generating brand names. Klein (2000) reported that young, predominantly migrant factory workers, often women, in free-trade zones in developing countries were subjected to long working days (between 12 and 16 hours) and military-style management, and were paid below-subsistence wages for low-skill, tedious, short-term work. She also recounted a wide range of 'horror stories' about the mistreatment and exploitation of workers and abuses of their human rights. The enormous power imbalance and distance between the multinational brands and the factory workers – situated as they are at opposite ends of the often long subcontracting chain – was identified by Klein as underlying the appalling working conditions.

The apparent power of brands and marketing is reflected in the bans and restrictions that have been placed on the marketing of harmful or potentially harmful products such as tobacco and alcohol. Furthermore, the harmful nature of their products undermines the credibility of any attempts to demonstrate corporate social responsibility (see, for example, Hastings and Liberman 2009).

However, it is important to bear in mind that both marketing and branding are merely tools that may be harnessed for good or ill. While maligned if misused by business, marketing and branding can also be employed to serve socially responsible businesses, by not-for-profit organisations and in social marketing to improve health and social well-being. Indeed, Amnesty International won an award for its television advertisement showing how ordinary people have the power to prevent human rights abuses (Stock 2008). Marketing and branding are as relevant to charities as to businesses, because charities must compete against one another for donations, just as businesses must compete against each other for custom.

Fair trade marketing is another example of branding being put to use to improve human lives – in this case to help disadvantaged farmers and workers in developing countries by improving the prices they get, their working conditions, local sustainability and the trade terms they achieve (Fairtrade Foundation 2009a). The international FAIRTRADE mark is a registered certification mark and trademark that can be used on packaging for products certified in accordance with Fairtrade standards, as well as for promotional and campaigning purposes (Fairtrade Foundation 2009b). It is essentially a logo that co-brands a product, acting as a guarantee that fair trade standards have been met in its production. The standards are designed 'to ensure that the conditions of production and trade of all Fairtrade certified products are socially, economically fair and environmentally responsible' (Fairtrade Labelling Organisations International 2009). As a branding device, it is consistent with modern branding concepts, offering cognitive and emotional value by reassuring consumers that a product bearing the FAIRTRADE mark is ethically sourced. The number and range of goods bearing this FAIRTRADE certification label is increasing, and there are signs that fair trade is moving from a niche market into the mainstream. Before being taken over by Kraft, Cadbury converted its Dairy Milk chocolate brand to fair trade. Although Dairy Milk was Cadbury's bestselling product, the fact that the company had an extensive range of products that did not bear the FAIRTRADE label could dilute consumers' inferences about its support for human rights.

Brand identity and reputation

The emphasis in the literature has shifted away from the notion of 'brand image' (how a brand is currently perceived by external audiences) to the concept of 'brand identity', which, in the case of corporate branding, is a proactive projection of how the organisation wishes to be perceived and is created internally. Whereas brand image fluctuates, brand reputation is built up over time, is based on the evaluations of all stakeholders and is more stable. Reputation is particularly powerful when products are similar or cannot be seen (Herbig and Milewicz 1995).

Building on Kapferer's (1997) model of brand identity, de Chernatony (1999) developed an 'Identity–Reputation Gap Model of Brand Management', in which brand management is conceptualised as the process of aligning a brand's reputation with its identity to ensure that external perceptions of the brand match its internal formulation. Gaps between a brand's identity and its reputation can occur if the components of the brand's identity are incongruous, if the brand identity is inconsistently communicated or if external factors intervene, such as accidents, tampering or reports in the media. For example, a gap between Starbucks' brand identity and its reputation emerged when it was criticised in the media for wasting water with its 'running tap' policy even as it claimed high standards of environmental responsibility in its corporate social responsibility report (Balakrishnan 2008).

For the corporate brand identity to be communicated effectively, consistency is crucial (Abratt 1989). The aim is to produce a favourable brand reputation and create a competitive advantage. However, in the cases of Nike, Gap and Disney, one of the key things that tarnished their brands (when it was discovered that their producers were employing unethical labour practices) was the discrepancy between their espoused brand identities and the reality of the way the goods bearing their brand names were manufactured.

To remain successful, brands need to be managed and actively sustained. As awareness of social issues and the monitoring of businesses' activities have grown, so brands and their organisations have needed to demonstrate social responsibility, and those that have attracted censure have undertaken strenuous efforts to remedy the problems and make social responsibility part of their identity. For example, Nike's responsibility is identified on its website as follows:

> Nike sees corporate responsibility as an integral part of how we can use the power of our brand, the energy and passion of our people, and the scale of our business to create meaningful change.
>
> The opportunity is greater than ever for corporate responsibility principles and practices to deliver business returns and become a driver of growth, to build deeper consumer and community connections and to create positive social and environmental impact in the world. (Nike 2009)

Brands and organisations are also being forced to take responsibility for their supply chain and to make the conditions under which their goods are manufactured more transparent. For example, on its website Gap proclaims:

As with most other companies that sell apparel, we don't own the garment factories that make our clothes. But we do share responsibility
for the conditions under which our clothes are made. Our commitment
to safe and fair working conditions extends beyond our employees and
stores to include the partners in our supply chain. (Gap 2009)

A favourable reputation is especially important where products are
complex, intangible (a service) or similar to those of competitors, and can
be an important factor in selecting a brand. Increasingly, corporations
need to have a good reputation for social responsibility, as well as for
the quality of their offering. Yet some scepticism surrounds the sincerity
of organisations' claims relating to social responsibility. For example, in
a critique of CSR by the campaign group Corporate Watch (2006) it was
suggested that CSR was a response by corporations to anti-corporate
activism and merely a means of repairing their damaged reputations and
assuming control of the issue. The reputation-management consultant
and writer Andrew Griffin acknowledged that 'CSR is very much part of
reputation risk management', though he did claim that CSR had only a
'marginal effect' as a strategy for managing the risks to a corporation's
reputation (Griffin 2008: 137). Yet, whereas Corporate Watch views companies as attempting to assume leadership of issues over which they have
been criticised, others believe that NGOs have hijacked CSR in order to
try to make companies solve the world's problems (Cowe 2003).

The growth of CSR

It is not just those organisations striving to restore their reputations
that attempt to demonstrate their ethical credentials. It is common
today for successful companies to make explicit reference to CSR on
their websites. For example, some of the Fortune 500 companies (based
on *Fortune* magazine's 2007 list of the top 500 companies in the world)
that mention CSR in their 'About...' web pages include: Canon, Fedex,
Indian Oil and National Australia Bank. The growth of CSR reporting
is evident in the large number of reports available on websites such as
CorporateRegister.com and CSRwire.com.

In addition to *Fortune* magazine's annual lists of the 'World's Most
Admired Companies' and '100 Best Companies to Work For', there are
various ratings of organisations based on assessments that include ethics and CSR as components. The *Ethical Consumer Magazine*'s Ethiscore
(www.ethiscore.org) assigns ratings to corporations, large and small,
across the world, based on their behaviour with regard to the environment, people (including human rights), animals, politics and product

sustainability. *Corporate Responsibility Magazine* (formerly *Business Ethics*), publishes an annual list of the '100 Best Corporate Citizens' (www.thecro.com/?q=be_100best). Conversely, exposing the detrimental social and environmental impact of large corporations is one of the stated aims of not-for-profit groups like Corporate Watch (www.corporatewatch.org.uk) in the UK and CorpWatch (www.corpwatch.org) in the USA. Similarly, SourceWatch (www.sourcewatch.org) provides a directory of the 'people, organisations and issues shaping the public agenda', whose primary purpose is 'documenting the PR and propaganda activities of public relations firms and public relations professionals engaged in managing and manipulating public perception, opinion and policy' (Source Watch 2009a).

Reputation management

Reputations are built up over time, but can be lost quickly. Once lost, they can be very difficult to re-establish. When faced with a situation that is potentially damaging to its reputation, these days an organisation will often have to respond immediately (Griffin 2008). Whereas in the past, organisations might have had time to decide how to handle any emerging crisis, developments in technology mean that news now spreads very rapidly indeed. Furthermore, stories are disseminated through unregulated as well as formal channels, and can remain online indefinitely. To protect their reputation, organisations need to be prepared and reputation management is essential. Publishing corporate social responsibility reports is not sufficient. In fact, the reputation-management consultant Andrew Griffin considers such reports 'a waste of time and trees', read mainly by sceptics and based on negative assumptions, since they are designed to address real or potential criticisms of the corporation in question (ibid.: 152). He claims that:

> reputation is not just about ethics, sustainability and responsibility. Reputation is about everything that an organization does, how it does it and how its customers and other audiences think, feel and act as a result. (ibid.: 18)

Considering 'other audiences' or *stakeholders* – 'any group or individual who is affected by or can affect the achievement of the organization's objectives' (Freeman 1984: 46) – is crucial. Stakeholder groups include owners, creditors, employees, suppliers, customers, the government, NGOs, the regional/national community and the local community. The ways in which an organisation interacts with any of these groups can affect its reputation – for example, the way an organisation treats its staff or the way its staff behave towards customers in the course of its everyday business, or the way its marketing activities are perceived by any stakeholder group. Griffin (2008) points out that even when only a small section of society is negatively affected by a corporation's activities, this can lead to wider condemnation by a larger section of society. Stakeholders differ in the criteria they use to assess reputation, and organisations need to be aware of this.

Griffin (ibid.) argues that the hardest threats to an organisation's reputation to manage are *issues* resulting from the organisation's own activities, rather than physical *crises* created by external events. This is because, in the latter case, the spotlight is likely to be shared, the organisation is not likely to be blamed and procedures for dealing with potential physical crises are usually in place. Griffin notes that organisations in product-based industries are better prepared to cope with issues and crises than are service organisations, which are far more reliant on their reputations. Issues management involves identifying and eliminating gaps between a corporation's internal policies and actions, so that they fit external stakeholders' perceptions (Margaritis 2000).

More broadly, Griffin urges corporations to adopt a more assertive, proactive mindset and to build reputation management into the whole business, instead of treating it as an add-on. However, there can be tension between a corporation's CSR activities and its public communication of them. In Denmark (and possibly other welfare states), although the public expects companies to practise CSR, it does not like companies to shout about their CSR activities (Morsing et al. 2008). Morsing et al. conclude that the perceived trustworthiness of CSR communications depends on employees' involvement in and commitment to CSR policies. Without what they term this 'inside-out approach', the authors report that CSR communication is viewed as mere management rhetoric. Their research indicates that companies should balance detailed CSR communication (facts, figures, statistics, etc.) directed at stakeholders who are knowledgeable about CSR with public communication through third-party experts such as employees and the media (which they term 'endorsed CSR communication'). In services marketing, staff play a crucial role in conveying the corporate brand, so the support of staff will affect the credibility of an organisation's external communication of its CSR activities.

Griffin's approach to reputation management is to encourage corporations to be less apologetic and more assertive in 'gaining control of issues, crises and corporate social responsibility' (the subtitle of his book on reputation management). He is correspondingly sceptical that 'companies embarked on the CSR journey out of some sort of Damascene conversion to social justice or sudden realisation that it was the right thing to do' (Griffin 2008: 137). Undoubtedly, however, there are people working on CSR initiatives who clearly genuinely and ardently believe in the value of these initiatives. People and organisations differ in their views of CSR and business ethics; three different perspectives are examined in the next section.

Justifications for corporations' social responsibilities

There are three main perspectives on the justification for corporations' social responsibilities.

1. Acting ethically is the only right way for an organisation to behave According to this ethically driven view, organisations should behave in a socially responsible way for no other reason than that it is the right way to behave. Mintzberg (1983: 3) described this perspective as the 'purest form' of social responsibility and considered it to be the only convincing argument for CSR, despite the challenges. He argued:

> Social responsibility – that most naïve of concepts – represents our best hope, perhaps our only real hope, for arresting and reversing that trend [toward impersonalism and utilitarianism in our organizations]. Without responsible and ethical people in important places, the society we know and wish to improve will never survive. (ibid.: 14)

2. Doing what is right, fair and just is expected of an organisation Following a tide of highly publicised environmental disasters and financial and labour-related scandals, organisations' activities are subjected to considerable scrutiny by their stakeholders and society. Concern about corporations' social performance has become reflected in the notion of the 'triple bottom line' of economic prosperity, environmental quality and social justice (Elkington 1997). A variety of global standards for non-financial reporting and principles have been developed, including the Global Reporting Initiative (2009) and the UN Global Compact (2009). Although corporate social reporting is not required in most countries, many large corporations do provide reports on their social behaviour, though it should be said that the extent to which businesses promote CSR and the CSR issues they emphasise differs from country to country (Chen and Bouvain 2009).

3. It is in an organisation's best interests to behave ethically This perspective is one of 'enlightened self-interest' and represents 'the business case for CSR'. While there have been mixed findings about the relationship between financial and social performance, Smith (2003) concluded that the balance of evidence supported a link between the two. Beyond financial incentives, having a good reputation as an ethical organisation (or *corporate brand*) represents an asset that enables premium pricing and is attractive to potential and existing employees, as well as to other organisations considering business dealings (de George 1993). In contrast, revelations of unethical behaviour can be damaging and tend to linger. Even if unethical behaviour has not been exposed publicly, sooner or later immoral strategies or practices that deeply trouble an organisation's employees will spell trouble for that organisation. Another argument, common in business, irrespective of the topic, is that if organisations do not 'put their own house in order', then the government may step in and impose more severe conditions.

In theory, inconsistencies between the different components of a brand's professed identity and between its brand identity and its reputation should undermine any false claims about CSR. Indeed, as noted in the Corporate Watch review, the gap between Enron's CSR claims and the reality became apparent after its collapse. Yet Corporate Watch also cited examples of corporations that purported to be leaders in CSR, but whose other business activities were at odds with notions of social responsibility. However, in the two examples offered, one company used endorsed branding rather than corporate branding and the other was a business-to-business (rather than consumer) corporate brand in an industry that is notorious for pursuing profits at the expense of indigenous people and the environment. It remains to be seen how corporations with such discrepancies will fare in the long term.

At the crux of the tensions between law, business and society in relation to human rights and corporate social responsibility lies the issue of whether or not social responsibility is voluntary. The justifications above vary in the level of discretion accorded to business to act ethically. The first perspective suggests that business is compelled to behave in a socially responsible way on moral grounds. The second perspective recognises that there is social pressure on corporations to behave in a socially responsible way, although acting ethically is *expected* rather than *required*. Finally, the third perspective implies that behaving in a socially responsible way is discretionary, but is to corporations' advantage. However, if the expectations in the second perspective translate into *market* pressure, this may 'require' a corporation to behave responsibly on business grounds. Corporations also have the discretion to decide how they focus their attention on behaving responsibly. The question of discretion is a theme that will recur throughout the remainder of this chapter.

The business case and advantages to the corporate brand from behaving in a socially responsible way have now been outlined. However, the question of whether a corporation is a moral agent requires further consideration.

Whether corporations can be held morally responsible depends on whether they can also be regarded as moral agents. Just as it is hard to reach agreement about the legal and normative responsibilities of corporations with regard to human rights, so the question of whether a corporation is a moral agent has been the subject of much philosophical debate. However, it is important to establish the moral agency of organisations for them to be regarded as having moral responsibilities towards human rights, given the often discretionary way in which corporate social responsibility is treated.

In his review of the debate, Moore (1999) identified the issues of intentionality and allocation of blame and punishment with regard to any wrongdoing (*mens rea*) as key in establishing moral agency with respect to corporations. French (1979) reasoned that intentionality could be ascribed to corporations on the basis that they have what he called an internal decision structure, comprising a hierarchical chart showing levels and positions of power within the corporation and a policy outlining corporate decision rules. French's arguments also suggest that moral responsibility could be attributed to corporations' acts, because the acts and the intentions behind those acts could only be ascribed to the corporation, rather than to individual members. According to French (1995), as well as intentionality, moral agency also requires the ability to make rational decisions and to change intentions and actions that harm others or the corporation itself. A problem, however, with treating corporations as moral agents is that innocent members of the corporation may suffer as a result of the misdeeds of the corporation, through the impact on the corporation itself. Furthermore, although members still have an individual moral responsibility, attribution of moral agency to the corporation may mean that members at fault for those misdeeds escape blame and punishment. While a counter-argument to the suffering of innocent members is that membership of a corporation involves accepting shared responsibility and thus shared blame (Moore 1999), the possibility that the guilty may escape commensurate punishment has been used to contest the moral agency of corporations (Velasquez 1985).

The two principal arguments against viewing corporations as moral agents are that (i) the moral responsibilities of individuals cannot be transferred to collectives, and (ii) as already mentioned, collectives either cannot be punished or cannot be punished appropriately (Moore 1999). In opposition to French, Velasquez (1985) argued that moral responsibility rests not with corporations but with those individual members who actually carry out any acts, as he considered them to be autonomous in their intentions and not controlled directly by the corporation. Ladd (1970) considered that decisions deemed to be corporate could only relate to economic matters and not social issues, unless they had some bearing on the economic well-being of the corporation. However, economic concerns are often at the root of many human rights abuses. Another argument that has been made against the moral agency of corporations is that, unlike real persons, corporations have no motivating emotions and thus cannot care; though such a view nowadays could be considered at odds with the modern branding conceptions discussed earlier, in which emotion has become an essential component of strong brands (Kapferer 2008). However, Goodpaster (1987) used reasoning similar to French's rationale for intentionality to make a case that corporations' policies or structures for decision-making can be influenced by individual members' moral agency.

From his review of the debate, Moore (1999: 339) concluded that the case for treating corporations as moral agents was 'more convincing' than was the case against doing so, and that 'the acceptance of corporate moral agency seems to be a better reflection of "reality" in the sense of how most people interpret the world around them'. It also makes intuitive sense to hold organisations responsible for their actions. Given the size and power of many multinational companies, it would be alarming if such bodies could evade the moral responsibility borne by individuals simply because being a collective obscured the attribution of blame. Furthermore, as Wettstein (2009: 138) reasoned:

> One cannot consistently defend the unconditional nature of human rights as ethical imperatives and at the same time leave their corresponding obligations up to the discretion of companies. If we accept human rights as undeniable and inherent moral entitlements of all human beings, then we cannot allow for any exceptions in regard to respective obligations. To exempt corporations from direct moral responsibility in regard to human rights means to question the legitimacy and ethical standing of human rights in general.

Companies are 'artificial persons', described in law as 'legal persons'. Although companies incorporated in England are owned by shareholders, the company itself owns company assets and employs directors, who have a fiduciary duty to act in the best interests of the company. Moore (1999: 339) identified corporations as having a threefold liability in law: (i) the corporation may be criminally liable; (ii) individuals in the corporation may be liable as 'perpetrators or accomplices'; and (iii) senior officers of the corporation may be liable under statutes, even though they might not be criminally liable under ordinary principles or it might otherwise be difficult to prove their guilt.

The nature of corporations' social responsibilities

If we accept the moral agency and responsibility of corporations, the next question is: 'What are organisations' responsibilities towards society?' The question of whether or not corporate social responsibility is discretionary is also reflected in the different ways in which CSR has been defined, as is evident in the following definitions of CSR:

> ... a commitment to improve community well-being through discretionary business practices and contributions of corporate resources. (Kotler and Lee 2005: 3)

> ... it is how a company carries out its mainstream business operations that determines whether or not it is socially responsible. (Marsden 2001: 46)

> ... [the] configuration of the principles of social responsibility, processes of social responsiveness, and policies, programs, and observable outcomes as they relate to the firm's societal relationships. (Wood 1991: 693)

Kotler and Lee's definition explicitly regards CSR as 'discretionary', a position that is at odds with the notion of moral obligation outlined by Wettstein (2009). Indeed, in their book *Corporate Social Responsibility. Doing the Most Good for Your Company and Your Cause*, the rationale for CSR focuses on its benefits to the organisation's health (Kotler and Lee 2005). They describe six 'options for doing good': (i) cause promotions (whereby a corporation makes financial or in-kind contributions to promote awareness or concern about a social cause); (ii) cause-related marketing (in which a corporation contributes an agreed percentage of its revenues from product sales to a specific cause); (iii) corporate social marketing (in which a corporation supports the development and/or implementation of a behaviour-change campaign designed to improve public health, social well-being or the environment); (iv) corporate philanthropy (the payment of direct contributions, financial or in-kind resources to a charity or cause); (v) community volunteering (whereby a corporation supports or encourages its employees to contribute their time to helping local community organisations or causes);

and (vi) socially responsible business practices (discretionary business practices and investments that support social causes) (Kotler and Lee 2005: 23–4). Such interpretations of CSR focus on the moral distribution of an organisation's profits, rather than on ethical consideration of how those profits were generated (Ulrich 2008).

In contrast, Marsden (2001) argued that CSR is not about disinterested giving, and nor is it necessarily about donating large percentages of a corporation's profits. Instead he viewed CSR as being about a corporation's business activities as a whole: how a corporation conducts its business and earns its profits.

Chen and Bouvain (2009) noted that Wood's (1991) definition integrates a lot of earlier work on CSR. What is striking is that it involves a commitment to the ethical principles, processes and outcome of CSR. It is not enough to adhere to one or other of these: all three are seen as essential components of CSR to ensure translation of principles into demonstrable outcomes.

Kotler and Lee (2005) discerned an increase in corporate giving and reporting of CSR initiatives, the development of 'a corporate social norm to do good' and a shift from regarding giving as an obligation to treating it as a strategy. Concern about the latter has been voiced by Maak (2008: 356), who rued the transformation of CSR into 'SCR – strategic corporate responsibility' – and the deterioration of corporations' social or moral obligation into 'a mere market opportunity to achieve competitive advantage'. Undoubtedly such business-based perspectives persist. However, in his review of CSR, Wettstein (2009: 132) observes that:

> The focus has shifted from only looking at how corporations distribute their profits to how they generate it. As such, CSR is concerned with a much larger range of ethical problems inherent (i.e. not external) and directly connected to a company's core business processes.

From a marketing perspective, it is the consistency between a corporate brand's identity components that matters. If an organisation's approach to CSR conflicts with any other aspects of its business, it will undermine the credibility of the brand's created identity, forging a gap between the brand's identity and its reputation. Corporate brands need to ensure that their core business processes take account of the larger range of ethical problems and are consistent with their CSR communications and the distribution of their profits, otherwise they will be greeted with scepticism.

In terms of the *types* of social responsibilities that are attributed to corporations, Carroll's (1991) well-known model represented corporate social responsibility as a pyramid of four domains of responsibility, as shown in Figure 3.1. The four domains were: a required economic responsibility to be profitable; a responsibility to adhere to legal requirements; an expected responsibility to be ethical (this relates to activities or practices not codified in law but that are expected or prohibited by society); and a desired philanthropic responsibility to be a good corporate citizen (Schwartz and Carroll 2003).

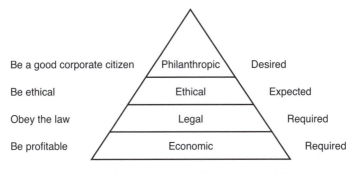

Be a good corporate citizen	Philanthropic	Desired
Be ethical	Ethical	Expected
Obey the law	Legal	Required
Be profitable	Economic	Required

Figure 3.1 Carroll's (1991) pyramid of responsibilities (based on Schwartz and Carroll 2003)

However, in Carroll's 1991 version of the model, social responsibility is regarded as discretionary, albeit desirable, and being 'a good corporate citizen' is expressed in terms of philanthropy – in other words, how profits are distributed, rather than how profits are earned. Furthermore, Carroll did not intend the pyramid to imply that philanthropy was the highest level; indeed he considered economic and legal responsibilities to be the most fundamental, and viewed philanthropic responsibilities as less important than the other three (Schwartz and Carroll 2003).

In a later version of the model – the 'Three-Domain Model of Corporate Social Responsibility' (Schwartz and Carroll 2003) – the economic, legal and ethical domains are represented instead as a Venn diagram of overlapping circles, to remove any suggestion of a hierarchy and to recognise the mutuality of the CSR domains. The philanthropic domain is subsumed into ethical and/or economic responsibilities, according to whether philanthropic activities are purely ethically motivated, purely economically motivated or a combination of both. The separate philanthropic category was removed, partly because Carroll considered that it might be inappropriate to categorise philanthropic activities as 'responsibilities', owing to 'their voluntary or discretionary nature' (ibid.: 505), and partly in recognition of the fact that philanthropic activities might sometimes be economically motivated. These revisions mean that ethically motivated philanthropy is no longer treated as discretionary, but is categorised as 'expected' in the ethical domain.

Even though under the Companies Act 2006 (Chapter 2, Section 172) in the UK directors are now required to have regard to the social and environmental impact of their decisions, this is subordinated to directors' duty 'to promote the success of the company'.

The Organisation for Economic Co-operation and Development (OECD) Guidelines for Multinational Enterprises treat corporate social responsibility as discretionary. The Guidelines 'provide *voluntary* principles and standards for responsible business conduct consistent with applicable laws' (OECD 2008: 9, emphasis added). The OECD is a group of thirty countries[2] whose governments are committed to democracy and the market economy, brought together to: 'support sustainable economic growth; boost employment; raise living standards; maintain financial stability; assist other countries' economic development; and contribute to growth in world trade' (OECD 2009). The 'general policies' listed in the Guidelines are of particular relevance with regard to human rights. These include a statement that enterprises should 'respect the human rights of those affected by their activities consistent with the host government's international obligations and commitments' (OECD 2008: 14). Specific guidelines are also provided relating to disclosure, employment and industrial relations, environment, combating bribery, consumer interests, science and technology, competition and taxation. The Voluntary Principles on Security and Human Rights (VPSHR 2000) also provide voluntary guidelines, in this case for companies in the extractive sectors, to maintain the safety and security of their operations, while ensuring respect for human rights.

Although rights imply corresponding duties, not all human rights have legal backing and, as just discussed, many human rights guidelines for business are voluntary. The issue of how corporations' social responsibilities should be managed provides the final focus of this chapter.

How should corporations' social responsibilities be managed?

Goodpaster and Matthews (2001) provide an overview of the differing perspectives on corporate responsibility. They discern three views on this issue, which they term: the 'invisible hand', the 'hand of government' and the 'hand of management'.

The 'invisible hand' According to this view, the way society functions means that corporations do most good by pursuing their own interests, so corporations have a moral responsibility to pursue their own interests. Corporate morality is thus considered to be best achieved through the market system. Milton Friedman famously argued:

[There] is one and only one social responsibility of business – to use its resources and engage in activities designed to increase its profits so long as it stays within the rules of the game, which is to say, engages in open and free competition, without deception or fraud. (Friedman 1962: 133)

The 'hand of government' This view regards government intervention as needed to make sure that corporations behave morally, and corporations' responsibilities should be limited to political and legal compliance. John Kenneth Galbraith maintained that corporations should follow only economic objectives, but the government and law should make sure that these objectives serve the common good (Goodpaster and Matthews 2001).

The 'hand of management' This third view claims that social responsibility should be managed by corporations themselves. Edward Freeman argued for the adoption of a stakeholder perspective, in which managers are regarded as having responsibilities to all the stakeholders of a corporation.

However, in a recent essay that sought to put an end to the 'Friedman–Freeman debate', Freeman claimed that his views were not incompatible with those of Milton Friedman, and that 'the so-called debate may be only a difference about the best way to understand how business works and could work, and a difference about what the "theories" are about' (Freeman 2008: 166). He described stakeholder theory as 'a very simple idea about how people create value for each other. It's a theory about what good management is' (ibid.: 166). Integrating their views, Freeman (ibid.) argued that 'Friedman could have written':

The primary responsibility of an executive is to create as much value as possible for stakeholders because that's how you create as much value as possible for shareholders. Where there's conflict between stakeholders and shareholders, executives have to rethink the problem so the interests go together. No stakeholder interest stands alone here. Where interests conflict, the job of the manager is to figure out how to redefine things so as to create more value for both. Sometimes this involves making tradeoffs in the real world. When that happens, the executive has to figure out how to make the tradeoffs and figure out how to improve the tradeoffs for both sides. Managing the stakeholders is about creating as much value as possible for stakeholders without resorting to tradeoffs, or fraud and deception. (ibid.: 166)

This implies that management is in a position to ensure that the human rights of an organisation's stakeholders are observed. However, this does not mean that all managers will recognise this, particularly in view of the differing perspectives on corporate social responsibility that have been discussed. Who then should ensure that corporations fulfil their human rights duties: the market, the government or corporations? There are limitations with each, as will now be examined.

Leaving market forces to weed out organisations that neglect their social responsibilities or infringe human rights assumes that consumers and buyers have sufficient and accurate information about organisations, and that ethical considerations will direct their purchase decisions. However, sufficient and accurate information is not always available or readily accessible, and consumers are often faced with conflicting information about brands. Although, as a segment, ethical consumers are increasing, ethical purchase *intentions* may not translate into actual purchase behaviour. Market forces may also encourage a 'race to the bottom', as corporations vie to offer the most competitive prices, with the result that ethical considerations may be set aside in a bid to cut costs. Furthermore, markets consist of segments of consumers, rather than society as a whole, and while campaign groups and journalists, for example, may influence consumers' purchases to varying extents, the impact of market forces depends on the acceptance or rejection of brands by subsections of society.

Governments cannot necessarily be relied upon to act disinterestedly as guardians of human rights. This is demonstrated for example in Borneo, with tribes trying to protect the endangered forests of the Malaysian state of Sarawak in which they live from companies granted licences by the Sarawak state government to exploit the rainforest by felling it to grow oil palms for biofuel, cooking oil, margarine and soap (Sheridan 2009). Furthermore, governments have to balance the needs of a wide range of constituents. In democracies, they rely on votes to stay in power, providing a strong incentive to please the majority, to the potential disadvantage of smaller groups. Furthermore, some writers have questioned the effectiveness of legal enforcement of CSR. Paine (1999: 202) argued that 'the law is an important but insufficient guide to ethical conduct'. Just because something is legal does not necessarily mean that it is ethical. Mintzberg (1983: 13) argued that 'legalistic approaches only set crude and minimum standards of behaviour, ones easily circumvented by the unscrupulous'. Griffin (2008: 143) was of the opinion that: 'Turning CSR into regulation would be a disaster. It would be hugely counterproductive, as it would turn the concept of doing "good business" into little more than a dull box-ticking exercise.' From a branding perspective, it would also lessen the scope for brand differentiation based on CSR.

A key concern in expecting corporations to manage their social responsibilities through self-regulation is that those corporations may find their interests to be in opposition to some other group's human rights. For example, see the discussion of the case *Doe* vs. *Unocal Corp* in Chapter 10 of this volume, which examines human rights issues in the construction of the Yadana Natural Gas Pipeline. In the case of corporations that produce harmful or addictive products, such as tobacco, asking them to respect human rights may be deemed nonsensical.

In the USA, tobacco companies are reported to be considering appealing against the legislation that regulates tobacco products and tobacco marketing activities – ironically on the grounds that the advertising restrictions infringe their constitutional right to free speech (*Economist* 2009). Also in the USA, Nike attempted (unsuccessfully) in 2002 to use the First Amendment's guarantee of free speech, in order to challenge a complaint about the way it represented its labour practices in a public relations campaign (ReclaimDemocracy.org 2007). Gerard Hastings, professor of social marketing, has remarked: 'There are some things that need doing that businesses will not sign up to' and voluntary regulation is like 'allowing foxes into the chicken coop provided they sign up to vegetarianism' (Hastings 2009). Other concerns include the enormous power of organisations and corporate lobbying, which, for example, reportedly diluted the outcomes of the 1992 Earth Summit (Bruno 1992).

Given these limitations, neither market forces, nor the government, nor corporations represent perfect vehicles for protecting human rights. In the absence of an ideal instrument, all three are probably required, though better coordination between them may be needed. In a draft report about the right to water, the Institute for Human Rights and Business reasoned:

> It is possible to build a case for corporate responsibility based on the normative notions of morality, ethics, fairness, and non-discrimination. But without legal backing, the commitments do not become concrete. While moral and ethical notions can help clarify, and indeed guide

many companies towards best-practices, they do not address the central problem of lack of access to all. (Institute for Human Rights and Business 2009: 11)

This highlights the need for multiple measures to safeguard human rights. Mintzberg (1983) argued that, despite the challenges, social responsibility was essential for society's survival, and that, if corporations dismissed it, their behaviour would deteriorate to the bare minimum sustained merely by legislation and external pressures. Perhaps the tensions between law, business and society and their ongoing debates will help to ensure that human rights and corporate social responsibility remain a focus of concern for all parties.

Conclusion

Branding provides a means for organisations to engage with their stakeholders and express their position with regard to CSR. Genuine commitment to CSR will be reflected in consistency between the various components of a brand's identity and between its identity and its reputation. Organisations' perspectives on the justification and nature of their social responsibilities should also be evident in the formulation of their brand identity. For example, organisations that view CSR primarily in terms of philanthropy, without considering the ethics of their operations, are likely to consider CSR to be discretionary.

This chapter has examined the tensions between law, business and society in relation to human rights and corporate social responsibility from a marketing perspective. While the issue of discretion permeates the debates, this chapter has argued that: (a) ethical theory suggests that rights (and by extension CSR) are not discretionary, so corporations should behave ethically because it is the right thing to do; (b) corporations can be considered moral agents; (c) CSR is about the ways in which a corporation earns its profits, not just what it does with those profits; and (d) all stakeholders have a role in managing corporate social responsibility.

Notes

1 The term 'organisation' is used to make discussions relevant to as broad a category of formal collective groups as possible. However, the term 'corporation' is used where for-profit businesses are the focus of discussion.

2 OECD member countries: Australia, Austria, Belgium, Canada, the Czech Republic, Denmark, Finland, France, Germany, Greece, Hungary, Iceland, Ireland, Italy, Japan, Korea, Luxembourg, Mexico, the Netherlands, New Zealand, Norway, Poland, Portugal, the Slovak Republic, Spain, Sweden, Switzerland, Turkey, the United Kingdom and the United States.

References

Aaker, D. A. (1991) *Managing Brand Equity. Capitalizing on the value of a brand name*, New York: Free Press.

Abratt, R. (1989) 'A new approach to the corporate image management process', *Journal of Marketing Management*, 5(1): 63–76.

AMA (2007) 'Definition of marketing', available at: www.marketingpower.com/AboutAMA/Pages/DefinitionofMarketing.aspx

Balakrishnan, A. (2008) 'Starbucks wastes millions of litres of water a day', *Guardian*, 6 October, available at: www.guardian.co.uk/uk/2008/oct/06/water.drought

BBC News (2009) 'Woolworths returns as online shop', BBC News, available at: http://news.bbc.co.uk/go/pr/fr/-/1/hi/business/8117433.stm

Berthon, P., J. M. Hulbert and L. F. Pitt (1999) 'Brand management prognostications', *Sloan Management Review*, 40(2): 53–65.

BMW (2009) 'Experience JOY', available at: www.bmw.co.uk/bmwuk/experience/?experienceKey=JOY

Bruno, K. (1992) 'The corporate capture of the Earth Summit', *Multinational Monitor*, 7 (July/August), available at: www.multinationalmonitor.org/hyper/issues/1992/mm0792_07.html

Carroll, A. B. (1991) 'The pyramid of corporate social responsibility: Toward the moral management of organizational stakeholders', *Business Horizons*, 34(4): 39–48.

Chen, S. and P. Bouvain (2009) 'Is corporate responsibility converging? A comparison of corporate responsibility reporting in the USA, UK, Australia and Germany', *Journal of Business Ethics*, 87: 299–317.

Corporate Watch (2006) 'What's wrong with corporate social responsibility?', available at: www.corporatewatch.org.uk/?lid=2670

Cowe, R. (2003) 'Morals maze', *Guardian*, 7 May, available at: www.guardian.co.uk/society/2003/may/07/guardiansocietysupplement7

de Chernatony, L. (1999) 'Brand management through narrowing the gap between brand identity and brand reputation', *Journal of Marketing Management*, 15: 157–79.

de Chernatony, L. and F. Dall'Olmo Riley (1998) 'Defining a "brand": beyond the literature with experts' interpretations', *Journal of Marketing Management*, 14: 417–43.

de Chernatony, L., F. Harris and F. Dall'Olmo Riley (2000) 'Added value: Its nature, roles and sustainability', *European Journal of Marketing*, 34(1/2): 39–56.

de George, R. T. (1993) *Competing with Integrity in International Business*, Oxford: Oxford University Press.

Doyle, P. (1989) 'Building successful brands: The strategic options', *Journal of Marketing Management*, 5(1): 77–95.

Economist (2009) 'Marlboro Country no more', *Economist*, 20 June.

Elkington, J. (1997) *Cannibals with Forks: The triple bottom line of 21st century business*, Oxford: Capstone.

Fairtrade Foundation (2009a) 'FAQs: What is Fairtrade?', available at: www.fairtrade.org.uk/what_is_fairtrade/faqs.aspx

— (2009b) 'The FAIRTRADE Mark', available at: www.fairtrade.org.uk/what_is_fairtrade/fairtrade_

certification_and_the_fairtrade_
mark/the_fairtrade_mark.aspx

Fairtrade Labelling Organizations
International (FLO) (2009)
'Aims of Fairtrade Standards',
available at: www.fairtrade.net/
aims_of_fairtrade_standards.
html

Fombrun, C. and C. van Riel (1997)
'The reputational landscape',
Corporate Reputation Review,
1(1/2): 5–13.

Freeman, R. E. (1984) *Strategic Management: A Stakeholder Approach*,
Boston, MA: Pitman.

— (2008) 'Ending the so-called
"Friedman-Freeman" debate',
Essay II in B. R. Agle, T. Donald-
son, R. E. Freeman, M. C. Jensen,
R. K. Mitchell and D. J. Wood,
'Dialogue: Towards superior
stakeholder theory', *Business
Ethics Quarterly*, 18(2): 153–90.

French, P. A. (1979) 'The corporation
as a moral person', *American
Philosophical Quarterly*, 16(3):
207–15.

— (1995) *Corporate Ethics*, Fort
Worth, TX, Dallas: Harcourt Brace.

Friedman, M. (1962) *Capitalism and
Freedom*, Chicago, IL: University
of Chicago Press.

Gap (2009) 'Social responsibility:
Goals and progress', available
at: www.gapinc.com/GapIncSub-
Sites/csr/Goals/SupplyChain/
SC_Overview.shtml

Goodpaster, K. E. (1987) 'The principle of moral projection', *Journal
of Business Ethics*, 6: 329–32.

Goodpaster, K. E. and J. N. Matthews
(2001) 'Can a corporation have a
conscience?', in W. M. Hoffman,
R. E. Frederick and M. S. Schwartz
(eds), *Business Ethics: Readings
and cases in corporate morality*,
4th edition, New York: McGraw-
Hill.

Goodyear, M. (1996) 'Divided by a
common language: Diversity and
deception in the world of global
marketing', *Journal of the Market
Research Society*, 38(2): 105–21.

Griffin, A. (2008) *New Strategies for
Reputation Management: Gaining
control of issues, crises and corporate social responsibility*, London:
Kogan Page.

Harris, F. (2001) 'Internal factors
affecting brand performance',
PhD thesis, Open University.

Harrison, R., T. Newholm and
D. Shaw (2005) *The Ethical
Consumer*, London: Sage Publica-
tions.

Hastings, G. (2009) 'E. M. Forster
meets the Lambrini girls', profes-
sorial lecture, Open University
Business School, 20 October.

Hastings, G. and J. Liberman (2009)
'Tobacco corporate social responsibility and fairy godmothers:
The Framework Convention on
Tobacco Control slays a modern
myth', *Tobacco Control*, 18(1):
73–4.

Herbig, P. and J. Milewicz (1995)
'The relationship of reputation
and credibility to brand success',
Journal of Consumer Marketing,
12(4): 5–10.

Institute for Human Rights and
Business (2009) *Business,
Human Rights & the Right to
Water: Challenges, Dilemmas
& Opportunities. Roundtable
Consultative Draft Report*,
available at: www.institutehrb.
org/pdf/Draft_Report-Business_
Human_Rights_and_Water.pdf

Kapferer, J. N. (1997) *Strategic
Brand Management. Creating and
sustaining brand equity long term*,
London: Kogan Page.

— (2008) *The New Strategic Brand
Management: Creating and*

sustaining brand equity long term, 4th edition, London: Kogan Page.

Keller, K. L. (1998) *Strategic Brand Management. Building, measuring and managing brand equity*, Upper Saddle River, NJ: Prentice Hall.

King, S. (1991) 'Brand-building in the 1990s', *Journal of Marketing Management*, 7(1): 3–13.

Klein, N. (2000) *No Logo*, London: Flamingo.

Kotler, P. and N. Lee (2005) *Corporate Social Responsibility. Doing the most good for your company and your cause*, Hoboken, NJ: John Wiley & Sons, Inc.

Ladd, J. (1970) 'Morality and the ideal of rationality in formal organisations', quoted as excerpts in T. Donaldson and P. Werhane (eds) (1988) *Ethical Issues in Business, A Philosophical Approach*, New Jersey: Prentice Hall.

Lury, G. (1998) 'Beware the brand-watchers', *Marketing*, 15 October.

Maak, T. (2008) 'Undivided corporate responsibility: Towards a theory of corporate integrity', *Journal of Business Ethics*, 82: 353–68.

Macrae, C. (1999) 'Brand reality editorial', *Journal of Marketing Management*, 15: 1–24.

Margaritis, W. (2000) 'Reputation management at FedEx', *Corporate Reputation Review*, 3(1): 61–7.

Marsden, C. (2001) 'Making a positive impact on society', in *Corporate Social Responsibility: Partners for progress*, Paris: OECD Publications.

Mintzberg, H. (1983) 'The case for corporate social responsibility', *Journal of Business Strategy*, 4(2): 3–15.

Mitchell, A. (1994) 'In good company', *Marketing*, 3 March: 22–4.

Moore, G. (1999) 'Corporate moral agency: Review and implications', *Journal of Business Ethics*, 21: 329–43.

Morsing, M., M. Schultz and K. U. Nielsen (2008) 'The "Catch 22" of communicating CSR: Findings from a Danish study', *Journal of Marketing Communications*, 14(2): 97–111.

Nike (2009) 'Nike responsibility', available at: www.nikebiz.com/responsibility/

OECD (2008) *OECD Guidelines for Multinational Enterprises*, available at: www.oecd.org/dataoecd/56/36/1922428.pdf

— (2009) 'About OECD', available at: www.oecd.org/pages/0,3417,en_ 36734052_ 36734103_1_1_1_1_1,00.html

Olins, W. (1989) *Corporate Identity. Making business strategy visible through design*, London: Thames and Hudson.

Paine, L. S. (1999) 'Law, ethics and managerial judgement', in R. E. Frederick (ed.), *A Companion to Business Ethics*, Oxford: Blackwell.

ReclaimDemocracy.org (2007) 'Kasky vs. Nike: Just the facts', available at: www.reclaimdemocracy.org/nike/kasky_nike_justfacts.html

Schwartz, M. S. and A. B. Carroll (2003) 'Corporate social responsibility: A three-domain approach', *Business Ethics Quarterly*, 13(4): 503–30.

Sheridan, M. (2009) 'Blowpipes thwart Borneo's biofuel kings', *Sunday Times*, 30 August.

Smith, N. C. (2003) 'Corporate social responsibility: whether or how?' *California Management Review*, 45(4): 52–76.

Source Watch (2009a) 'Welcome to Source Watch', available at: www.sourcewatch.org/index.php?title=SourceWatch

— (2009b) 'Unocal', available at: www.sourcewatch.org/wiki. phtml?title=Unocal

Stock, M. (2008) 'Pure TV brilliance from Amnesty International', *Marketing*, 26 November.

Ulrich, P. (2008) *Integrative Economic Ethics. Foundations of a civilized market economy*, Cambridge: Cambridge University Press.

Velasquez, M. G. (1985) 'Why corporations are not morally responsible for anything they do', in J. R. Desjardins and J. J. McCall (eds), *Contemporary Issues in Business Ethics*, California: Wadsworth.

VPSHR (2000) 'Voluntary Principles on Security and Human Rights', available at: www.voluntary principles.org/files/vp_fact_sheet. pdf

Wettstein, F. (2009) 'Beyond voluntariness, beyond CSR: Making a case for human rights and justice', *Business and Society Review*, 114(1): 125–52.

Wood, D. J. (1991) 'Corporate social performance revisited', *Academy of Management Review*, 16(4): 691–718.

4 | Transforming labour standards into labour rights

PIYA PANGSAPA AND MARK J. SMITH

Introduction

> If a business cannot afford to be ethical ... then they cannot afford to be in business. (Neil Kearney, the late General Secretary of the International Textile, Garment and Leather Workers' Federation)

The economic growth rates of developed and rapidly developing countries since the 1980s have, to a large degree, been a result of a global sweatshop economy. As transnational companies seek to maximise profits, competitiveness and market share (sometimes with artificial cost cuts), so suppliers are compelled to offer them the lowest possible price. Besides the pressures to keep wage costs low, there are questions about working hours, improving working conditions, the right to organise and strike, as well as health and safety in the workplace. In the global recession that started in 2008, there has been even more pressure to keep costs low, in order to maintain the low prices of goods purchased in the developed world. As this process has accelerated, and a greater share of the human population has been drawn into waged labour, so the call to transform labour standards into labour rights has become even more urgent and necessary. The argument developed here is that labour rights should be central to business ethics. Labour advocates and labour organisations feel that independent monitoring and verification of factories can only be effective if codes of responsible conduct are properly implemented, and that some kind of process must be initiated at the level of the supplier. This has proved to be difficult in practice because of certain restrictions imposed by the outsourcing company on the suppliers and the confidentiality of internal surveys. As a result, it is common practice in many factories (for instance, in China, India and Thailand) to falsify their records (Lee 2007).

Workers also explain that, if they tell labour inspectors what conditions are really like, the factory would risk losing orders and so they would be out of a job. At the same time, workers say that company inspectors are actually concerned about product quality, rather than the working conditions of the labourers. The retailers argue that the consumer would not pay the extra cost of the goods they purchase if wage levels were raised in countries at the end of the global chains. The factory owners, who need the work orders to stay in business, argue that they are forced to accept such low prices from the wholesalers, which is why they cannot afford to pay workers higher wages. The suppliers and wholesalers themselves have to negotiate with the companies that often have the advantage in setting the prices, which is why they try to achieve the best possible deal from the supplier. At the same time, managers from European and North American companies are unable to make the connection between low wages and workers' willingness to work overtime. Everyone blames the respective government for not enforcing labour regulations and for not punishing companies that violate the law.

The idea of corporate responsibility has had some concrete effects, but much depends on the willingness of a company to develop robust codes of conduct and to monitor its own activities and those of its subsidiaries, as well as contracted outsourced manufacturers and suppliers. To address this, we first need to examine the debates over labour standards and labour rights.

Understanding labour standards

The general debate on international labour standards (ILS) centres on whether there should be a universal set of standards that can be enforced (Basu et al. 2003; Heintz 2007; Dehejia and Samy 2002; Chau and Kanbur 2001; Flanagan and Gould 2003; Fields 2003) and on the differential effects of universal legislation on labour standards in different countries. According to Engerman, the argument for imposing ILS has been to protect those who are, either legally or economically, unable to protect themselves (Engerman 2003: 11).

Opponents of ILS argue that their implementation or imposition harms poor countries, since the competitive advantage of developing countries lies in low wage production (Heintz 2007). In addition, ILS are seen by many governments in developing countries as a form of disguised protectionism on the part of the rich nations (Dehejia and Samy 2002). At the same time, 'proponents of the idea of ILS point to the dangers of ... the "race to the bottom" and thus, in the absence of cooperation, individual countries cannot raise international standards without jeopardising production and employment' (Heintz 2007: 65). In effect, Engerman (2003) points out that labour standards can be divided broadly into three categories:

1 rules concerning wages, working hours and overtime rates;
2 rules dictating acceptable work conditions; and
3 rules that specify the arrangements and relations between employer and employee.

While trade sanctions have been suggested as a way of enforcing compliance with ILS, these are unlikely to affect the responsible actors, and the higher costs involved would run counter to World Trade Organization (WTO) rules.

Dehejia and Samy (2002) highlight a 1996 OECD study which found 'no evidence that countries with low labour standards achieved a better performance than countries with high labour standards'. This implies that the concerns developing countries have that ILS will adversely impact their comparative advantage are unfounded. More realistic indicators of labour standards, Dehejia and Samy suggest, are the existence of civil liberties in general and the degree of unionisation, as well as surveys on working hours and leave. They conclude that labour standards are best seen as

> ultimately a matter of domestic policy choice, and comparative advantage is enhanced by diversity of standards, not by an artificial harmonization or 'straitjacketing' of countries into a particular country's favoured standard. (ibid.: 33)

Flanagan takes a similar stance, pointing out that 'ratification is driven by a country's dominant social values and the pre-existing levels of labour rights and conditions'. As such, ratification does not lead to improvements in domestic labour policies, and therefore the 'link between trade and total ratifications does not translate into improved labour rights and working conditions' (Flanagan 2003: 47). Fields also states that developing countries have different standards, and that changes should be country specific (Fields 2003: 73–4), while Cleveland (2003) highlights the lack of political will and inadequate enforcement mechanisms that characterise many societies.

When examining voluntary codes of conduct and certification procedures, Posner and Nolan (2003: 209–10) argue that companies prefer to adopt those that 'require compliance with national laws and argue that applying human rights norms are not their business'. More positively, for Chau and Kanbur (2001: 146), ratifying these conventions is not random and meaningless, for the 'evidence suggests that, on average, countries think about ratification, balance the costs and benefits, and, when they ratify, they have higher standards than when they do not'. In addition, Kaufmann (2007) focuses on the lack of a clear legal framework for labour standards or rights in the context of international economic institutions, and in particular on the fact that the standards are not framed as legally binding instruments, but rather as soft law or expert advice. Similarly, Lee (1997) argues that:

> the ultimate guarantee of the full observance of [core labour standards] is the political will to achieve this on the part of all countries, reflected in actual policies and programmes. Thus the strengthening of the institutional mechanisms at the international level for bringing this about must remain an overriding objective.

Heintz argues that ILS can indeed help workers 'only if they are appropriately designed, implemented, and enforced'. He further suggests that we need to recognise the 'potential negative impacts of higher labour costs on employment ... the institutional context in which global production is organised, and to design policies and strategies that take these factors into account' (Heintz 2007: 66–7).

Labour standards and labour rights

One of the problems in this area is the tendency to treat labour rights and labour standards as synonymous. This is largely a result of campaign activities: when unions and NGOs ask governments to address the activities of a company, they tend to use the rhetoric of 'rights discourse' – for example, that a reduction in pay or redundancy without fair compensation is a violation of the rights of workers. This gives the claim more force, regardless of whether such actions are subject to legal adjudication and enforcement in the country in question. The discussion of labour standards tends to be more broadly applied when exploring the treatment of working people across national boundaries (or regional boundaries if we consider the European Union). Yet even here, there is a tendency to conflate standards and rights. The variability of national regulations on labour – and even on the definition of such key terms as 'forced labour' or 'child labour' – adds to the confusion, as does the description of minimum wages in medium-sized and large-scale enterprises in the US Fair Labor Standards Act 1938 (and in subsequent amendments, Acts 1996, 2007). Yet just as it is important to highlight duties and obligations, so it is also important to develop some conceptual clarity here.

If we consider the definition of labour standards adopted by the OECD (following the ILO), then international labour standards embrace numerous aspects of labour markets, ranging from minimum wages

Box 4.1 What are international labour standards?

International labour standards are legal instruments drawn up by the ILO's constituents (governments, employers and workers) setting out basic principles and rights at work. They are either *conventions*, which are legally binding international treaties that may be ratified by member states, or *recommendations*, which serve as non-binding guidelines. In many cases, a convention lays down the basic principles to be implemented by ratifying countries, while a related recommendation supplements the convention by providing more detailed guidelines on how it could be applied. Recommendations can also be autonomous, i.e. not linked to any convention (ILO 2009: 14).

'A set of worker rights provided and enforced by national governments of different countries, the levels of which are both a reflection of these countries' preferences and the extent to which they comply with international conventions (from the International Labour Organization) which they have signed. The level of labour standards chosen by a particular country is ultimately a function of that country's level of economic development, and is therefore a domestic policy choice which means that one should expect diversity in labour standards as the norm ... Theoretically, it establishes the conditions under which and the reasons why countries might opt for a given level of labour standards that go beyond just the concern for human rights' (Dehejia and Samy 2002: 2–3).

and equal pay to health and safety regulations. These standards can be classified into six main categories:

1 respect for fundamental human rights;
2 protection of wages;
3 employment security;
4 working conditions;
5 labour market and social policies; and
6 industrial relations.

According to this definition, ILS are merely guidelines that are non-binding and that may be changed at any time. They are often seen as loose commitments that are almost aspirational, rather than as mandatory requirements. Since employers are not compelled to abide by these guidelines, they may violate labour standards, and they do not have to change their practices because there is no legal retribution. Labour rights, on the other hand, would involve rights and duties (rather than standards) that entail entitlements and obligations (see Table 4.1). Workers may be entitled to a minimum wage, but this does not guarantee that they will *receive* a minimum wage, as they do not have the right to demand a minimum wage by law. In the UK, for example, workers have the right to expect a minimum wage because it is established in law – they should not be paid less than the minimum wage and they should not be let go indiscriminately.

TABLE 4.1 Responsibility in context

	Capacities to act (enablement)	Liabilities to others (constraint)
Informal	Entitlements	Obligations
Formal	Rights	Duties

Source: Smith and Pangsapa 2008

In practice, however, much depends on the conditions of employment and on the relations between employers and employees in each context. The ILO (a tripartite body representing governments, workers and employers) generates conventions concerned with labour standards at the international level, but also makes recommendations on minimal labour rights regarding free association and organisation, collective bargaining, equal opportunity and treatment, as well as on the prohibition of forced labour. The ILO also provides technical assistance for unions and non-unionised workers worldwide on legal matters, employment policy, health and safety and financial security. We are not proposing that labour standards and rights should be seen as mutually exclusive. We argue that each has a role – in fact, the success of one depends on the effectiveness of the other. When a contractual relationship between employer and employee is subject to statutes that demand compliance and that provide mechanisms for both sides of the relationship to ensure compliance (or to resolve grievances before an agreed and impartial judge), then it is more accurate to talk of the rights and duties of actors. However, rights and duties, as part of a context that can be described as the 'rule of law', do not operate in a social vacuum.

The former British Lord Chancellor Lord Hailsham once described the rule of law as a gigantic confidence trick designed to conceal its delicate character and fragility: it only works as a set of legal principles and through due process if the citizens or subjects that law regulates see the rule of law as authoritative and broadly legitimate. If this becomes questionable, Hailsham argued, the social fabric begins to come apart at the seams. Such an account is a traditional conservative view of law and society, which is bonded together by small platoons of voluntary associations and a legacy of compromises between the different groups in the social hierarchy. Nevertheless, it is a useful pointer to the important role played by cultural context in the interpretation of law and how it is applied.

Many state governments formally subscribe to ILO conventions, but forced labour and various other violations continue to exist (see Table 4.2). So, having clearly defined rights and duties in both developed and developing societies does not guarantee the elimination of exploitative practices such as these, especially where the cultural context sees these kinds of exploitation as either natural or inevitable. As a result, we also need to pay greater attention to those common-sense values of culture that are taken for granted and to their interaction with legally specified rights and duties. The practical application of rights relies on the willingness of actors to claim them, depending on their sense of entitlement to such claims (see Table 4.1). Willingness to claim rights does not automatically imply their practical application. In short, we should distinguish between 'claiming' one's rights and 'exercising' them. The former implies the capacity to act (rights and entitlements), by virtue of possessing knowledge of one's rights and entitlements and choosing to assert/declare them. When we exercise rights, we acquire specific duties and obligations related to each right. For example, the right to free speech entails duties to avoid 'hate speech', discriminatory language or the promotion of acts of terror, as well as duties to avoid slander and libel. In addition, there are obligations to use moderate and civil language and, while we may rightly criticise others, we have an obligation not to walk up to their front door and shout through their letterbox. Liabilities to others are invoked, based on binding constraints on the exercise of those rights, in both formal and informal ways.

Of course, entitlements can exist where rights have not yet been established or where they are unlikely to be applied, providing a key source of motivation (alongside grievances) for workers' movements in poor-governance situations. Similarly, actors can have obligations even when duties have not formed or where they are not enforced. The undertakings made by companies as part of their commitments to corporate responsibility are often better understood as obligations,

TABLE 4.2 Human rights and labour standards violations today

Type	Definition	Countries
Slavery	Physical abduction followed by forced labour	Congo, Liberia, Mauritania, Sierra Leone, Sudan
Farm and rural debt bondage	When workers see all their wages go to paying for transportation, food and shelter because they've been 'locked into debt' by unscrupulous job recruiters and landowners – and they can't leave because of force, threats or the remote location of the worksites.	Benin, Bolivia, Brazil, Côte d'Ivoire, Dominican Republic, Guatemala, Haiti, Mexico, Paraguay, Peru, Togo
Bonded labour	Another form of debt bondage, it often starts with the worker agreeing to provide labour in exchange for a loan, but quickly develops into bondage as the employer adds more and more 'debt' to the bargain.	Bangladesh, India, Nepal, Pakistan, Sri Lanka
People trafficking	When individuals are forced or tricked into going somewhere by someone who will profit from selling them or forcing them to work against their will, most often in sexual trades. Many countries are both 'origins' and 'destinations' for victims.	Albania, Belarus, Bosnia and Herzegovina, Brazil, China, Colombia, Côte d'Ivoire, Czech Republic, Dominican Republic, Ecuador, France, Ghana, Haiti, Honduras, Hungary, Israel, Italy, Republic of Korea, Laos, Latvia, Malaysia, Moldova, Myanmar, the Netherlands, Nepal, Nigeria, Philippines, Poland, Romania, Russia, Thailand, Ukraine, United Kingdom, United States, Vietnam, Yugoslavia
Abuse of domestic workers	When maids and other domestic servants are sold to their employers or bonded to them by debts.	Benin, Côte d'Ivoire, France, Haiti, throughout the Middle East
Prison labour	The contracting out of prison labour or forcing of prisoners to work for profit-making enterprises.	Australia, Austria, China, Côte d'Ivoire, France, Germany, New Zealand, Madagascar, Malaysia, United States
Compulsory work	When people are required by law to work on public construction projects such as roads and bridges.	Cambodia, the Central African Republic, Kenya, Myanmar Sierra Leone, Swaziland, Tanzania, Vietnam
Military labour	When civilians are forced to do work for government authorities or the military.	Myanmar

Source: http://www.usatoday.com/news/world/2001-05-25-labor-chart-usat.htm

rather than as a matter of duty. In some contexts, obligations can become formalised as duties. Consider the right to free speech again. If citizens using this right ignore their obligations, as in the case of hate speech, it is likely that formal duties will be established to proscribe such forms of expression.

Similarly, the twentieth century is littered with examples of enterprises ignoring the health and environmental effects of their activities on their employees and local communities. As a result, both public and private organisations now have duties related to such practices. For example, in the EU, companies have a 'duty of care' for managing the waste products that result from their activities, and a strict regulatory regime ensures that corporate actors comply with this (or face legal penalties for environmental crime). In developing societies, even though environmental protection legislation exists, it does not always carry the same implications for companies, and in many cases it is the outsourced manufacturers that are seen as directly responsible for waste management. Much then depends on whether corporate executives have developed a sense of obligation for the conditions of work in outsourced manufacturers and for the effects of these activities on such other constituencies as local communities or the environment.

The case for labour rights

The establishment of 'labour rights' requires independent third-party inspection and enforcement powers exercised by local, national and transnational political authorities, in conjunction with international and local labour organisations acting as stakeholders in the political and legal processes. The growth of labour standard violations in the global supply chain highlights a significant drawback when considering the effectiveness of union local campaigns and civic engagement (even where transnational activism is proving to be effective, for example, the Clean Clothes Campaign and US Students against Sweatshops). While human rights have a longer and more established history (intergovernmental bodies take seriously the issues that arise over human rights violations), ILS are much more difficult to monitor and enforce. When governments and private corporations seek to ensure labour standards, they tend to regard them as minimal requirements on conditions, safety and wage levels. In addition, the codes of responsible conduct adopted by corporations vary a great deal, and there remains considerable flexibility in the interpretation of labour standards within the terms of the UN Global Compact and the established practices of transnational, outsourced and subcontracting companies.

When workers succeed in being recognised through unions, the success is often short-lived, for soon afterwards production is relocated so that outsourced manufacturers can employ non-unionised workers. Some transnational brand companies quickly distance themselves from these violations by cutting loose client manufacturers in developing societies and seeking advantageous market conditions elsewhere, thus shifting their responsibilities to outsourced companies.

The purpose of campaigns such as that undertaken by the Gina Bra workers in Thailand was to improve wages and conditions – not to leave all those involved unemployed and have production transferred by the Clover Group to South China. Manufacturing companies in developing societies (including intra-regional developing-country firms) are forced to keep costs low while, at the same time, they must appear to live up to the codes of the brand corporations. This generates false accounting to conceal child labour, actual wage levels, long overtime hours and poor conditions. As a result of these underlying pressures, while monitoring and auditing systems have been developed, they are often partial and ineffective. Weak and compromised social and environmental auditing keeps workers in sweatshops and continues bad practices in terms of health and safety for both employees and local communities. It also encourages companies to employ one of the most vulnerable groups – migrant labour (simply because stateless migrants have few, if any, citizenship rights in many countries).

Presently, the international system endorses labour standards, but not labour rights (in the same sense as human rights). Standards do not have the same moral and political force as rights. In many developing countries, especially those with significant sweatshop economies (often under the guise of special economic zones, free trade zones or development zones), rights may be expressed constitutionally, but are frequently ignored. Rights need to be more than empty-shell statements; they require vigilance and the capacity to act or make claims. These may include commitments to a minimum wage, limits on working hours, child labour and other protection against exploitation. The issue here is how labour standards can be hardened into something that requires people to act, and that requires employers to have duties to their workers. How can a 'duty of care' be formalised? A key to this development is a greater awareness of the importance of obligations within the global supply chain, so that rights are established, thus carrying corresponding duties on actors not to inflict harm (Smith and Pangsapa 2008).

Due to the ability of companies to move where they want and when they want, nationally legislated labour rights, so far as they exist, are treated as if they were guidelines, whereas international statements on labour standards are often a way of avoiding the issue. Labour standards are informally binding arrangements, not formally binding contracts where failure to fulfil duties can be remedied through the due process of law. In other words, the central question is how can we formalise what is informal? Approaching the issue in this way provides an impetus for forward thinking and action.

Governments argue that they cannot enforce labour rights because companies will move elsewhere. At the same time, companies argue that this is the responsibility of the state and they can only do so much. In the end, labour rights are ignored and labour standards are frequently breached, especially when outsourced manufacturers subcontract to other developing-country firms (Pangsapa and Smith 2008). There has to be a compact between states and transnational companies to take labour rights seriously. If labour rights are formally expected and properly enforced, then workers know they can expect to be treated fairly by an impartial judge in any dispute with employers. In Thailand, migrant workers successfully demanded their rights using national legislation, providing a good example of embryonic labour rights in a developing country. This does not imply that exploitation would go away if companies started to make a serious effort to respect rights and fulfil duties, but having such mechanisms in place would make it more difficult (and costly) for companies if they do not live up to their commitments.

Transnational movements for change

This section explores some of the most prevalent violations of labour standards in the global supply chain and looks at evidence to promote both labour standards and rights. These violations exist throughout the developing world, as well as many in industrial sectors in developed societies (interestingly these tend to be most evident where migrants from developing countries provide the labour power). We associate labour exploitation in the production of Western consumer goods with factories in Asia – since most goods are 'Made in China'. However, even sub-Saharan Africa is not immune. One recent research report on outsourcing to Africa suggests: 'foreign investors have been able to circumvent local labour laws, as well as internationally agreed labour standards as a result of trade agreements and incentive programmes offered by the host country' (De Haan and Vander Stichele 2007: 55).

De Haan and Vander Stichele cite cases where serious labour infringements in factories have only been brought to light after local unions collaborated with international labour advocacy organisations (for example, in the case of Nien Hsing, a Taiwanese supplier of denim to such major brand-name companies as Calvin Klein, DKNY, Tommy Hilfiger, Nautica, Mudd Jeans and Gap). Similarly, a factory in Lesotho was investigated by SOMO (a Dutch non-profit research and advisory bureau) and the Trade Union Research Project (TURP) in 2001/02. The garment industry trade union LECAWU worked with other advocacy groups, including the Clean Clothes Campaign, Maquila Solidarity Network and the African office of the International Textile, Garment and Leather Workers' Federation (ITGLWF), to improve working conditions and get the union recognised. The Ethical Trading Action Group (ETAG) in Canada pressured the Hudson's Bay Company, a known buyer of Nien Hsing garments. Campaigning efforts were also targeted at Gap, which was urged to pressure Nien Hsing to improve working conditions. Instead of persuading it to use its influence to improve conditions, these actions led the Hudson's Bay Company to stop sourcing from the factories in question. Gap, on the other hand, started to work with its supplier, and kept the campaigning coalition updated on progress (ibid.: 47–8).

A mixture of labour standards and human rights violations were also documented at Asian-owned factories in Swaziland, including forced overtime, verbal abuse, sexual intimidation, unhealthy and unsafe conditions, unreasonable production targets and anti-union repression. 'In 2001, when asked about their influence, the Department of Labour in Swaziland admitted that in an attempt to keep investors happy it did not pursue labour law violations to its fullest ability' (ibid.: 55). The Kenya Human Rights Commission's (KHRC) Labour Rights Project believes that business must be fundamentally ethical in its treatment of host communities (KHRC 2009). As an advocate for workers' rights, the KHRC mounted a campaign against the fruit producer Del Monte's corporate human rights abuses. This pilot project demonstrated how workers at the end of the global supply chain can make alliances with consumers at the top of the chain to uncover and make public human rights violations of workers (including the death of a worker who was denied first aid at the company clinic). Gross violations and abuses of the workers at the factory were reported by the KHRC's Monitoring and Research Programme, which prompted other Kenyan civil organisations to join in the campaign as well. The Del Monte case in Kenya is an example of effective campaigning achieved through the involvement of workers, local and international civil society, local enterprises and consumers (ibid.).

In Latin America, the problem in many countries is 'noncompliance with labour legislation and ineffective enforcement by government authorities' (Cook 2006: 46). Countries in the region have generally seen a weakening of employment protection during periods of economic reform (ibid.: 54). As Cook explains: 'not all labor protections are necessarily labor *rights*' in the Latin American context. This is a crucial distinction, 'because some labor provisions defended by unions may not be related to labor rights at all and in fact may even restrict the rights of other workers' (ibid.: 40). We also need to bear in mind the flexible nature of labour legislation in Latin America on issues like working hours and overtime (ibid.: 50). Cook also notes that it is important to distinguish between individual employment law and collective labour law, as these correspond to the different aims of Latin American governments, and also between labour legislation in the public and the private sectors, since a separate statute governs public-sector employees in most Latin American countries (ibid.: 39).

In the Dominican Republic, gross violations of labour rights are widespread across different sectors: Haitian migrant workers are targeted on sugar and coffee plantations; child labour is used on family farms and in the sex and tourism trade; and sweatshop labour is exploited in the textile, clothing and footwear factories, where workers are prohibited from organising (Shrank 2006: 4–5). A Human Rights Watch report on El Salvador documents serious violations of workers' human rights, including delays in paying wages, failure to pay overtime, denial of mandatory bonuses and vacation payments, taking workers' social security contributions (thus preventing workers from receiving health care) and egregious tactics that violate workers' right to freedom of association. The report states that the few protections that do exist are barely enforced, and with only thirty-seven labour inspectors covering a workforce of roughly 2.6 million, monitoring and enforcement is difficult. Moreover, labour law violations are sometimes committed by employers in collaboration with state authorities. Workers who seek redress through the country's labour courts face a long drawn-out process (Human Rights Watch 2003).

Similarly, in Guatemala, the international women's human rights organisation MADRE reports that labour laws are rarely enforced in the hundreds of sweatshop factories around Guatemala City, where women assemblers are abused, sexually harassed and suffer long-term health problems, and where those who attempt to organise often risk their lives. Labour rights in Mexico are regulated by the Federal Labour Law, which establishes minimum rights and obligations for workers and employers, such as provisions on wages, working hours, rest days, holidays, vacation and social security (Diaz 2009). Throughout Central America, the forty-eight-hour week is typical.

In the economic powerhouse of the twenty-first century, the same issues are manifest. On 1 January 2008, the Chinese government passed into law new protective workplace legislation that requires all employers to comply with minimum wage and safety regulations in written employment contracts (Jackson 2007; Canaves 2009). The new law, which, among other protective measures, places more stringent regulations on working hours, wages and working conditions, 'gives legal protection to a vast majority of workers who had no way to protect their rights under the old system' and is especially significant for the 130 million migrants who have long endured the widespread abuse and exploitation 'endemic in boom-time China' (Kahn and Barboza 2007). But even with stricter protective measures in place, workers' legal rights may not be enforced by local governments that also 'lack power to influence factory owners' (Jackson 2007).

So at issue is whether the Chinese government will be able to provide adequate enforcement of the new law, especially when there was no enforcement of the regulations already in place (ibid.). The 1995 labour law limited the working week to forty hours and overtime to thirty-six hours per month, but in reality the majority of workers put in 130 to 140 hours per week, getting little sleep and no breaks. As *Ethical Corporation* magazine notes, 'the Chinese see human rights as subordinate to economic development, and not something in which external interference is appreciated' (Blyth 2004). But increasingly, as a response to effective public campaigning, major multinational companies (like Nike, Adidas or Gap) that take codes of conduct seriously will look to suppliers that are prepared to comply with the new legislation. In any event, passage of the new law has resulted in a remarkable surge in labour arbitration and dispute cases in migrant-dominant manufacturing hubs, such as Guangdong province's Pearl River Delta (Pomfret 2009). The local arbitration office in the city of Guangzhou, for example, received more than 60,000 grievances from January through November 2008 – 'about as many as it handled over the previous two years combined' (ibid.). Companies fear that the new law will increase the cost of doing business in China, but recent factory closures have been prompted not by the new regulations, but by the global economic downturn. Over 15,000 factories in Guangdong province shut down their operations in the first ten months of 2008, leaving millions of workers out of work and without compensation (Canaves 2009). A common scenario is illustrated by the following:

After their factory closed last month, workers from the Shatangbu Yifa Rubber & Hardware Factory in Shenzhen filed for the back pay and severance promised under a contract required by the new law. The Hong Kong-based owner disappeared, according to Shenzhen officials. That left many migrant workers stranded without enough money to return to their hometowns hundreds of miles away. About a third of the factory's 300 workers went to the Shenzhen government to request a speedy resolution of their case. 'We are aware of our rights, but we don't have enough time to go to court. We just want to get paid and go home before the holiday,' said one worker, referring to the Lunar New Year celebration. (ibid.)

Similarly, in Southeast Asia, the governments of Thailand, Cambodia and Vietnam all have labour legislation in place – the Thai Labour Protection Act of 1998, the Cambodian Labour Law for the Garment Industry, the Labour Code of the Socialist Republic of Vietnam 1994 – but lack of enforcement means that Thai law, for example, does not adequately protect workers' labour rights. Women workers are often forced to work overtime hours for which they are paid 20 cents an hour (with the usual shift being eight hours) although current minimum pay rates per day have now reached US$6 in Bangkok (which is still less than the minimum rate *per hour* for UK workers). In one specific case, women from a factory discovered during their lunch break that the overtime wages they were making were lower than the wages other women doing comparable work were receiving at other factories nearby. This was the first time the workers realised they actually had rights under law, and they set out to claim them (Pangsapa 2007).

Despite these low rates, textile and garment factories have increasingly relocated to special economic zones in border towns in north-eastern Thailand. In such contexts, they produce ready-made apparel for brand-name companies through outsourcing arrangements, by hiring migrant workers, mainly from neighbouring Burma/Myanmar, at typically less than half the daily rate of pay in Bangkok. These migrant workers in Thailand are also usually employed throughout the country in low-paying occupations, commonly described as '3-D jobs' (dangerous, dirty and difficult). Both documented and undocumented migrant workers remain unprotected, due primarily to the lack of concrete measures to monitor, implement and enforce laws regarding working and living conditions. Migrant workers in all sectors face common problems: low wages; harmful working conditions and poor living conditions; discrimination and harassment; and lack of access to basic provisions, such as medical care and legal assistance. Pregnancy provides grounds for deportation (Pang-sapa 2009). Even if more effective forms of monitoring and compliance are established in factory production, for many of the most vulnerable workers (such as stateless migrants who work in smaller units, often for subcontractors) neither national legislation nor codes of responsible conduct are likely to make a significant difference. This paints a fairly bleak picture, but there is some hope that the ILO is making progress on integrating ILS with labour rights at the national level.

The ILO and the Cambodian experiment

The ILO is one of the oldest international organisations, founded in 1919, based on the belief that universal, lasting peace depends on the decent treatment of working people. As Murray (2002: 36) puts it:

> [The] ILO was created to bolster the regulatory role of states by help-ing them to ensure that workers were not exploited through the unre-strained power of capital, and to protect society as a whole from the upheaval of worker revolution in response to such conditions.

The ILO's mission is, therefore, rooted in the promotion of social justice and internationally recognised human rights and labour rights, and it is the international body responsible for drawing up and oversee-ing international labour standards. Working with its member states, it tries to ensure that labour standards are respected in practice as well as in principle. Within all three bodies of the ILO – the International Labour Conference, the Governing Body and the International Labour Office – government representatives, employers and workers are brought together to shape policies and programmes. In the ILO's eight conven-tions there are four fundamental principles relating to labour rights at work:

- freedom of association and the effective recognition of the right to collective bargaining;
- the elimination of all forms of forced or compulsory labour;
- the effective abolition of child labour; and
- the elimination of discrimination in respect of employment and occupation.

It also monitors other key issues in relation to labour standards, such as employment security, wages, working hours, maternity protection, occupational health and safety, and labour inspection. On the positive side, with 182 member states, the ILO is the international community's main arbiter on labour issues, and it promotes social dialogue among governments, employers and workers in the establishment and implementation of important policies that guide labour legislation. The ILO also provides technical assistance to over eighty countries, with more than a thousand programmes on labour law reform, labour administration and dispute settlement, collective bargaining and organising, and awareness-raising. Even in the case of Burma, the ILO reached an understanding with the Burmese government that would enable victims of forced labour to seek redress by filing complaints with ILO officials in Rangoon (Pangsapa 2009). The organisation also plays an essential role in conducting research and analysis on labour issues, generating reports, specialised studies, periodicals, magazines and journals. The ILO's magazine *World of Work*, for instance, addresses such key gender issues as maternity protection, education and balancing work and family. Its recommendations on childcare, child trafficking, violence in the workplace and an ageing workforce have been incorporated into policy in many contexts.

In Cambodia, the ILO is more directly involved in a unique experiment in developing countries as part of the Better Factories Cambodia (BFC) programme, which is aimed at improving working conditions in the garment industry. The BFC involves independent monitoring, with the coordination of management, stakeholders, international buyers and international and domestic labour organisations. The programme has developed an information management system (IMS) that enables it to automatically generate reports for individual factories, indicating current compliance, documenting progress over time and making recommendations for improvement. This means that information about factory practices is available to the companies that make outsourcing decisions. As Kolben (2006) notes, 'buyers would evaluate companies and make sourcing decisions based in part on the information generated by the ILO. Indeed, some would not do business in a factory that had not been inspected.'

What is particularly novel about this model is that it combines the state-focused, public law approach of a trade agreement with a mechanism that generates information for the market for labour rights-compliant garments. The project has been so successful in the view of Cambodia's government, unions and garment manufacturers that it has garnered funding from the World Bank to continue a monitoring initiative as a means of improving its competitive advantage after the Multi-Fibre Agreement (MFA) (Kolben 2006: 258–9). Companies that subscribe to the IMS in Cambodia include Gap, H&M and Nike. This project has been effective because any factory in Cambodia that wishes to obtain an export licence is required to participate in the programme (so the programme excludes many smaller subcontract factories). Based on three or four consecutive visits to twenty-six participating factories, the ILO monitoring team found no evidence of forced labour, discrimination or child labour, but did report problems pertaining to wages, overtime work, freedom of association, lawful strike action and occupational health and safety. At the same time, international buyers concerned about working conditions often use the ILO reports to help them monitor (not enforce) compliance with labour standards in their supply chains. Cambodia shows a combination of transnational corporations and developing-country firms playing different roles in outsourcing production, yet progressing towards compliance with labour standards. In Cambodia, at least, there is evidence of more participation and effective monitoring on behalf of companies and the state in partnership, despite the lack of a fully fledged civil society.

However, while ILO conventions are designed to place obligations on states (Murray 2002: 33), governments are also obliged to maintain their competitive edge in a rapidly globalising economy. This has limited the ILO's success in persuading them to adopt regulatory powers over workers' rights. From the perspective of the ILO, cross-border migration (such as that of Cambodian migrants in Thailand) is seen as beneficial to Cambodians and investors, because migration helps to generate employment in a given region, despite the failure to address labour standards. This standpoint is best captured in the ILO's Decent Work for All agenda. The ILO's Asia Pacific members have pledged a commitment to the Asian Decent Work Decade (2006–15) – an agenda that has more to do with increasing employment opportunities (which complements state development policies) than it has with ensuring decent conditions for workers.

Of the five regional priority areas set out in the Asian Decent Work Decade agenda, only one area (protecting migrant workers) is concerned with social protection. Another long-standing criticism of the ILO is its lack of power to enforce its conventions, even though there are mechanisms in place to pressure countries to abide by the ratified conventions (such as the Committee of Experts on the Application of Conventions and Recommendations of the ILS unit that requires member countries to submit detailed reports explaining the measures they have taken). We argue that the organisation's main limitation lies in its ability to transform labour standards into labour rights. The ILO promotes labour standards and can initiate partnership arrangements, but as a UN agency it also needs to maintain its neutrality and does not possess the mandate to enforce labour rights – not even in the Better Factories Cambodia project. This remains the responsibility of state governments, and many remain unwilling to enforce those labour rights that are already on the statute book. One suggestion for addressing this is to establish a 'World Labour Organization' (along the lines of the World Trade Organization). Given the limitations of what the ILO can do in terms of advancing labour rights, we want to stress that, for labour standards to be transformed into labour rights, everyone needs to accept the underlying notion. The broader acceptance of labour rights would also translate the looser obligations of companies into duties that can be enforced. This reality, however, makes it difficult for states (and firms) to live up to the commitment to respect and promote workers' labour and human rights, and much still remains to be done.

Conclusion: from advocacy to partnership

> Much work needs to be done to ensure that corporate social responsibility becomes more than a passing fad and translates into real protection for workers. (Human Rights First n.d.)

The fact that transnational companies have broadly accepted labour standards is absolutely necessary as a first step in the formalisation of labour rights, just as the idea that employers should have obligations towards their workforce is absolutely essential in generating a more formalised duty of care on the part of company decision-makers for all those who work for the company. It is not just a matter of rights; it is also a matter of duties. Otherwise the rights will be undermined and whittled away. In raising awareness among consumers in developed countries about labour standards violations in developing countries, local, regional and international labour advocacy groups have been effective in publicising often shocking stories about the working and living conditions of the women, men and children who 'labour behind the label'. For 'labour rights' to become properly established, however, we need not just binding international agreements, but also legal provisions at other levels. And these require third-party inspection and enforcement powers to be exercised by independent bodies, in conjunction with political authorities, labour organisations and other stakeholders (such as local community bodies) in a judicial process. Successful implementation requires enforcement and attractive incentives (for example export licences) such as we saw in the Cambodian case.

Campaign groups that have been concerned with advocacy now have to shift their *modus operandi* to become partnership organisations willing to collaborate with political authorities and companies and to develop ongoing stakeholder consultation mechanisms. This is already starting to occur. International and regional organisations like the International Textile, Garment and Leather Workers' Federation (ITGLWF) and the Clean Clothes Campaign are umbrella organisations, involved in influencing policy-making, coordinating activities, lobbying and providing technical assistance and training to workers. The ITGLWF is a global umbrella organisation, encompassing 217 national unions of workers in the textile, apparel and leather industries in 110 countries. International coalitions of trade unions have used ILO standards and procedures to assess company practices and to put pressure on governments and companies, and have negotiated sixty framework agreements with transnational private corporations. In Bangladesh, the ITGLWF has cooperated with unions, politicians, NGOs and companies to develop the 'child labour free' RugMark for carpet retailers and wholesalers, as part of the ILO international programme for the elimination of child labour. The ITGLWF also needs to maintain its advocacy role in developed societies, in order to ensure that the import of uncertified rugs is minimised.

The Clean Clothes Campaign (CCC) is a global alliance of trade unions and NGOs in twelve European countries that supports garment workers. It relies on a partner network of more than 200 organisations and unions, and cooperates with labour rights groups in the United States, Canada and Australia. The organisation's Better Bargain project focuses on the policies and practices of major global retailers, such as Wal-Mart, Tesco, Carrefour, Aldi and Lidl – referred to as 'giant' retailers. The CCC has been successful thanks to its urgent appeals system, which reacts to workers' requests by sending out appeals for action through its extensive network. Workers have reported improvements in health and safety standards, and sustained campaigning has prompted many companies to adopt their own codes of conduct – or at least to work towards being more responsible. The CCC regards this as a positive first step in the whole process of abolishing sweatshop conditions in the global garment industry. Beyond these two promising examples, NGO activities vary; but they are united in their commitment to end labour standards violations and improve the conditions of workers in the global clothing industry. The main activities of some NGOs – such as the Fair Labor Association, Worldwide Responsible Accredited Production (WRAP) and the Worker Rights Consortium – involve monitoring and inspecting factories.

While these initiatives adopt a more proactive approach to dealing with labour standards violations through monitoring and inspection activities, other NGOs provide support for workers on the ground, using their well-organised consumer campaigns to lobby governments and put pressure on transnational companies. These include the Campaign for Labor Rights, Labour Behind the Label and Human Rights First.

The Campaign for Labor Rights works to mobilise grassroots activists in alliance with anti-sweatshop struggles around the world, and provides assistance to workers who are trying to organise.

Labour Behind the Label is a group that supports garment workers' efforts around the world. It actively puts pressure on companies and lobbies governments to implement protective worker legislation, and collaborates with other campaigns across Europe. Labour Behind the Label responds to urgent appeals from workers and, as the UK platform for the Clean Clothes Campaign, is currently investigating the impact of Tesco, Asda/Wal-Mart and Sainsbury's (the UK's top three retailers) on workers.

Human Rights First, an international human rights organisation, is committed to pursuing labour rights as human rights. In 2005, Human Rights First testified before the Congressional Human Rights Caucus on corporate responsibility, and in 2006 it testified before the same caucus on human rights and brand accountability, with a focus on how multinationals can promote labour rights. As the Human Rights First website says:

> Enabling consumers to become well-informed about specific company practices – piercing the veil between brand names and a web of abusive contractors and suppliers – creates the kind of market pressure that strongly encourages corporate compliance with international human rights standards in a regular and systematic way. (Human Rights First n.d.)

All these labour advocacy groups are committed to ending labour standards violations and are united on basic fundamental principles concerning a worker's right to earn a living wage, the right to work in a clean and safe environment, and the right to collective bargaining. Compliance with labour standards and accountability have been achieved through effective lobbying and campaigning, as well as through independent third-party inspection and enforcement. All these groups are actively engaged in raising awareness among consumers, and continue to work and to make alliances with international and local labour organisations in their collective effort to end labour rights violations. The range of actors involved in this field highlights the complexity of the problem, for there are various levers that can work to support labour standards and rights. In some cases, this might involve generating bad publicity to damage the intangible assets of a company. In other cases it may involve demands for companies to desist from practices that are harmful to workers, communities and the environment (such as the use of chemicals in manufacturing that have been banned in developed societies). However, to make further progress on labour rights, and to prevent companies from simply moving the problem to another location, advocacy groups are seeking a stakeholder role in company and policy decisions, so that the rules of the game in the global supply chain are changed for good.

References

Basu, K., H. Horn, L. Roman, J. Shapiro (eds) (2003) *International Labor Standards: History, Theory, and Policy Options*, Maldon: Wiley-Blackwell.

Benítez, I. (2007) 'GUATEMALA: Labour rights mean little in maquila factories', *Inter Press Service*, 14 August, available at: http://ipsnews.net/news.asp?idnews=38886

Blyth, A. (2004) 'Corporate responsibility in China – a cross section of business issues and practices', *Ethical Corporation*, 11 March, available at: www.ethicalcorp.com/content.asp?ContentID=1773

Canaves, S. (2009) 'Factory closures strain China's labor law', *Wall Street Journal,* 17 January, available at: http://online.wsj.com/article/SB123215043508192065.html#

Chau, N. H. and R. Kanbur (2001) 'The adoption of international labor standards conventions: Who, when, and why?', in *Brookings Trade Forum*, Washington, DC: The Brookings Institution Press.

Cleveland, S. H. (2003) 'Why international labor standards?', in R. J. Flanagan and W. B. Gould IV (eds), *International Labor Standards: Globalization, trade, and public policy*, Stanford, CA: Stanford University Press.

Cook, M. L. (2006) *The Politics of Labor Reform in Latin America: Between flexibility and rights*, University Park: Pennsylvania State University Press.

De Haan, E. and M. Vander Stichele (2007) *Footloose Investors: Investing in the garment industry in Africa*, Amsterdam: SOMO – Centre for Research on Multinational Corporations.

Dehejia, V. H. and Y. Samy (2002) *Trade and Labour Standards: Theory, new empirical evidence, and policy implcations*, CESifo Working Paper No. 830, CESifo Conference on Globalization, Inequality and Well-Being.

Diaz, F. L. (2009) 'Mexican Labor Law', available at: http://laboris.uqam.ca/babillard/mexlaborlaw.htm

Elliot, K. A. and R. B. Freeman (2003) *Can Labor Standards Improve Under Globalization?*, Washington, DC: Peterson Institute.

Engerman, S. L. (2003) 'The history and political economy of international labor standards', in K. Basu, H. Horn, L. Roman and J. Shapiro (eds), *International Labor Standards: History, theory, and policy options*, Maldon: Wiley-Blackwell.

Fields, G. (2003) 'International labor standards and decent work: Perspectives from the developing world', in R. J. Flanagan and W. B. Gould IV (eds), *International Labor Standards: Globalization, trade, and public policy*, Stanford, CA: Stanford University Press.

Flanagan, R. J. (2003) 'Labor standards and international comparative advantage', in R. J. Flanagan and W. B. Gould IV (eds), *International Labor Standards: Globalization, trade, and public policy*, Stanford, CA: Stanford University Press.

Flanagan, R. J. and W. B. Gould (eds) (2003) *International Labour Standards: Globalization, trade, and public policy*, Stanford, CA: Stanford University Press.

French, P. (2004) 'China is different – companies need to do their homework', *Ethical Corporation*, 5 October, available at: www.ethicalcorp.com/content.asp?ContentID=2882

Gandotra, V. and S. Patel (eds) (2009) *Women, Working Conditions and Efficiency: The Indian experience*, New Delhi: New Century Publications.

Glantz, A. and N. Nguyen (2006) 'Vietnam's labor strife worsens: Series of strikes, protests over pay, working conditions', *Chronicle Foreign Service*, 30 May.

Heintz, J. (2007) 'Rethinking global labor standards: Controversies, constraints, and possibilities', *Good Society*, 16(2).

Human Rights First (n.d.), available at: http://www.humanrightsfirst.org/workers_rights/index.asp

Human Rights Watch (2003) 'Deliberate indifference: El Salvador's failure to protect workers' rights', available at: www.hrw.org/en/reports/2003/12/03/deliberate-indifference

ILO (2005), *A Global Alliance against Forced Labour: Global report under the follow-up to the ILO Declaration on fundamental principles and rights at work*, Geneva: ILO.

— (n.d.) 'Decent work in Asia', available at: http://www.ilo.org/asia/decentwork/lang--en/index.htm

— (2009) *Rules of the Game: A brief introduction to international labour standards*, Geneva: ILO.

Jackson, R. (2007) 'Chinese labour laws – New workplace rules need better policing', *Ethical Corporation*, 3 July, www.ethicalcorp.com/content.asp?ContentID=5204

Kahn, J. and D. Barboza (2007) 'China passes a sweeping labor law', *New York Times*, 30 June, available at: www.nytimes.com/2007/06/30/business/worldbusiness/30chlabor.html

Kaufmann, C. (2007) *Globalization and Labour Rights: The conflict between core labour rights and international economic law*, Oxford: Hart Publishing.

KHRC (Kenyan Human Rights Commission) (2009) 'Labour rights project: A case for corporate social responsibility', available at: www.khrc.or.ke/subsubsection.asp?ID=5

Kinetz, E. (2009) 'Indian textile workers sliding back into poverty', *Associated Press*, 20 June, available at: www.timesdispatch.com/rtd/ lifestyles/health_med_fit/article /I-TEXT0529_ 200906 18-182806/274628/

Kolben, K. (2006) 'The new politics of linkage: India's opposition to the workers' rights clause', *Indiana Journal of Global Legal Studies*, 13(1): 225–59.

Lakshman, N. (2008) 'An industry that's fraying fast', *BusinessWeek*, No. 4066.

Lal, D. (2008) *Reviving the Invisible Hand: The case for classical liberalism in the twenty-first century,* Princeton, NJ: Princeton University Press.

Lee, C. K. (2007) *Against the Law: Labor protests in china's rustbelt and sunbelt*, Berkeley: University of California Press.

Lee, E. (1997) 'Globalization and labour standards: A review of issues', *International Labour Review*, 136(2) (Summer): 173–89.

Locke, R. M., F. Qin and A. Brause (2007) 'Does monitoring improve labor standards? Lessons from Nike', *Industrial & Labor Relations Review*, 61(1).

Lu, J. L. (2009) 'Effect of work intensification and work extensification on women's health in the globalised labour market', *Journal of International Women's Studies*, 10(4): 111–26.

Menona, N. and Y. Rodgers (2009) 'International trade and the gender wage gap: New evidence from India's manufacturing sector', *World Development*, 37(5): 965–81.

Murray, L. (2002) 'Labour rights/corporate responsibilities: The role of ILO labour standards', in R. Jenkins, R. Pearson and G. Seyfang, *Corporate Responsibility and Labour Rights: Code of conduct in the global economy*, London: Earthscan.

Pangsapa, P. (2007) *Textures of Struggle: The emergence of resistance among garment workers in Thailand*, Ithaca, NY and London: ILR/Cornell University Press.

— (2009) 'When battlefields become marketplaces: migrant workers and the role of civil society and NGO activism in Thailand', *International Migration*, 47(4).

Pangsapa, P. and M. J. Smith (2008) 'Political economy of Southeast Asian borderlands: Migration, environment, and developing-country firms', *Journal of Contemporary Asia*, 38(4): 485–514.

Pomfret, J. (2009) 'Chinese labour laws buckle as economy darkens', *Mail & Guardian*, 28 January, www.mg.co.za/article/2009-01-28-chinese-labour-laws-buckle-as-economy-darkens

Posner, M. and J. Nolan (2003) 'Can codes of conduct play a role in promoting workers' rights?', in R. J. Flanagan and W. B. Gould IV (eds), *International Labor Standards: Globalization, trade, and public policy*, Stanford, CA: Stanford University Press.

Scheuerman, W. E. (2001) 'False humanitarianism?: US advocacy of transnational labour protections', *Review of International Political Economy*, 8(3): 359–88.

Shrank, A. (2006) 'Labor standards and human resources: A natural experiment in an unlikely laboratory', Department of Sociology, University of New Mexico, Albuquerque, prepared for 'Observing Trade: Revealing International Trade Networks and Their Impacts', available at: www.princeton.edu/˜ina/gkg/confs/schrank.pdf

Smith, M. J. and P. Pangsapa (2008) *Environment and Citizenship: Integrating justice, responsibility and civic engagement*, London and New York: Zed Books.

5 | Violent corporate crime, corporate social responsibility and human rights

GARY SLAPPER

Introduction

This chapter examines the way in which law can be used to enhance corporate social responsibility and to encourage corporate compliance with human rights principles. A fundamental human right, enshrined in most human rights codes and conventions, is the 'right to life'. In countries that have embedded human rights law into their domestic law, this right is generally enforceable only against *public* or *governmental* authorities or organisations performing public functions. Although some governments are bound by their law or constitutions to uphold human rights through law and its enforcement, commercial companies are not generally governed directly by human rights law. It is, however, arguably very important that the application of the right to life should extend into the commercial world, because more people are killed worldwide by industrial accidents and diseases each year (2.2 million) than are killed in wars (HSE 2004; Takala 2005: 5).

The phrase 'industrial accident' has a sort of dry, obscure quality to it. What we are talking about, however, are human stories in which one day men and women go to work but do not return home, because they have been impaled, burnt alive, electrocuted, crushed by machinery, drowned, buried alive, decapitated, frozen, gouged, suffocated, smashed in high-altitude drops, burnt in acid vats or poisoned by noxious gas. Most of those deaths are completely avoidable.[1]

One important theme and argument of this chapter is that, as human rights laws do not cover most commercial activity directly, and as commercial activity kills so many people each year,[2] criminal laws dealing specifically with corporate crime (as opposed to human rights laws) can help improve the corporate social responsibility of many commercial organisations, and thus endorse human rights realisation.

Although there is a prodigious and rapidly growing literature on 'corporate social responsibility', and although tens of thousands of companies across the world have already adopted corporate social responsibility undertakings, there is no single agreed template or index of the principles or precepts that are at the core of CSR. A company could therefore put in its official documents or on its website a declaration of, say, six key objectives for its corporate social responsibility, and, however odd these choices may appear to some experts in the field, they could not be classified as officially 'wrong' under any single universally adopted code. So company experts, academics and members of the general public could, in fact, quarrel about what are the key objectives within the corporate social responsibility agenda. One principle, however, seems indisputable: in order to be a socially responsible corporation, an organisation must not kill its customers or members of the public either intentionally[3] or through its gross negligence.

Article 2 of the European Convention on Human Rights and Political Freedoms refers to the 'right to life' thus:

> Everyone's right to life shall be protected by law. No one shall be deprived of his life intentionally save in the execution of a sentence of a court following his conviction of a crime for which this penalty is provided by law.

That right is currently incorporated into the national law of many countries. The International Covenant on Civil and Political Rights (ICCPR) is a treaty that was adopted by the United Nations General Assembly in 1966 and came into force from 1976. Part III, Article 6 of the treaty states that:

> Every human being has the inherent right to life. This right shall be protected by law. No one shall be arbitrarily deprived of his life.

As of January 2010, the Covenant had 165 national parties. In the UK, for example, it is incorporated through the Human Rights Act 1998.

If it can be argued that, whatever else might be included in an organisation's corporate social responsibility obligations, as a minimum there must be the undertaking not to negligently endanger life and limb, then the same is true of its ethical obligations. Currently, there are over 2,300 books in English about ethical business,[4] and an enormous range of ideas about what should be included among the core principles of ethical business. One point, though, is incontestable: that a *sine qua non* (an indispensable condition) of ethical business is that its conduct should not subject its customers, members of the public or employees to unwarranted risk of injury or death.

This chapter focuses on corporate crime committed by corporate bodies such as transport companies, engineering companies and construction companies (which all have high death and injury rates), and examines the legal ways in which the issue is being tackled. The British justice system will be used for purposes of illustration. The chapter also utilises some comparative material from other jurisdictions, and examines whether there is a need for a more global legal approach to promoting corporate social responsibility. Securing corporate compliance with the law (even though corporations are not generally public bodies and therefore commonly not within human rights law) is highly desirable and of great social consequence. For example, there are over 2 million companies in the UK, and the way in which they behave affects almost every part of the lives of all citizens.

The global nature of corporate risk-taking

Law within many national jurisdictions is already changing to accommodate both the commercial and the human rights demands for greater international uniformity.[5] Such change has occurred because lawyers in private practice and government service have been educated in a way that allows them to see the world and its legal challenges from international perspectives.

Of the world's hundred largest economic entities, fifty-one are companies and forty-nine are countries (Anderson and Cavanagh 2000; Robbins et al. 2003). This is a world in which the power and reach of large transnational corporations is something that requires the development of a jurisprudence different from that which emerged in an earlier era, with a different landscape of legal subjects.

Historically, in many European countries, medieval regional governance begot the law and governance of regional kingdoms. The principles of modern state sovereignty developed in the seventeenth century in Europe and begot the hegemony of national law, albeit with some concessions to international treaties.[6] Globalisation can and will beget laws that apply on a global basis.[7] It is clear that this immediately raises questions about what one means by 'laws', what transnational enforcement mechanisms are possible and practicable, how such a phenomenon can be made compatible with the autonomy of nation states, and many more similar points. None of those points, however, poses an insuperable obstacle to some form of global law. Comparable objections were made at various stages in the development of European Union law from the 1960s, but European law now has a substantial and demonstrable impact across a European population of over 400 million people in twenty-seven culturally and economically diverse nations.

As corporate globalisation progresses (with hundreds of separate companies each becoming operational across many parts of the world), the effectiveness of individual jurisdictional safeguards against crime, financial malpractice and health and safety dangers becomes severely attenuated, because risk can be simply shifted to the jurisdiction of least resistance. In effect, this means that the most hazardous risks hurt the developing communities – the very countries that are least able to cope with the disasters when they do materialise. There was some evidence, for example, that the defective chemical plant in Bhopal (where over 5,000 people were killed)[8] had been established in India after it had been refused authorisation in Canada.[9]

As was noted in the introduction, globally more people are killed each year (and over generations) at work or through the operation of commerce than are killed annually in wars. The harms that aberrant companies commit have many more victims than do the crimes of individuals. If an individual commits criminal damage, then a window is broken or a wall is sprayed in graffiti. If an individual drives recklessly, then a person or a few people might be killed. By contrast, if a chemical company is run recklessly, then colossal damage is inflicted on the environment; or if a railway company runs an unsafe operation and a major train disaster occurs, hundreds might die.[10] In August 2008, a Spanair jet crashed in Madrid, killing 153 people. It was not, though, an entirely unforeseen event: in the month before the crash, the airline's workers warned management repeatedly that passengers' safety was being put at risk by the 'chaotic' way in which the airline was being run. The Spanish pilots' union SEPLA sent a series of emails to the airline's management, stating that the airline's day-to-day operations were a disaster. In April 2007, in an email to Lars Nygaard, the chief executive of Spanair at the time, a union representative wrote:

> The lack of resources and their quality on the ground, the repeated AOGs [grounded aircraft] in the fleet, the scarcity of crews and the system of movement of crew members mean that the general feeling is one of operational chaos that places the passengers at risk.

The next month the union again wrote to management, saying: 'The operation continues to be a disaster and is getting worse by the day' (Catan 2008).

If a motor company sells unsafe cars, the victims are many and widespread. As the German sociologist Ulrich Beck (1992) has argued, in the modern world, the eventuation of commercial risk (in cases involving things like chemical explosions or pesticides) can injure people across a wide geographical area – and over history, since the harms last for many years.

The law does not, and should not, prohibit all forms of risk-taking. It should, however, encourage corporate decision-makers to get the balance right[11] between excessive caution and excessive imperilment of workers and the public at large. As Lord Justice Asquith said:

> ... if all the trains in this country were restricted to a speed of five miles an hour, there would be fewer accidents, but our national life would be intolerably slowed down. The purpose to be served, if sufficiently important, justifies the assumption of abnormal risk.[12]

In many legal systems (such as the English), exposing someone to an *unjustified* risk will be the basis for a manslaughter charge if death results. Sometimes, of course, we subject ourselves to a *justified* lethal risk, as in surgery or if we work as emergency rescuers; if death results in those sorts of situations, it will not normally be a crime, provided there has been no gross negligence in the surgery or by the emergency service employer. So, part of working out whether a death has resulted from a crime entails looking at why the person doing something dangerous was doing it. The more socially useful and necessary it is to do, the less likely it will be seen as unlawful if death results. Thus, if you throw a piece of concrete from a high-rise car park, there is no possible good that can come from such conduct. It will amount to an unjustified risk, and will thus be indictable as manslaughter if someone is hit and killed. Cutting someone open carries an even greater risk of death, but if the incision is made by a surgeon as part of emergency medical treatment, the conduct can easily be seen as a justified risk.

Beck (ibid.) argues that the social nature of risk has radically changed in our times. Unlike nineteenth-century society, where members of the ruling class lived geographically apart from workers, and where the catastrophes (though often causing great carnage) were limited to 'contained' destruction and injury (poisoned food, factory deaths, etc.), today's risks put huge swathes of the *general population* in peril. Radioactive and chemical disasters like Chernobyl[13] and Bhopal injure, displace or kill thousands of people in the short term – and then, as the atmosphere absorbs and redistributes the poison, another longer wave of deaths occurs. The toxic flow does not discriminate between rich and poor. If poisonous gas clouds contaminate a city, they contaminate both wealthy and impoverished districts. The toxic flow does not respect national boundaries, and nor does it evaporate in a matter of hours.

Oddly, however, the law has not really reflected this social and technological change and the increased magnitude of many modern corporate risks. As we move further into the twenty-first century, the way these sorts of industrial risks are policed and occasionally punished is still a largely nineteenth-century affair.

Legal implications of the global nature of risk

As so many corporations are large, powerful and transnational, they can easily locate operations or commercial activity in any given jurisdiction. There will thus be an incentive for some to choose jurisdictions that offer the least legal control. The danger in any country easing the tightness of its control can be seen in relation to avoidable financial disasters that have occurred recently. For example, in the UK this was highlighted by Sir Ken Macdonald QC, the former Director of Public Prosecutions, who observed that:

> ... financial deregulation undoubtedly released great energy and wealth into the markets and did so in part by giving bankers and financiers more space. But this space had another effect. It created a growing distance between wealthy and powerful individuals and the agencies designed to police their behaviour.

> Not sensing the danger in this, our two main political parties supported looser regulation over many years ... the scale of failure is laid bare by one inevitable consequence clear for all to see: too many people and too many institutions function as though they are beyond the reach of the criminal law. (Macdonald 2009)

It is therefore desirable that, in respect of conduct that has transnational dimensions (such as international trade or corporate crime), jurisdictions across the world should, as far as possible, acquire uniform law or legal principles. There might well be different ways in which different nations would achieve the desired results (different types of laws, different principles, and differing enforcement procedures and apparatus); but diverse approaches can nonetheless provide functional equivalency – they can protect life. The current state of play concerning the law related to corporate homicide across the countries of the world is, however, that it is highly varied and does not produce uniform levels of safety.

There is a growing global acceptance that the criminal law is an appropriate instrument[14] with which companies can be encouraged to become compliant with the provisions of human rights law – in particular those precepts that protect the right to life. Professor John Ruggie, the United Nations Special Representative of the Secretary General on human rights and transnational corporations and other business enterprises, published a report in 2009 which, in part, underlines the need for the criminal law to play a role in the enhancement of human rights in the context of corporate social responsibility. The report expounds a three-pillar framework for corporate accountability for human rights outlined in an earlier report (Ruggie 2008).[15] The 2009 report sets out the assumptions and notes that:

> The framework rests on three pillars: the State duty to protect against human rights abuses by third parties, including business, through appropriate policies, regulation, and adjudication; the corporate responsibility to respect human rights, which in essence means to act with due diligence to avoid infringing on the rights of others; and *greater access by victims to effective remedy*, judicial and non-judicial. The three pillars are complementary in that each supports the others. (Ruggie 2009: paragraph 2; emphasis added)

It also notes:

> ... the growing international harmonization of standards for international crimes that apply to corporations under domestic law, largely as a by-product of converging standards applicable to individuals; an emerging standard of corporate complicity in human rights abuses; *the consideration by some States of 'corporate culture' in deciding criminal responsibility or punishment* [see later in this chapter, under 'Is it Manslaughter?']; and an increase in civil cases brought against parent companies for their acts and omissions in relation to harm involving their foreign subsidiaries [see later in this chapter under 'Conclusions']. (ibid.: paragraph 20; emphasis added)

The law, though, if it is to work well, must be properly resourced, and this is not always the case. As Ruggie notes:

> As regards criminal proceedings, even where a legal basis exists, if State authorities are unwilling or unable to dedicate the resources to pursue allegations, currently there may be little that victims can do. (ibid.: paragraph 96)

We will now consider the law in the UK as an illustration and case study of how one government has responded to the phenomenon of corporate manslaughter.

The UK Corporate Manslaughter and Corporate Homicide Act 2007

To examine and explore the issues related to prosecuting organisations for homicide (a general legal term for killing), this section will focus on a relatively new law, most of which came into force in 2008 in the UK. It is the most recent type of dedicated legislation on this theme in the world.[16] A corporation was prosecuted in the United States as far back as 1904,[17] and France enabled corporations to be prosecuted for any crime from January 2006. The UK law, however, digests most of the issues encountered in other jurisdictions. I shall examine key elements[18] of the Corporate Manslaughter and Corporate Homicide Act 2007 and evaluate its potential for being adopted or adapted in other jurisdictions. Is this law likely to improve the social responsibility of corporations?[19] Before turning to the working of the Act, it is helpful to note something of the legislation's genesis. The Act resulted from a decade of governmental consultations with industry, commerce and legal reform groups.

The story might begin, though, with the case of Glanville Evans. On 5 July 1964, Mr Evans, a twenty-seven-year-old welder, was killed when the bridge at Boughrood that he was demolishing collapsed and he fell into the River Wye. The company that employed him had evidently been reckless in instructing him to work in a perilous way, but an attempt to convict it for manslaughter at Glamorgan Assizes at Cardiff failed on the merits of the case. Nonetheless, Mr Justice Streatfeild fully accepted the propriety of the charge of corporate manslaughter against Northern Strip Mining Construction Co. Ltd.[20] Notwithstanding this imaginative precedent,[21] the offence was rarely prosecuted in subsequent decades.

At common law, it was very difficult to convict companies, even when there had been public outrage at the gross negligence involved in a disaster (Home Office 2000: 3). This was because, in order to convict a company, it was necessary to find at least one director or senior member in whom all the legally required blame could be located. The doctrine, known as the 'identification principle', required the discovery of someone whose will could be identified as that of the company's and in whom all fault lay. As companies commonly have responsibility for matters related to safety distributed across more than one directorial portfolio, getting a conviction was difficult. Everyone with apparently relevant responsibility claimed to know only a fragment of a danger that materialised and killed people. It was not permissible to incriminate the company by aggregating the fragmented faults of several directors.[22]

The relatively new Corporate Manslaughter and Corporate Homicide law aims to criminalise corporate killing without the need to demonstrate that the entire guilt could be found in at least one individual. If a company can enjoy benefits by virtue of being an aggregate of people, it should be able to take the blame, in aggregate, if its corporate conduct causes death by gross negligence. This principle is generally recognised in law, and expressed in the maxim *Qui sentit commodum debet sentire et onus* (he who has obtained an advantage ought to bear the disadvantage as well).

The scale of the problem

In the UK, about 300 people (employees, self-employed people and members of the public) are killed each year in incidents[23] or through the operation of commerce.[24] Long-term deaths are excluded from the discussion here. These include circumstances where a company might have been responsible for recklessly causing a condition (like asbestosis or mesothelioma) that may take many years to cause death. Since the Law Reform (Year and a Day Rule) Act 1996, it has been possible to prosecute companies under the common law, even if the gap between a grossly negligent infliction of serious harm and consequential death is longer than a year and a day,[25] but those cases, while just as serious as those being considered here, raise some legal problems that are not appropriate for inclusion in this chapter. However, commercially caused deaths on the roads, whose number has been estimated at up to a thousand a year (Work-Related Road Safety Task Group 2001: v), will be within the ambit of this discussion. This is part of a wider social phenomenon.

In the UK, over 40,000 people were killed in commercially related circumstances between 1966 and 2008,[26] but only thirty-four companies were prosecuted for homicide (Slapper 1999; Home Office 2005).[27] Between 1992 and 2005, some 3,425 workers were killed at work in fatal accidents (HSC 2005: 15). It has been estimated that in around 70 per cent of cases where death has resulted from corporate activities, the company involved is to blame; where the level of blameworthiness reaches 'gross negligence', the company would be open to a charge of corporate manslaughter (HSE 1988: 4). In national research conducted over four years across a variety of cities and towns, a detailed examination of evidence and case materials indicated that about 20 per cent of all work-related deaths afforded a strong prima facie case of corporate manslaughter. That equates to about fifty corporate manslaughter prosecutions a year, or about one a week (Slapper 1999: chapters 3 and 4). In fact, there are annually only about three such prosecutions. The Act creates a new offence of corporate manslaughter (called 'corporate homicide' in Scotland) which applies to companies and other incorporated bodies, government departments and similar bodies, police forces and certain unincorporated associations.[28]

Who should be prosecuted?

In the UK, historically the law developed to recognise only *individual people* as legal persons appropriate to stand trial when facing general criminal charges; companies could not be put on trial. Today it is recognised that organisations are capable of committing crimes. This raises the question of which sorts of organisation should be within the purview of a law on homicide.

The UK Corporate Manslaughter and Corporate Homicide Act addresses this in section 1. The new law applies to commercial companies (both with and without shareholders) and a variety of organisations, including charities. The new offence will apply where a charity or voluntary organisation has been incorporated (for example, as a company or as a charitable incorporated organisation under the Charities Act 2006). A charity or voluntary organisation that operates as any other form of organisation to which the offence applies, such as a partnership with employees, will also be liable to the new offence (Ministry of Justice 2007: 7).

The offence set out in section 1(3) is not contingent on the personal guilt of one or more individuals. Liability depends on a finding of gross negligence in the way in which the activities of the organisation are run. The offence is committed where, in particular circumstances, an organisation owes a duty to take reasonable care for a person's safety, and the way in which activities of the organisation have been managed or organised amounts to a gross breach of that duty and causes the person's death. How the activities were managed or organised by 'senior management' must be a 'substantial element' of the gross breach.

The term 'senior management' is defined in section 1(4) to mean those persons 'who play significant roles' in (a) deciding how the whole or a substantial part of the organisation's activities are to be managed or organised or (b) the actual managing or organising of the whole or a substantial part of those activities. This covers both those in strategic or regulatory compliance roles, and those in the direct chain of management.

Upon conviction, the sanction is an unlimited fine (section 1(6)), although the court will also be empowered to impose a 'remedial order' (a court order to remedy whatever organisational fault caused the death or deaths) (section 9) and a publicity order (section 10) on a convicted organisation. In general, the amount of the fine must reflect the seriousness of the offence, and the court must take into account the financial circumstances of the offender.[29] The Court stated in one case (*Howe*) that the fine should 'reflect public disquiet at the unnecessary loss of life'[30] where a death has occurred, although it is not possible to incorporate a financial measure of the value of human life in the fine imposed for an offence.[31]

The Sentencing Advisory Panel has suggested a level of fine of between 2.5 and 10 per cent of a convicted company's average annual turnover during the three years prior to the offence. The starting point, assuming a publicity order is also being made against the organisation, would be 5 per cent of turnover (SGP 2007: paragraph 60). Turnover is the aggregate of all money received by an organisation during the course of its business over an annual period. It is comparable with the income of an individual, which is typically the primary measure used to assess an individual offender's ability to pay a fine.[32] It is also the measure already used by the Office of Fair Trading (OFT) when imposing financial penalties on companies that have infringed competition law (OFT 2004). Ten per cent of global turnover is also the maximum fine the European Commission can impose for breaches of European Community competition law.[33]

This will be a significant departure from previous sentencing policy. Research conducted for the Centre for Corporate Accountability (CCA) showed that the majority of large companies convicted of health and safety offences involving the death of a worker or member of the public are fined at a level which is less than a 700th of their annual turnover. If individuals earning an average annual income of £24,769 were sentenced at this level, they would be fined just £35. The research also showed that the fines imposed on most of these companies were only 1 per cent of their gross profits. The research, published in 2008, examined companies convicted for death-related health and safety offences since 1 January 2006 – and compared the fines imposed against the convicted company's turnover and gross profits (CCA 2008).

When should an organisation owe a legal duty of care?

The UK law founded the crime of corporate killing on the idea that no case can result in a conviction unless it can be first proved that the defendant company owed a duty of care to the person or people it allegedly killed. The new offence applies only in circumstances where an organisation owed a duty of care to the victim. In that respect, it is the same as the remaining individual crime under the common law offence of gross negligence manslaughter.[34] That necessary relationship between the defendant organisation and victim underlies the broad scope of the offence. The sorts of duty of care that are commonly owed by corporations (set out in section 2 of the Act) include the duty owed by an employer to his employees to provide a safe system of work, and by an occupier of buildings and land to people in or on the property. Duties of care also arise out of the activities that are conducted by corporations, such as the duty owed by transport companies to their passengers. These duties sit in an elementary way within commonly accepted versions of human rights. Ruggie, for example, notes that: 'the corporate responsibility to respect human rights ... in essence means to act with due diligence to avoid infringing on the rights of others' (Ruggie 2009: paragraph 2).

Is it manslaughter?

It is relatively easy to measure the conduct of an individual against that of a notional 'reasonable person'; it is considerably harder to judge the conduct of an organisation like a commercial company against a relevant standard. Section 8 of the Act is a very innovative provision. Before turning to that section, it is important to recite its context. Earlier in the Act, section 1(4)(b) sets out the test for assessing whether the breach of duty involved in the management failure was 'gross'. The test asks whether the conduct that constitutes this failure 'falls far below what can reasonably be expected of the organisation in the circumstances'. Whether the standard has been so breached will be an issue for the jury to determine. The common law offence of gross negligence manslaughter asks whether the conduct in question was 'so negligent as to be criminal'. When the common law was used to prosecute companies for manslaughter, it was the jury that had to decide whether the corporate carelessness in question went: 'beyond a mere matter of compensation between subjects and showed such a disregard for the life and safety of others as to amount to a crime against the State and conduct deserving of punishment'.[35]

Lord Mackay said that the decision as to whether negligence is culpable at a criminal level is 'supremely a jury question'.[36] Now, however, to assist in the determination of an organisation's culpability, section 8 sets out a number of matters for the jury to consider. These put the management of an activity into the context of the organisation's obligations under health and safety legislation, the extent to which the organisation was in breach of these, and the risk to life that was involved. First, section 8(2) says that the jury *must* consider whether the evidence shows that the organisation failed to comply with any health and safety legislation that relates to the alleged breach, and if so: (a) how serious that failure was; and (b) how much of a risk of death it posed.

Section 8 also provides for the jury to consider the wider context in which these health and safety breaches occurred:

8 (3) The jury may also—

(a) consider the extent to which the evidence shows that there were *attitudes, policies, systems or accepted practices within the organisation* that were likely to have encouraged any such failure as is mentioned in subsection (2), or to have produced tolerance of it;

(b) have regard to any health and safety guidance that relates to the alleged breach. [emphasis added]

This is a most interesting development. Section 8(3)(a) means that the attention of juries is being focused upon what might be called the 'corporate culture' of the organisation standing trial for homicide, with the particular question of whether this culture was conducive to the unsafe practices that resulted in death. When considering breaches of health and safety duties, juries may also consider official guidance (section 8(5)) on how those obligations should be discharged. Guidance does not provide an authoritative statement of required standards, and therefore the jury is not required to consider the extent to which this is not complied with. However, where breaches of relevant health and safety duties are established, guidance may assist a jury in considering how serious the breach was. These factors are not exhaustive and section 8(4) provides for the jury also to take account of any other relevant matters.

'Naming and shaming' as punishment

Criminal sanctions can in themselves constitute an effective censure (and thus help educate people about the need for precaution), but only if they are widely known. Historically, most corporate crime is poorly reported, and so little or no social censure follows. The idea of publicly stigmatising commercial offenders, though, is not new. The nineteenth-century Bread Acts in Britain permitted magistrates to order the publication of the names of those found guilty of adulterating bread.[37] Section 10 of the 2007 Act empowers a court to order a convicted organisation to publicise, in a manner specified by the court, the fact of its conviction, specified particulars of the offence, the amount of any fine imposed, and the terms of any remedial order that has been made.

Prior to making an order, the court is required to consult any relevant enforcement authorities and to have regard to any representations made by the prosecution and defence. The order must specify the period within which the publicity must be made and may require the organisation to give evidence that it has complied with the order to a specified regulator. Non-compliance with an order is an offence triable on indictment only and punishable with an unlimited fine. The menace of this sanction should act as a serious deterrent because, unlike the publication of some Anti-Social Behaviour Orders (ASBOs),[38] which might be 'badges of rebellion' to certain delinquents, the corporate offender has nothing to gain and everything to lose from the publication of its conviction for homicide.

There might, however, be some limitations on the potency of adverse publicity. The Ford Motor Company was not convicted of manslaughter in the USA following a prosecution for that crime in 1987 arising from the highly dangerous vehicle, the Pinto (Cullen et al. 1987). Nonetheless, the case revealed that the company's concern for safety was alarmingly less rigorous than it could have been. Perhaps as many as 500 people died or received serious burn injuries as a result of Pinto cars bursting into flames after only minor rear-end collisions. There was written evidence that the company, having recognised that the Pinto had been dangerously designed, had calculated that it would be cheaper to leave the vehicle on the roads and pay compensation to predicted numbers of crash victims and their bereaved, than it would be to recall the vehicle and adapt it. Acquittal can be seen as in some ways technical – the defence was able to raise a doubt about the competence of the drivers who died in the particular incident that led to the prosecution. Despite the awful publicity, however, there was no evidence that, following the case, the profits of Ford in the USA were adversely affected by the courtroom exposure of the company's evidently less-than-perfect attitude to the safety of its customers.

Evaluation of the Corporate Manslaughter and Corporate Homicide Act 2007

At the heart of the new legislation is the replacement of the old common law's 'identification doctrine' with a new test of liability. This test does not require the prior identification of a particular individual director or senior manger prosecutable for manslaughter before consideration of the prosecution of the organisation. This can be seen as an advance, since it assists in the process of the law being able to visit criminal culpability on an organisation *qua* organisation. Removal of the element of individual liability from the test of corporate culpability is a positive step and should make it easier to prosecute organisations whose corporately reprehensible conduct has resulted in death.

The new test does, however, require some significant connection between the gross failure that caused the death and the *senior management* of the organisation. This is because a 'substantial' element of the gross failure resulting in the death must be at a senior management level (section 1(3)). This new test thus still contains a flavour of the old identification principle. This is odd, as it was that very principle that was key to why the old law was widely seen as inadequate (CCA 2007).

One danger highlighted by a leading legal academic, Prof. C. M. V. Clarkson, is that the new 'senior manager' test could encourage companies to pass health and safety responsibilities to non-senior managers, so as to shield the company from criminal liability (House of Commons 2005: paragraph 133; Clarkson 2007: 19). In anticipation of the legislation, Clarkson noted, there was indeed evidence that some companies were delegating health and safety responsibilities down to more junior employees (House of Commons 2005: paragraph 135). Clarkson argues that a further problem with the approach is that it replicates one of the main problems with the previous common law on corporate manslaughter, in that it applies inequitably across small and large organisations (ibid.: paragraph 150). He contends:

> It will clearly be easier to identify senior management failings in small companies. In essence, this senior management test is little more than a broadening of the present identification doctrine under which, instead of identifying one senior directing mind, one aggregates the actions and culpability of several senior persons. It is unfortunate that the Law Commission approach was not adopted whereby the definition of a management failure removed the need to identify persons representing the senior management and placed the emphasis on the *activities* of the company: 'the way in which its activities are managed or organised'. This would place the focus where it should be: on the activities and organisational practices of the company. (Clarkson 2007: 19)

Looked at in this way, the legislation creates a set of rules whose workings are alarmingly similar to those that the government said it wished to replace, having taken ten years to plan such a change. Another weakness is that the law might encourage companies to subcontract dangerous work to avoid criminal liability. It should be remembered, however, that even if no senior management member holds particular responsibility for the aspects of safety whose deficiency caused death, the very omission to make that safety a boardroom concern could *itself* be a substantial element of breach by senior management.

Where warranted by the facts of a case, directors can still now be prosecuted personally for manslaughter, and they can be prosecuted pursuant to section 37 (via section 33) of the Health and Safety at Work etc. Act 1974. The Act was amended by the Health and Safety (Offences) Act 2008, and today directors can be imprisoned for up to two years for many offences under the 1974 Act.

Conclusions

In its regulatory impact assessment for the legislation, the UK government estimated that the new offence would result in only ten to thirteen prosecutions for corporate manslaughter each year (Home Office 2006: paragraph 25).[39] Whether one regards that number as regrettably high or low, or apparently about right, it should not be hoped that any particular number of companies will be convicted of the new crime. A better hope would be that the new law results in no convictions. It should be that, as a result of the new law, companies at large take better care than they do now. They might be more alert to the need for safety through fear of the consequences of prosecution (now that it is easier to convict organisations of killing) or through simple enlightenment that comes from reading about why the law was passed. Either way, the result will be socially beneficial. That the responsibility might be procured under threat of punishment is, in one sense, of no consequence. It does not matter if good comes from the threat of a reasonable penalty imposed on a lawbreaker. Most people, for example, do not drive recklessly on the highways because it would be irresponsible and dangerous to do so; a minority might only comply with safety rules because they fear conviction if they break the law – but the driving laws are desirable, even though they are, in effect, only influencing a minority.

This chapter has argued that the Act will be likely to create a better approach to safety in a great many workplaces. Additionally, another recent law might well act as a catalyst in the process of improving safety practice and consciousness. Section 172 of the Companies Act 2006 imposes clear duties on directors, and this, in combination with the clear power of shareholders over the company also afforded by the Act,[40] might well serve to focus directorial minds more sharply on health and safety issues. Section 172 states:

... Duty to promote the success of the company

(1) A director of a company must act in the way he considers, in good faith, would be most likely to promote the success of the company for the benefit of its members as a whole, and in doing so have regard (amongst other matters) to—

(a) the likely consequences of any decision in the long term,

(b) the interests of the company's employees...

(e) the desirability of the company maintaining a reputation for high standards of business conduct...

If by focusing the attentions of careless companies on safety issues, the new law reduces the annual unnecessary death toll, it will have done something remarkably good.

However, one major question in many jurisdictions will be whether there is sufficient political will to bring corporations within the criminal law of homicide. Are governments and legislators sufficiently independent of commercial interests? A Bureau of Corporations was set up by Theodore Roosevelt in America in 1903, with the purpose of marshalling public opinion against various corporate malpractices. The Bureau was to investigate companies and also to maintain an inquiry on an industry-wide level. However, it was disbanded after a very short time because of the need to obtain election funds from some of the largest corporations.

This chapter has dwelt on the criminal law and its uses to promote corporate social responsibility. However, there are some ways (modest at present) in which civil law is used to vindicate the human rights of citizens in various countries. This is because, apart from a growth in domestic *criminal* liability of corporations, there has also been, in many states, not just an increase in civil litigation against companies causing injury and death, but also the advent of *domestic liability* for corporate torts that are committed *abroad*. Civil litigation has been taken against corporations in their home jurisdiction, even where the act of negligence has been committed by them in the developing world. In the United States, actions have been brought under the Alien Claims Tort Act 1789, and while none of these cases has gone to judgment, some have settled. For example, in *Doe* v. *Unocal*, a Californian court permitted Burmese villagers to bring a claim against Unocal in respect of human rights abuses related to a pipeline in which Unocal had invested. Another case arose in Colombia: in 2002, the families of three deceased Colombian labour leaders and the union they belonged to, Sintramienergética, sued Drummond Company, Inc. and its wholly owned subsidiary Drummond Ltd in the United States Federal Court. The claimants alleged that Drummond had hired Colombian paramilitaries to kill and torture the three labour leaders in 2001 (Gumbel 2002). Some aspects of this litigation are still under appeal.

This chapter began by noting that the more corporations operate globally, the greater the need for certain types of law to have global effect. Corporate social responsibility and the commercial recognition of human rights principles such as 'the right to life' can only really be achieved on a global basis. After all, 'human' refers to a species, not to a nationality. And therein lies the dilemma, as the enforcement of law and the vindication of rights can only be carried out against organisations *nationally*, given that there is no world legal system.

Notes

1 With the reasonable provision of training, or the reasonable provision of equipment, or with reasonable work systems the deaths could be avoided. What is 'reasonable' will undoubtedly vary from country to country, but it has not proved impossible to unify expected standards of practice in such activity as international air pilot practice, and it should not, in general terms, be impossible across most branches of work.

2 For example, the ILO figures show that, for 2001, India (with an economically active population of 443,860,000) had an estimated 40,133 deaths from fatal accidents and 261,891 deaths from industrial diseases. The figures for China (with an economically active population of 740,703,800) were 90,295 industrial accident deaths and 368,645 deaths from work-related industrial diseases.

3 The only exception is (arguably) an organisation like Dignitas (based in Switzerland), which assists with voluntary suicides.

4 Influential texts include: Crane and Matten (2003, 2006) and Fisher and Lovell (2008).

5 I recognise that there is a greater pressure for the internationalisation and uniformity of commercial law than for the internationalisation and uniformity of human rights. International commerce drives the assimilation of commercial law, whereas cultural and historical differences among nations mean that human rights measures enjoy a differential reception across countries.

6 The 'Peace of Westphalia' arose from two peace treaties signed on 15 May and 24 October 1648, ending both the Thirty Years' War in the Holy Roman Empire and the Eighty Years' War between Spain and the Republic of the Seven United Netherlands. The treaties were developed by a prototype modern diplomatic conference, and they originated a new order in Europe founded on the principle of state sovereignty. See Gross (1948).

7 By this I mean the phenomenon whereby (through international travel, international telephony and pre-eminently the internet) companies trade and customers buy from sources across the planet, unmindful of national boundaries; human rights becomes a pan-global jurisprudence, and the art, sport, culture, news and politics of any nation become accessible to people of all nations.

8 The true number of dead is disputed. The Indian government counted 5,370. However, one organisation believes the total was about 8,000, a figure based on the number

of shrouds sold to cover the dead (*The Times*, 21 November 2004).

9 See, for example, Jones (1988: 9, note 3).

10 See, for example, transport disasters in which hundreds are killed, such as the capsizing of the *Herald of Free Enterprise* off Zeebrugge in 1987 (in which 192 people were killed) or of the *Estonia*, which sank in the Baltic in 1994, killing 852.

11 What is 'right' will depend upon many variables including factors such as the commercial and industrial context, and the culture of any nation in question; there are, though, certain minimum standards (as in air travel) that could be established internationally. It might be that some nations would want to derogate from any established international standard, but they could be required to explain why to the world if they wished to do so.

12 *Daborn* v. *Bath Tramways Motor Co Ltd and Trevor Smithey* [1946] 2 All ER 333 at 336.

13 The major nuclear reactor disaster in the Ukraine. See *The Times*, 29 April 1986 and 10 April 1996; and Culbert (2003). In the eleven days following the Chernobyl catastrophe on 26 April 1986, more than 116,000 people were permanently evacuated from the area surrounding the nuclear power plant.

14 Criminal law, though, is by no means the only instrument. Civil proceedings can also be used. See the Drummond Company, Inc. case below.

15 See analysis from Černič (2009).

16 Other countries have introduced laws enabling companies to be prosecuted, but these have mostly been general laws, e.g. in Finland in 1995, South Africa in 1995, Australia (some states) from 1995, Romania in 2006 and Austria in 2006.

17 In 1904, a New York court held that a corporation could be indicted for manslaughter. The case arose from an incident in which 900 people travelling by the steamboat *General Slocum* drowned in an attempt to escape the flames when fire erupted on the ship. The issue before the court was whether the Knickerbocker Steamboat Company, the corporate owner of the *General Slocum*, was liable for manslaughter. The court said yes, holding that '[t]he corporation navigated without [life preservers], and caused death thereby'. The court stated that under the relevant law it was 'not necessary to show intention to kill'. *United States* v. *Van Schaick* (1904) 134 Fed. 592.

18 Only a selection of the sections are digested here, and I have focused on those that are relevant to the general concerns of this book.

19 Even if so, it should be noted that the Act applies only to deaths in the UK or caused by an injury sustained in the UK.

20 See *The Times*, 2, 4 and 5 February 1965.

21 In *R* v. *Cory Bros* [1927] 1KB 810 a company had been indicted for an incident during the miners' strike, after a miner was killed by an electrified fence; but Mr Justice Finlay ruled that a corporation could not be prosecuted for a crime involving violence.

22 *R* v. *HM Coroner for East Kent ex parte Spooner* per Bingham LJ, (1989) 88 Cr. App. R. 10 at 16.

23 These are often prejudged as 'accidents', though that immediately displaces the possibility of serious blame.

24 Health and Safety Commission Annual Reports, 1995/96–2007/08.

25 Section 1 says: 'The rule known as the "year and a day rule" (that is, the rule that, for the purposes of offences involving death and of suicide, an act or omission is conclusively presumed not to have caused a person's death if more than a year and a day elapsed before he died) is abolished for all purposes.' Prosecutions of such cases must be by or with the consent of the Attorney General.

26 This does not include the many thousands killed on the roads in work-related incidents (by lorry drivers, coach drivers, etc.) where ill-maintained vehicles or harmful work rotas are implicated in the cause of the accident; nor does the figure include the thousands of deaths from chronic diseases such as asbestosis.

27 Also HSE deaths at work data in HSE annual reports 2000–07.

28 A full version of the Act can be found at: www.uk-legislation.hmso. gov.uk/acts/acts2007a

29 Criminal Justice Act 2003, s 164.

30 *Howe and Son (Engineers) Ltd* [1999] 2 All ER 249 at 254.

31 *Howe and Son (Engineers) Ltd* [1999] 2 Cr App R (S) 37; and see *Friskies Petcare Ltd* [2000] Cr App R (S).

32 Tesco was fined £15 million for a fatal gas explosion in 2005. Had the new criteria been applied, the fine would have been five times higher (applying a mid-range figure) and the global turnover of some UK companies is in the order of £300 billion, so a court would be obliged to consider a fine of £3 billion. The CBI and Brehony and Daniels (2009:

89) highlight the preposterousness of such a fine but, in reality, a sentencing guideline is, after all, only a guideline.

33 Regulation 1/2003; www. europa.eu. Cited in SGP (2007: paragraph 57).

34 The 'common law' is that set of principles and precepts declared by senior judges when they give judgments in cases and evolved over centuries. It is organic, and develops by the application of old principles to new situations, or the development of new principles. In Britain it has been developing from the eleventh century. It works alongside statute law passed by the legislature, although statutory law is the superior form if the two sources afford different answers to any point.

35 Per Lord Hewart CJ in *R* v. *Bateman*, quoted with approval by Lord Mackay in *R* v. *Adomako* [1994] 2 All ER 79 at 84d; both cases were indictments against individual doctors.

36 *R* v. *Adomako* [1994] 2 All ER 79 at 87c.

37 *The Times*, 31 July 1822.

38 A British civil sanction against low-level offenders, such as those who commit criminal damage or act antisocially towards others in the community. The penalty for disobeying an ASBO is the imposition of a criminal sanction.

39 This would represent more than double the current number of prosecutions (fewer than five a year).

40 For example, derivative claims in section 260.

References

Anderson, S. and J. Cavanagh (2000) *The Top 200 Corporations*, Institute for Policy Studies report, December 2000, available at:

www.corporations.org/system/top100.html

Beck, U. (1992) *Risk Society: Towards a new modernity*, London: Sage.

Brehony, P. and I. Daniels (2009) 'Kill Bill 2?', *New Law Journal*, 23 January.

Catan, T. (2008) 'Pilots' union warned "chaotic" Spanair passengers were at risk', *The Times*, 23 August.

CCA (Centre for Corporate Accountability) (2007) 'Is the Corporate Manslaughter and Homicide Bill 2006 worth it?', Statement by the Centre for Corporate Accountability, 14 May.

— (2008) *The relationship between the levels of fines imposed upon companies convicted of health and safety offences resulting from deaths, and the turnover and gross profits of these companies*, Research Report, London: CCA.

Černič, J. (2009) 'John Ruggie's 2009 report on Business and Human Rights', *International Law Observer*, May 28, available at: http://internationallawobserver. eu/2009/05/28/john-ruggies-2009-report-on-business-and-human-rights/

Clarkson, C. M. V. (2007) 'Corporate Manslaughter: Need for a special offence?' Paper delivered to the Society of Legal Scholars conference on 'Criminal Liability for Non-Aggressive Death', University of Leicester, 19 April 2007.

Crane, A. and D. Matten (2003) *Business Ethics*, Oxford: Oxford University Press.

— (2006) *Business Ethics: Managing corporate citizenship and sustainability in the age of globalization*, Oxford: Oxford University Press.

Culbert, E. (2003) *Zones of Exclusion: Pripyat and Chernobyl*, New York: Steidl.

Cullen, F..T., W. Maakestad and G. Cavender (1987) *Corporate Crime Under Attack*, New York: Anderson Publishing.

Fisher, C. and A. Lovell (2008) *Business Ethics and Values: Individual, Corporate and International Perspectives*, London: Pearson.

Gross, L. (1948) 'The Peace of Westphalia 1648–1948', *American Journal of International Law*, 42(1): 20–41.

Gumbel, A. (2002) 'US firm sued after mine union leaders' deaths', *Independent*, 25 March.

Home Office (2000) *Reforming the Law on Involuntary Manslaughter: The government's proposals*, London: Home Office.

— (2005) *Corporate Manslaughter: The government's Draft Bill for Reform*, Cm 6497, London: Home Office.

— (2006) *Corporate Manslaughter and Corporate Homicide: A Regulatory Impact Assessment of the Government's Bill*, 20 July, London: Home Office.

House of Commons (2005) Home Affairs and Work and Pensions Committees, *Draft Corporate Manslaughter Bill, First Joint Report of Session 2005–06*, Vols I–III, London: House of Commons.

HSC (Health and Safety Commission) *Statistics of Fatal Injuries, 2004/05* (2005), London: HSC.

HSE (Health and Safety Executive) (1988) *Blackspot Construction*, London: HSE.

— (2004) *The Work of the Health and Safety Commission and Executive, House of Commons, Work and Pensions Committee, Fourth Report of Session 2003–4*, Vol. III, Written

Evidence, House of Commons, 14 July, Ev219.

Jones, T. (1988) *Corporate Killing: Bhopals will happen*, London: Free Association Books.

Macdonald, K. (2009) 'Give us laws that the City will respect and fear', *The Times*, 23 February.

Ministry of Justice (2007) *A guide to the Corporate Manslaughter and Corporate Homicide Act 2007*, available at: www.justice.gov.uk/guidance/docs/guidetomanslaughterhomicide07.pdf

OFT (Office of Fair Trading) (2004) *OFT's Guidance as to the Appropriate Amount of a Penalty*, available at: www.oft.gov.uk/shared_oft/business_leaflets/competition_law/oft423a.pdf

Robbins, S. P., A. Odendaal and G. Roodt (2003) *Organisational Behaviour*, South Africa: Pearson.

Ruggie, J. (2008) *Protect, Respect and Remedy: A framework for business*

and human rights', UN Doc. A/HRC/8/5, 7 April.

— (2009) *Business and Human Rights: Towards operationalizing the "protect, respect and remedy" framework* , UN Doc. A/HRC/11/13/, 22 April, available at: www2.ohchr.org/english/bodies/hrcouncil/docs/11session/A.HRC.11.13.pdf

SGP (Sentencing Guidelines Panel) (2007) *Consultation Paper on Sentencing for Corporate Manslaughter*, London: SGP.

Slapper, G. (1999) *Blood in the Bank*, Aldershot: Ashgate.

Takala, J. (2005) *Introductory Report: Decent Work – Safe Work*, Geneva: International Labour Organization.

Work-Related Road Safety Task Group (2001) *Reducing At-Work Road Traffic Incidents*, November, available at: www.orsa.org.uk/guidance/pdfs/dykes_report.pdf

6 | Access to medicines: intellectual property rights, human rights and justice

KEREN BRIGHT AND LOIS MURAGURI

Introduction

Conceptually and philosophically, intellectual property rights (IPRs) are about power relations. These power relations are shown in particularly stark terms in the field of health. Discourse often refers to 'the 90/10 gap' – that is, approximately 90 per cent of all medical research is directed towards diseases affecting only 10 per cent of the world's population. The true figures are probably bleaker than this. According to a report issued by the Global Forum for Health Research (GFHR), malaria, pneumonia, diarrhoea and tuberculosis make up about 21 per cent of the global disease burden, yet they receive 0.31 per cent of all public and private spending on health research (GFHR 2007: 122). The pharmaceutical industry, premised as it is on profit return, invests in diseases with a large market that can bear higher prices, and sidelines research into diseases with a low rate of profit return, typically those in the developing countries. These are often described as the neglected diseases and include blinding trachoma, yaws, cholera, leprosy, dengue and schistosomiasis.

Three types of tension can be identified in the interface between intellectual property rights and the human right to health. First is the tension of applying intellectual property rights, which are essentially private rights,[1] to the provision of medicines, which may be private goods but have welfare (public goods) implications. Second, there is the tension of balancing the inventor's need to recover the substantial research and development costs against ensuring that these inventions are accessible to the poor. Last, there is the overarching tension of power asymmetry between the pharmaceutical industry and those with limited access to medicines.

This chapter is concerned with the dynamics between the intellectual property rights owned by pharmaceutical companies (and the discussion will focus primarily upon patents),[2] the human right to health and the access of the poor to 'essential medicines'.[3] We shall consider the responsibility of pharmaceutical companies in sharing scientific advances and the various initiatives undertaken by the public and private sectors, including 'pharma' (used here as shorthand for the pharmaceutical industry generally), to promote the right to health. We will argue that human rights concepts have shaped the use of intellectual property rights and the development of health-related organisational mechanisms in poorer countries.

This chapter is organised into three sections: the first examines the different traditions of patent law and human rights law and considers the relationship between them within the context of the main international human rights instruments; the second section considers the accountability of the pharmaceutical industry to society; and the third section provides an overview of the key developments that derive from the application of the human rights approach to IPRs.

Human rights and fairer access to medicines

The historical development of intellectual property rights and the historical development of human rights principles and laws derive from different traditions. Human rights law derives from the tradition of natural law, while intellectual property rights were developed through state-endorsed privilege, designed to foster commercial activity. In this section, we consider the weight given to the human right to health, as against the right to own patents accorded by various international instruments. We shall also consider whether the right to own patents is a human right, as well as an economic right.

The 1948 Universal Declaration of Human Rights (UDHR) gave us an aspirational moral code and a vision for an ethical rights-based society. The human right to health is set out in Article 25: 'Everyone has the right to a standard of living adequate for the health and well-being of himself and of his family, including ... medical care.' Additionally, Article 27 states that: 'Everyone has the right freely ... to share in scientific advancement and its benefits.'

However, while some human rights are absolute and unqualified (such as the right to life), the right to health is qualified by other articles that take account of the freedoms of others. Article 27 of the UDHR goes on to say that: 'Everyone has the right to the protection of the moral and material interests resulting from any scientific, literary or artistic production of which he is author.' This element of Article 27 is reinforced by Article 17: 'Everyone has the right to own property, alone as well as in association with others' and 'No one shall be arbitrarily deprived of his property.' Articles 17 and 27 appear to provide protection to pharma as holders of patents. These articles could be used to justify the exclusive and monopolistic protection provided to patent owners over the use of their invention for a world-standard term of twenty years. Patent owners would say that patents can only be granted for moral inventions,[4] and that they satisfy the other part of Article 27 ('Everyone has the right freely ... to share in scientific advancement and its benefits') by sharing information about their invention with the world at large. This is described as the 'intellectual property bargain'. Information about the invention, which may be a product or a process, is provided to the Intellectual Property Office or Patent Office, as part of the inventor's application for a patent. The information is a public good in the public domain, and is available for anyone to see on demand. In return, the patent holder enjoys exclusive rights to control the way their invention is used for a maximum period of twenty years.[5]

The European Court of Human Rights appeared to endorse this view when it decided in 2007 that intellectual property 'undeniably attracted the protection of Article 1 of Protocol No. 1 of the European Convention of Human Rights'.[6] Article 1, which focuses on the Protection of Property, states:

> Every natural or legal person is entitled to the peaceful enjoyment of his possessions. No one shall be deprived of his possessions except in the public interest and subject to the conditions provided for by law and by the general principles of international law.
>
> The preceding provisions shall not, however, in any way impair the right of a State to enforce such laws as it deems necessary to control the use of property in accordance with the general interest or to secure the payment of taxes or other contributions or penalties.

So pharmaceutical companies as 'legal persons' appear entitled to the peaceful enjoyment of their patents, although Article 1 also gives the state primacy in deciding when it should act in the public interest and in accordance with the principles of international law.

Patent holders should, however, be aware that Article 27 of the Universal Declaration of Human Rights does not say that 'the protection of the moral and material interests resulting from any scientific, literary or artistic production of which he is author' has to be enforced using existing intellectual property right systems; these rights could be protected by other means. Indeed, patents on medicines are a relatively recent phenomenon, as medicines were excluded from patent protection in many jurisdictions until the latter half of the twentieth century.[7]

It can certainly be questioned whether patents can be considered human rights (or instruments of human rights), given that they protect, in the main, corporate and business interests and that patent-holding pharma frequently price medicines at such a level as to make them inaccessible to the world's poor. Pharma also use patents defensively, by registering many patents in a particular field (a practice described as creating 'patent thickets') in order to protect their market position and to make it more difficult for their competitors to invent around these patents. It has been argued that, if patents are meant to serve the public interest, then patent regimes should do more to encourage research where public needs are greatest (Dutfield and Suthersanen 2008: 313–14). Indeed, Resolution 2001/21 of the UN Commission on Human Rights suggested exploration of whether the patent 'as a legal instrument' was compatible with the promotion and protection of human rights.

The expression of a need to balance the right to health against intellectual property rights has been contained within a number of instruments since the UDHR, such as the International Covenant on Economic, Social and Cultural Rights (ICESCR) and, in particular, Article 15 (1966).[8] The World Health Organization, too, recognises that 'Intellectual property rights are an important incentive for the development of new health-care products', but that 'This incentive alone does not meet the need for the development of new products to fight diseases where the potential paying market is small or uncertain' (WHO 2008: 6). Sometimes there may be a more dramatic see-saw between instruments, such as when the Agreement on Trade-Related Aspects of Intellectual Property Rights (TRIPS Agreement) in 1994 made it mandatory for all World Trade Organization (WTO) members, including developing countries, to make provision for patent protection for pharma products. Among those lobbying for the TRIPS Agreement were pharmaceutical companies that wanted to secure protection from competition by manufacturers of generic drugs. The TRIPS Agreement was followed later by the Doha Declaration on TRIPS and Public Health, which stated that the TRIPS Agreement 'can and should be interpreted and implemented in a manner supportive of the World Trade Organization Members' right to protect public health and, in particular, to promote access to medicines for all' (WTO 2001). The impact of the TRIPS Agreement and the Doha Declaration is explored in greater depth in the section below on 'Voluntary and compulsory licences'.

The narrative above could be seen as an impasse, in that the rights of different parties with competing interests seem too finely balanced. However, and possibly surprisingly, the aspirational and declaratory language of human rights has had a transformative effect on the asymmetrical power relations between pharma as patent holders and the poor for whom medicines are out of reach. The language of human rights has embedded values and provided a framework for the discourse of political and academic commentators, campaigners, the media and pharma, which have created a driving force for change.

Pharmaceutical industry accountability to society: responsibilities and obligations

Pharma does have responsibilities and obligations to both its shareholders and to society as a whole. Its shareholders expect it to generate sufficient profit to provide a return on their investment, meet the cost of research and development and attract new capital. It has been very successful in meeting these obligations and responsibilities, as it is the most profitable of all sectors of industry (Angell 2000; Henry and Lexchin 2002). With regard to accountability to society, pharma has, at the very least, legal obligations rooted in contract law, competition law and product liability law, and it has a duty of care to its consumers. It is required by regulators to provide drugs of sufficient quality, to provide accurate and reliable information about the conditions the drugs are designed to address and their side effects, and to exercise due concern for patient safety (Dukes 2002; Collier and Iheanacho 2002). From time to time, pharma fails spectacularly to meet these legal obligations, as was the case with Pfizer in 2009.[9]

Beyond these legal obligations owed by pharma to society, an interesting question is whether pharma has further responsibilities – or even obligations – to advance the realisation of the right to health. International human rights law addresses the obligations of sovereign states, but is unhelpfully silent on the rights–obligation relationship between companies and society. States have the primary obligation to meet all human rights; they have a duty to respect, protect and fulfil the rights of individuals. At best, international instruments recognise a *shared responsibility* to achieve the highest attainable standard of health. For example, the 2000 Millennium Declaration set human rights-based development goals to be attained by 2015. One of the Millennium Development Goals (MDGs) in relation to the right to health was 'in cooperation with pharmaceutical companies [to] provide access to affordable essential drugs in developing countries'.[10] The declaration does not, however, have the force of law and cannot therefore be said to impose legal obligations upon pharma to fulfil human rights or the MDGs. While a General Comment from the Committee on Economic, Social and Cultural Rights (CESCR) confirms this,[11] it also allocates responsibilities: 'While only States are parties to the Covenant and thus ultimately accountable for compliance with it, all members of society – ... civil society organizations, as well as the private business sector – have responsibilities regarding the realisation of the right to health' (CESCR 2000: paragraph 42).

The 'Human Rights Guidelines for Pharmaceutical Companies in Relation to Access to Medicines' prepared by the UN Special Rapporteur on the right to the highest attainable standard of health have continued the debate over responsibilities as against legal obligations.[12] The guidelines recognise the central role that pharma plays in providing access to medicines and propose the imposition of a legal obligation upon pharma. However, the guidelines are in draft and they are opposed by pharmaceutical companies, which argue that, although enhancing access to medicine is a shared responsibility, the guidelines 'divert attention and resources from the real problems and challenges' (Merck 2008).

The Committee on Economic, Social and Cultural Rights envisages each state's obligation to *protect* the human right to health as including measures to 'prevent third parties from interfering with article 12 [right to health] guarantees' (CESCR 2000: paragraph 33). As companies are third parties, a state is entitled to take measures against pharma if the latter impedes society's right to health. The Committee's General Comment declares (under a section headed 'Specific legal obligations') that: 'Obligations to *protect* include ... the duties of states to adopt legislation or to take other measures ensuring equal access to health care and health-related services provided by third parties' (ibid.: paragraph 35). Could the adoption of legislation include the imposition of legal obligations upon pharma? One must bear in mind, though, the status of a General Comment. UN General Comments are the official collective statement of the expert members of the treaty-supervising body and are not binding. However, they have strong moral and political force (Conde 1999), not least because of the expertise of body members. Accordingly, General Comments impose moral obligations upon states which can encompass legal measures against pharma, but these moral obligations do not appear to extend to pharma itself.

The pharmaceutical industry itself seems to accept that it has moral responsibilities, but stops short of describing these as obligations. The websites and annual reports of big pharma contain sections on corporate social responsibility, and sometimes on human rights. This could be viewed as pharma holding itself to account, possibly as a response to the emergence of an ethical investment market and as a way of counterbalancing the weight of bad press. Merck talks of its 'belief that pharmaceutical companies have a responsibility to offer assistance' (Merck 2008); GlaxoSmithKline (GSK) takes measures aimed at 'playing [their] part in helping to address' lack of access to life-saving medicines (GSK 2009a); while Pfizer acknowledges that 'as an industry [pharma] have an important role to play in improving access to medicines in the developing world' and that 'Pfizer has a responsibility to support developing countries directly' (Pfizer 2007).

While the moral and legal obligations of pharma in providing access to essential medicines have not yet been unequivocally established, the language of human rights has been used by many stakeholders in assessing the performance of pharma and in mediating the power asymmetry between it and society. As a consequence, there are increasing examples of the way in which human rights concepts are influencing the policies of pharma as regards their use of patents and the trade in medicines. The accepted norms of the sector appear to be changing, and there is competition within pharma in terms of the initiatives and partnerships they become involved in. The following section looks at some of these developments.

Developments in IPRs and the right to health

Public–private partnerships Encouragingly, the collaborations or partnerships between the public and the private sectors are increasing.[13] Health partnerships can potentially mitigate the exclusive nature of patent-protected drugs, as the private sector (often patent-holding pharma) works in collaboration with the public sector (whose mandate is more welfare oriented) to address complex health problems. Public–private partnerships (PPPs) can be said to provide mediation between IPR-protected products and the right to health.

PPPs are viewed as important conduits for health delivery, particularly in developing countries. They help build collective capacity to respond 'to turbulent conditions as creative solutions are needed that exceed the limited perspectives of each individual partner' (Saad et al. 1999: 498). PPPs provide an alternative model for research and development, and have the potential to close the gap between the demand and the supply of drugs, vaccines and diagnostics needed to treat (and ultimately eradicate) the diseases associated with poverty (Widdus and White 2004). Without PPPs, it could be argued that pharma involvement in addressing the diseases of poverty would be limited; PPPs therefore assist pharma in exercising its moral responsibilities.

In particular, global health partnerships are important social experiments that address issues such as product development, access to health products and services, and generally the global coordination of health research in particular diseases. They are an important facet of the 'social technologies' necessary to ensure the effective delivery of health products and services to the poor – that is, 'the mix of organisations as well as their institutional norms, values and culture within and external to organisations' (Chataway et al. 2009). Global health partnerships are increasingly funded by philanthropic foundations, such as those established by Bill and Melinda Gates or by Bill Clinton, which have been motivated by the inequality in health provision.[14] These partnerships and foundations are pioneering in their creativity in conducting collaborative research into the diseases of poverty. By the end of 2004, global health PPPs were responsible for nearly 75 per cent of neglected disease drug development projects (Moran et al. 2005).

One such global health product development PPP is the International AIDS Vaccine Initiative, which has been lauded for its efforts in bridging the gap between scientific potential and the needs of the developing world (Chataway and Smith 2005). Like most other product-development PPPs, this initiative directly addresses the availability of a vaccine, but goes further, as it proactively facilitates access to its vaccine through advocacy, by preparing communities for vaccine field trials and by identifying potential manufacturers.[15] Private sector partners involved in the initiative are exposed to the welfare aspects of realising the right to health.

Similarly, the Malaria Vaccine Initiative aims 'to accelerate the development of malaria vaccines and ensure their availability and accessibility in the developing world'.[16] This initiative works with other research institutes that are involved in malaria vaccine development. It has been known for some time that immunising against malaria is theoretically possible, but there have been financial and technical barriers to realising this.[17] The initiative identifies possible candidates for malaria vaccine and facilitates their development from the laboratory to clinical trials. GSK has developed a promising malaria vaccine, and Phase 3 trials of it began in 2009 in seven African countries.

Differential pricing and discounted purchasing Pharmaceuticals account for 20–60 per cent of health spending in developing and transitional countries, compared with 18 per cent in OECD countries (WHO 2004b). Developing countries account for about 20 per cent of the global pharmaceutical market, and most of these purchases are typically made by the wealthiest 10 per cent of the population (Watal 2001).[18] In developing countries, about 90 per cent of the population buys medicine 'out of pocket', making it the largest item of family expenditure after food (WHO 2004a). Ironically, when drugs are sold in developing countries, they are often sold at higher prices than in more developed countries (WHO Secretariat 2001).

The debate on differential pricing (where prices are varied according to national wealth or ability to pay)[19] has been underpinned by arguments relating to access to medicines and the human right to health. While the pharmaceutical industry agrees in principle to differential pricing (Kapp 2001), it has proved difficult to agree a mechanism to give differential pricing effect (Lopert et al. 2002). One such mechanism, which may possibly be applied from another sector of industry, is that of 'Ramsey pricing'. This is a form of price discrimination that is used to set prices in utilities. Ramsey pricing is a theory applied to address the high fixed costs associated with providing utilities; the idea is to establish how to allocate the costs among different consumer groups according to their ability to pay, in order to achieve the twin goals of efficiency and equity (Danzon 2001).[20]

Discussions about differential pricing at the international level have included the 2001 WHO/WTO workshop on Differential Pricing and Financing of Essential Drugs.[21] The workshop looked at the feasibility of differential pricing in theory and practice, including the limitations and challenges (WHO/WTO Secretariats 2001). The limited use of differential pricing has been attributed to difficulties in achieving effective market segmentation; difficulties in preventing unlawful diversion of the lower-priced products into higher-priced markets (arbitrage);[22] political and regulatory concerns that may possibly flow from there being lower prices in particular markets; and little pressure for differential pricing being brought to bear by the governments of developing countries (Watal 2001).

There have been a number of projects exploring the use of differential pricing at the industry, governmental and international levels. For instance, Novartis produces an anti-malarial drug that is supplied at different prices under two different names and with different distinctive packaging. One brand is marketed to the European travellers' market at the standard price, while the other is available to developing countries at about 25 per cent of the standard price. Merck has applied differential pricing to its anti-retroviral medicines in the least developed countries since 2001. Cipla, a leading Indian generics company, announced that it would make a complete cocktail of anti-retroviral medications available to African countries at a 98 per cent discount (Achieng 2001). This triggered a series of price cuts by leading brand-name pharmaceuticals, including Merck. GSK announced in 2009 that it would reduce the price of patented medicines to the least developed countries (Boseley 2009a). The company would cover its costs, but would take no more than 25 per cent of the price charged in developed countries (GSK 2009b). However, this may still be too expensive for the governments and the poor of those countries (Baker 2009).

The UK Working Group, which comprises representatives from the pharmaceutical industry, the WHO, EU and foundations, has sought to address 'ways of improving access to medicines through measures such as facilitating differential pricing arrangements and encouraging appropriate donations' (DFID 2002). The European Commission has a voluntary global tiered-pricing system for key pharmaceuticals in HIV/AIDS, tuberculosis and malaria that also includes mechanisms to prevent arbitrage (European Commission 2003). Although these initiatives have not been as successful as originally intended, they have nevertheless contributed to an understanding of how differential pricing can be made feasible.

The use of differential pricing to benefit the poor in developing countries remains limited. The availability of cheaper drugs in developing countries is instead mainly due to donations, competitive tenders, bulk purchasing and skilful negotiation. For example, the Global Alliance for Vaccines and Immunizations has negotiated prices as low as 1 per cent of US vaccine prices; by means of bulk buying, UNICEF and UNFPA (the United Nations Population Fund – the largest public sector purchaser of contraceptives) obtain reductions of up to 99 per cent of US prices for some contraceptives in developing countries.

Voluntary and compulsory licences As described above, the holder of a patent has an exclusive monopoly to exploit its subject matter – which can be either a product or a process – for a twenty-year term. The use of a patent may be disseminated more widely by the licensing of it to one or more parties. Permission to use the patent is granted in return for a payment or royalty, which may be one-off or periodic. Pharma will voluntarily license their patents if it is in their economic interest to do so; alternatively, the ethical imperative of public health crises may cause pharma to grant voluntary licences, either willingly or unwillingly, to generics companies in order to meet the upsurge in demand for essential medicines. The HIV/AIDS pandemic, with the death of millions in sub-Saharan Africa, has been a considerable force in this regard. Even so, negotiations over voluntary licences may take considerable time to complete, not least because there may be numerous patents with multiple owners in respect of a single product – hardly ideal in times of a public health crisis.

In contrast to a voluntary licence, a compulsory licence 'is a permit which effectively negates a patent' (Lexchin 1997), as a government allows another manufacturer to produce the pharmaceutical without the consent of the patent holder. This provides a mechanism of last resort to increase production capacity, encourage competition and reduce prices. This is such a draconian power that, while it is often threatened in order to achieve these aims, it is not commonly exercised.

Compulsory licensing to supply domestic markets is one of the flexibilities (or safeguards to combat the exclusivity of patent protection) included in the 1994 TRIPS Agreement. Article 31 of this Agreement sets out the extreme circumstances in which compulsory licences can be granted: national emergencies, other circumstances of extreme urgency, public (or government) non-commercial use, or where anti-competitive practices exist. In all other circumstances, the applicant should have first tried to negotiate a voluntary licence with the patent holder on reasonable commercial terms. Although the consent of the patent holder is overridden, they remain entitled to adequate remuneration, as provided by the TRIPS Agreement, and can continue to produce the patented medicines. As noted above, the TRIPS Agreement was formulated against a background of lobbying by pharmaceutical companies. As many national patent regimes already made provision for compulsory licensing where the patent had not been used for three years after it was granted, the 'flexibilities' (although in name suggesting otherwise) restricted the circumstances in which compulsory licences could be issued. The lobbying by pharma also resulted in the TRIPS Agreement making it mandatory for all World Trade Organization members, including the least developed countries, to make provision for patent protection for pharma products in order to curtail the activities of the generic drugs industry.

The Doha Declaration on TRIPS and Public Health was intended to allay public concern about the impact of TRIPS, and it clarified the flexibilities provided by the TRIPS Agreement. It declared:

> We agree that the TRIPS Agreement does not and should not prevent Members from taking measures to protect public health … we affirm that the Agreement can and should be interpreted and implemented in a manner supportive of WTO members' right to protect public health and, in particular, to promote access to medicines for all. (WTO 2001: paragraph 4)

The Doha Declaration affirmed that countries have the right to determine what constitutes a national emergency for the purposes of issuing a compulsory licence to supply domestic markets, and this would include public health crises such as those wrought by HIV/AIDS, tuberculosis and malaria (ibid.: paragraph 5(b)). The declaration also extended the transition period for the least developed countries to implement TRIPS, as regards the protection of pharmaceutical patents, until 2016.

One flaw that is visible in the flexibilities provided by TRIPS and the Doha Declaration is that they relate to the production and supply of generic medicines within domestic markets. This assumes the existence of a certain level of pharmaceutical expertise and manufacturing capability: India particularly has a significant generic medicines industry. However, the necessary manufacturing capability is invariably absent from the least developed countries, such as many in sub-Saharan Africa. So countries in most need of compulsory licensing to address their domestic public health crises would be least able to take advantage of it. A subsequent decision in 2003 on paragraph 6 of the Doha Declaration[23] goes further than the grant of compulsory licences in domestic markets, as it deals with compulsory licences to produce generic copies of medicines for export to the least developed countries or to developing countries with a proven lack of production capacity. The exporting country where the medicine does have patent protection must issue a compulsory licence to allow the export of generic medicines, and other importing countries have to issue compulsory licences to import the generic medicines. Furthermore, until 2016 a government in a least developed country does not need a compulsory licence to import if the medicine has no patent protection in that government's country.

While the 2003 decision does represent an initiative to address the plight of the least developed countries, its effectiveness so far remains in doubt. Take-up of the waiver to allow compulsory licensing is low: a high-profile example of Canada exporting generic anti-retrovirals for the treatment of HIV/AIDS in the least developed country of Rwanda in 2007 is often cited; but it also stands out, as there are not many other examples. There may be a number of possible reasons for this, including the fact that the compulsory licensing requirements under the waiver are extraordinarily complex and the consideration that many of the least developed countries are reluctant to compromise trading relationships with developed countries.

The HIV/AIDS pandemic in South Africa provides an illustration of the interplay between pharma, humanitarian organisations and governments, where compulsory licences have been used as both a threat and a draconian remedy. In 2003, the Competition Commission in South

Africa upheld a complaint against two pharmaceutical companies, GSK and Boehringer Ingelheim, for excessive pricing of their anti-retroviral medicines and anti-competitive sales practices. The Competition Commission recommended compulsory licensing for the manufacture of generic anti-retrovirals. At this point, GSK and Boehringer Ingelheim opted to negotiate and agreed to grant voluntary licences for the import into South Africa, and production within the country, of generic anti-retrovirals, and for their distribution throughout the forty-seven countries of sub-Saharan Africa (Nelson 2003: 2074). Thus the capacity to exploit compulsory licensing when there is a crisis in public health can bring the pharmaceutical companies to the negotiating table. The availability of compulsory licensing has also been used successfully by a number of other countries, including Thailand and Brazil.

However, we need to issue a few words of caution. While compulsory licensing is a useful bargaining tool for governments to have at their disposal in dealing with the pharmaceutical companies, a patent licence of itself may not be enough for the generic drug companies to replicate the medicines. For instance, a patent specification may not necessarily contain enough information to allow the medicine to be copied. Additionally, some of the information about a product or process may not be protected by the law relating to patents, but instead by the law relating to confidential information and trade secrets, which cannot be released into the public domain.

Patent pools Patent pools are where two or more patent holders license or give one another permission to use their patents. Patent pools are not new, since they first appeared in the nineteenth century in a commercial context. What is new is the developmental use of patent pools to bring affordable medicines to the world's poor. It is very much more cost-effective to license patents and technical information (which would normally be protected as trade secrets) as a complete package from a single entity than it is to license patents from each separate patent holder. A patent pool managed by a single entity would act as a catalyst to innovation and would enhance the development of medicines for neglected diseases. One proposal has included the establishment of an 'Essential Medicines Licensing Agency' to manage a patent pool (Knowledge Ecology International 2007). The patents within the pool could be licensed as a package to companies, public bodies, charities and NGOs. They could also be available to generic drugs companies, which would have the effect of fostering competition between them and lowering the prices of essential medicines.

The cost of setting up any patent pool would be high, so there is the question of funding. UNITAID was established in 2006 as an innovative financing mechanism for the provision of medicines for the treatment of HIV/AIDS, tuberculosis and malaria.[24] UNITAID's funding is currently derived from government contributions and, rather imaginatively, from taxes on airline tickets and carbon dioxide emissions.

Another issue for consideration is whether patent licences from those patent holders identified as candidates for the patent pool would be compulsorily or voluntarily obtained. The pharmaceutical companies would only countenance a voluntary system of patent pool licences, and even then could not be assumed to be willing participants, although the possibility of an enforced compulsory licence would encourage them to negotiate voluntary licences. In 2008, UNITAID announced that it was establishing a patent pool for medicines, which it envisages will be a voluntary system, where a patent holder could delimit both the territories of the licence and how it would be used (UNITAID 2008). UNITAID plans for its patent pool to be managed by a licensing agency. The pool will focus first on anti-retroviral medicines and will aim to reduce prices of existing anti-retrovirals, foster production of newer generic anti-retrovirals, and encourage more research and development into HIV treatments appropriate for children and more effective fixed-dose combinations for adults.

In an announcement made by its chief executive in February 2009, GSK was the first of the pharma to endorse the concept of patent pools as a strategy for tackling neglected diseases. GSK will put, over a period of time (which suggests that it first wants to see how other pharmaceutical companies and institutions respond), around 800 chemical products and processes relevant to neglected tropical diseases into a patent pool for the use of other researchers.

Oxfam, Médecins Sans Frontières, UNICEF, Christian Aid, UNITAID and many other humanitarian organisations have acknowledged this as a major step forward, but have also commented that GSK should go further and include HIV/AIDS drugs in UNITAID's patent pool (Bermudez and Douste-Blazy 2009; Boseley 2009b).

Advance market commitments As discussed above, current market mechanisms, including pharmaceutical patents, are inadequate as incentives for research into diseases affecting the poor. Advance market commitments have been proposed as a way in which the power asymmetry between drug manufacturers and users can be mediated. Advance market or purchase commitments combine market-based financing tools with public intervention: a commitment is made in advance to buy vaccines if and when they are developed. Arguably, this serves as an incentive for industry to increase investment in diseases that it would not otherwise invest in due to the lack of a market. Essentially, the pharmaceutical industry would still be driven by the profit model; the main difference is that governments in the developed countries, charitable bodies and international agencies would be subsidising the cost of the vaccines on behalf of the poor in developing countries. One novel feature is that participating companies would make binding commitments to supply the vaccines at lower and sustainable prices after the donor funds are used up.

The idea of advanced market commitments gained momentum after the publication of a report by the Centre for Global Development (Centre for Global Development 2005). In 2007, Canada, Italy, Norway, Russia, the United Kingdom and the Bill and Melinda Gates Foundation committed US$1.5 billion to launch the first advance market commitment, which targets pneumococcal diseases. The project formally began in 2009 (GAVI 2009).

Conclusion

In the landscape of health, the players are many and the power relations between them are evolving in response to the human rights framework, the resolutions and reports produced by the UN, WTO, WHO and charitable bodies, competition within pharma itself, and the many and varied public and private sector initiatives. It is a far more complex landscape than simply power asymmetry between the pharmaceutical industry and the world's poor.

This chapter has considered some of the ways in which access to medicines has been actually and potentially enhanced: public–private partnerships, differential pricing, voluntary and compulsory licences, patent pools and advance market commitments. Significant advances have been made, particularly in discourse between the pharmaceutical industry and many stakeholders, and agreements have been arrived at in principle. However, the precise ways in which some of these agreements can move from the theoretical to practical action have yet to be determined and realised. The agreements have not always been entered into willingly by the pharmaceutical industry, but are instead the result of a combination of shaming, generic competition, increased dialogue and creative thinking. Political change, the media, shifts in public opinion and the corporate social responsibility agenda have all played a part. The pharmaceutical industry has demonstrated that it is resilient enough to adapt to change in response to various pressures and initiatives. The concepts and language of human rights have been instrumental in achieving this.

Notes

1 Intellectual property rights such as patents are private rights, since, once assigned to a legal entity, the right holder can exclude others from their unauthorised use. When states and other public entities spend their revenue on medicines for free distribution, that is the point at which private goods may become public goods.

2 Generally, innovations can be protected by secrecy, by lead time or by IPRs, including patents. In the pharmaceutical industry, it is patents that are especially crucial in appropriating returns to research and development.

3 'Essential medicines' are formally defined and delimited by the World Health Organization, which has published the Essential Medicines List every two years since 1977. 'Essential medicines are those that satisfy the priority health care needs of the population ... exactly which medicines are regarded as essential remains a national responsibility' (www.who.int/countries/eth/areas/medicines/en/).

4 The Patents Act 1977 (as amended) section 1(3): 'a patent shall not be granted for an invention the commercial exploitation of which would be contrary to public policy or morality'. The Biotech Directive Art. 6(1) refers to 'inventions the publication or exploitation of which would be contrary to public order or morality'.

5 However, in cases where regulatory approval is delayed, Supplementary Protection Certificates are available to extend patent protection beyond the twenty-year term.

6 *Anheuser-Busch Inc.* v. *Portugal*, European Court of Human Rights, Grand Chamber, No. 73049/01, 11 January 2007.

7 For example, medicines were not patentable in Germany until 1968, Japan until 1976 and Spain until 1992.

8 It can be seen that the wording of the ICESCR (1966), quite closely follows that of the UDHR. ICESCR (1966), Article 15(1):

The State Parties to the present Covenant recognize the right of everyone:

a. To take part in cultural life;

b. To enjoy the benefits of scientific progress and its applications;

c. To benefit from the protection of the moral and material interests resulting from any scientific, literary or artistic production of which he is the author.

Article 12 places various obligations upon states, which include Art. 12(2)(c) The prevention, treatment and control of epidemic, endemic, occupational and other diseases; and Art. 12(2)(d) The creation of conditions which would assure to all medical service and medical attention in the event of sickness.

9 Pharmacia & Upjohn (Pfizer subsidiary) misbranded and illegally promoted some drugs, including the painkiller Bextra, for uses and dosages not approved by the US Food and Drug Administration due to safety concerns. Pfizer was found guilty of intent to defraud or mislead

and was required to pay a criminal fine of $1.3 billion. Pfizer also met civil claims by reimbursing $1 billion to health insurance schemes in respect of prescriptions claimed by consumers.

10 UN Millennium Development Goals, available at: www.un.org/millenniumgoals/global.shtml

11 This is a committee of independent experts which monitors implementation of the ICESCR by states. The committee's interpretation of Covenant provisions are termed 'General Comments'.

12 Annex to General Assembly 63rd session on the Right to Health; UN Document A/63/263, dated 11 August 2008. See www.essex.ac.uk/human_rights_centre/research/rth/docs/GA2008.pdf

13 See the global health partnerships database – formerly the Initiative on Public–Private Partnerships for Health (IPPPH) – which was set up by the Global Forum for Health Research and is currently maintained by the ESRC Innogen Centre, available at: www.health-partnerships-database.org/; see also the website of the International Federation of Pharmaceutical Manufacturers and Associations, which represents the research and development activities of the pharmaceutical, biological and vaccine industries, available at: www.ifpma.org

14 Described as 'Billanthrops' – see 'Billanthropy', *Economist*, 29 June 2006.

15 The latter activities are what may be described as 'social technologies' that accompany the 'physical' technology, i.e. the vaccine.

16 See the Malaria Vaccine Initiative website at: www.malariavaccine.org/

17 See the Malaria Vaccine Initia-

tive website at: www.malariavaccine.org/about-faqs.php

18 Friedman et al. (2003) provide a more conservative figure of 5 per cent in relation to Africa, the Indian subcontinent and the poorer countries of Asia.

19 This applies to patented pharmaceuticals, as well as to those that are not protected by IPRs.

20 Ramsey pricing is, however, not without its critics; see Scherer (2001) and Scherer and Watal (2002).

21 Held in Norway from 8–11 April 2001.

22 The scale of the problem was highlighted in Boseley and Carroll (2002). About a third of HIV/AIDS medicines supplied by GSK at a tiered price were found to have been diverted from African countries to Europe.

23 The decision on the paragraph 6 system of the Doha Declaration waiving obligations under Article 31(f) of the TRIPS Agreement was made by the General Council of the World Trade Organization on 30 August 2003.

24 UNITAID was established by Brazil, Chile, France, Norway and the United Kingdom with the aim of funding the purchase of medicines for HIV/AIDS, malaria and tuberculosis for distribution in poorer countries. It is hosted within the World Health Organization. It now has twenty-nine member countries and one foundation. For more information about UNITAID, see www.unitaid.eu

References

Achieng, J. (2001) 'Kenya: NGOs seek to import generic drugs from India', *Third World Network*, 22 February, available at: www.twnside.org.sg/title/generic.htm

Angell, M. (2000) 'The pharmaceutical industry: To whom is it accountable?', *N Eng J Med*, 342: 1902–4.

Baker, B. K. (2009) 'GSK access to medicines: The good, the bad and the illusory', *Health Gap Global Access Project*, 15 February, available at: www.healthgap.org/bakeronGSK.htm

Bently, L. and Sherman, S. (2001) *Intellectual Property Law*, Oxford: Oxford University Press.

Bermudez, J. and P. Douste-Blazy (2009) 'GSK: please extend patent pool to AIDS drugs', *The Lancet*, 373(9672).

Boseley, S. (2009a) 'Drug giant GlaxoSmithKline pledges cheap medicine for world's poor', *Guardian*, 13 February.

— (2009b) 'GlaxoSmithKline urged to pool its patents on HIV drugs', *Guardian*, 7 September.

Boseley, S. and R. Carroll (2002) 'Profiteers resell Africa's cheap AIDS drugs', *Guardian*, 4 October.

Buse, K. and G. Walt (2000a) 'Global public–private partnerships: Part I – A new development in health?', *Bulletin of the World Health Organization*, 78(4): 549–61.

— (2000b) 'Global public–private partnerships: Part II – What are the health issues for global governance?, *Bulletin of the World Health Organization*, 78(5): 699–708.

Centre for Global Development (2005) 'Making markets for vaccines: Ideas to action', available at www.cgdev.org/content/publications/detail/2869

CESCR (Committee on Economic, Social and Cultural Rights) (2000), 'Substantive issues arising in the implementation of the international covenant on economic, social and cultural rights, General Comment 14', 22nd Session, 11 August, UN doc. E/C.12/2000/4.

Chataway, J. and J. Smith (2005) *Smoke, Mirrors and Poverty: Communication, biotechnological innovation and development*, Innogen Working Paper No. 36, available at: www.genomicsnetwork.ac.uk/media/Innogen%20Working%20Paper%2036.pdf

Chataway, J., R. Hanlin, J. Mugwagwa and L. Muraguri (2009) *Global Health Social Technologies : Reflections on evolving theories and landscapes*, Innogen Working Paper No. 76, available at: www.genomicsnetwork.ac.uk/media/Innogen%20Working%20Paper%2076.pdf

Collier, J. and I. Iheanacho (2002) 'The pharmaceutical industry as an informant', *The Lancet*, 360(9343): 1405–9.

Conde, H. (1999) *A Handbook of International Human Rights Terminology*, Nebraska: University of Nebraska Press.

Danzon, P. (2001) 'Differential pricing: Reconciling R&D, IP and access', WHO-WTO Secretariat Workshop on Differential Pricing and Financing of Essential Drugs, Hosbjor, Norway, 8–11 April.

DFID (Department for International Development) (2002) *Report to the Prime Minister: UK Working Group on Increasing Access to Essential Medicines in the Developing World: policy recommendations and strategy*, 28 November, available at: www.eldis.org/vfile/upload/1/document/0708/DOC11518.pdf

Dukes, M. (2002) 'Accountability of the pharmaceutical industry', *The Lancet*, 360(9356): 1682–4.

Dutfield, G. and U. Suthersanen (2008) *Global Intellectual Property Law*, Cheltenham: Edward Elgar.

European Commission (2003) Council Regulation (EC) No. 953/2003 of 26 May 2003 to avoid trade diversion into the European Union of certain key medicines, available at http://eur-lex.europa. eu/LexUriServ/LexUriServ.do?uri= OJ:L:2003:135:0005:0011:EN:PDF

Friedman, M., H. den Besten and A. Attaran (2003) 'Out-licensing: A practical approach for improvement of access to medicines in poor countries', *The Lancet*, 361(9354): 341–4.

GAVI (2009) 'GAVI partners fulfill promise to fight pneumococcal disease', available at www. gavialliance.org/media_centre/ press_releases/2009_06_12_ AMC_lecce_kick_off.php

GFHR (Global Forum for Health Research) (2007) *The 10/90 Report on Health Research 2003 – 2004*, Geneva: GFHR.

Gibson, J. (2009) *Intellectual Property, Medicine and Health, Current Debates*, Farnham: Ashgate.

Gosseries, A., A. Marcianco and A. Strowel (eds) (2008) *Intellectual Property and Theories of Justice*, Basingstoke: Palgrave Macmillan.

GSK (2009a) 'GlaxoSmithKline statement in response to Paul Hunt's report on GSK' A/ HRC/11/12/Add.2, June, available at: http://198.170.85.29/GSK-response-to-Paul-Hunt-report-June-2009.pdf

— (2009b) 'GlaxoSmithKline's contribution to fighting HIV/ AIDS & improving healthcare in the developing world', available at: www.gsk.com/responsibility/ downloads/GSK-contribution-to-ddw.pdf

Henry, D. and J. Lexchin (2002) 'The pharmaceutical industry as a medicines provider', *The Lancet*, 360(9345): 1590–5.

Hollis, A. and T. Pogge (2008) *The Health Impact Fund: Making new medicines accessible for all*, New Haven, CT: Incentives for Global Health.

Kapp, C. (2001) 'Health, trade, and industry officials set to debate access to essential drugs', *The Lancet*, 357: 1105.

Kettler, H. and A. Towse (2002) *Public–Private Partnerships for Research and Development: Medicines and vaccines for diseases of poverty*, London: Office of Health Economics.

Knowledge Ecology International (2007) 'IGWG submission on collective management of intellectual property: The use of patent pools to expand access to needed medical technologies', 30 September, available at: www.iprsonline.org/ictsd/ Dialogues/2007-10-22/17%20 Ress-PatentPool.pdf

Lenk, C., N. Hoppe and R. Andorno (eds) (2007) *Ethics and Law of Intellectual Property, Current Problems in Politics, Science and Technology*, Farnham: Ashgate.

Lexchin, J. (1997) 'After compulsory licensing: Coming issues in Canadian pharmaceutical policy and politics', *Health Policy*, 40: 69–80.

Lopert, R., D. Lang, S. Hill and D. Henry (2002) 'Differential pricing of drugs: A role for cost-effectiveness analysis?' *The Lancet*, 359: 2105–7.

Merck (2008) 'Merck's response to the Human Rights Guidelines for Pharmaceutical Companies', 29 February, available at: 198.170.85.29/Merck-response-to-UN-Special-Rapporteur-Hunt-29-Feb-2008.pdf

Moran, M., A. L. Ropars, J. Guzman, J. Diaz and C. Garrison (2005) *The New Landscape of Neglected Disease Drug Development*, London: LSE/Wellcome Trust.

Nelson, K. (2003) 'GSK and Boehringer agree to generic AIDS drugs deal', *The Lancet*, 362(9401): 2074.

Nelson, R. (2008) 'What enables rapid economic progress: What are the needed institutions?', *Research Policy*, 37: 1–11.

Pfizer (2007) 'Access to medicines', available at www.pfizer.co.uk/Our-Responsibility/KeyIssues/Pages/Accesstomedicines.aspx

Saad, M., K. Rowe and P. James (1999) 'Developing and sustaining effective partnerships through a high level of trust', in L. Montanheiro et al. (eds), *Public and Private Sector Partnerships: Furthering development*, Sheffield: SHU Press.

Scherer, F. (2001) 'The economics of parallel trade in pharmaceutical products', WHO-WTO Secretariat Workshop on Differential Pricing and Financing of Essential Drugs, Hosbjor, Norway, 8–11 April.

Scherer, F. and J. Watal (2002) 'Post-TRIPS options for access to patented medicines in developing countries', *JIEL*, 5(4): 913–39.

Stiglitz, J. (2006) 'Give prizes not patents', *New Scientist*, 16 September.

UN (2008) 'The report of the UN Special Rapporteur on the right to the highest attainable standard of physical and mental health', UN doc A/63/263, 11 August.

UNITAID (2008) 'UNITAID moves towards a patent pool for medicines', Press release, 9 July.

Watal, J. (2001) 'Workshop on differential pricing and financing of essential drugs', WHO-WTO Secretariat Workshop on Differential Pricing and Financing of Essential Drugs, Hosbjor, Norway, 8–11 April.

WHO (2004a) *Equitable Access to Essential Medicines: A framework for collective action*, Geneva: World Health Organization.

— (2004b) *The World Medicines Situation*, Geneva: World Health Organization.

— (2008) *Global Strategy and Plan of Action on Public Health, Innovation and Intellectual Property*, WHO, 61st World Health Assembly, available at: http://apps.who.int/gb/ebwha/pdf_files/A61/A61_R21-en.pdf

— (2010) 'Essential medicines', available at: www.who.int/topics/essential_medicines/en/

WHO Secretariat (2001) 'More equitable pricing for essential drugs: What do we mean and what are the issues?', WHO-WTO Secretariat Workshop on Differential Pricing and Financing of Essential Drugs, Hosbjor, Norway, 8–11 April.

WHO/WTO Secretariats (2001) *Report of the Workshop on Differential Pricing and Financing of Essential Drugs*, Geneva: WHO/WTO, available at: www.wto.org/english/tratop_e/TRIPS_e/hosbjor_report_e.pdf

Widdus, R and K. White (2004) *Combating Diseases Associated with Poverty: Financing strategies for product development and the potential role of public–private partnerships*, Geneva: Initiative on Public–Private Partnerships for Health/Global Forum for Health Research.

Widdus, R. (2001) 'Public–private partnerships for health: Their main targets, their diversity, and their future directions', *Bulletin of the World Health Organization*, 79: 713–20.

— (2003) 'Public–private partner-ships for health require thoughtful evaluation', *Bulletin of the World Health Organization*, 81: 235.

WTO (2001) 'Declaration on the TRIPS Agreement and public health', 20 November, WT/MIN(01)/DEC/W/2.\

7 | Foundations – actors of change?

HELEN YANACOPULOS

Introduction

Foundations have been prominent actors in international politics since they were created at the beginning of the twentieth century. While the Ford Foundation, the Rockefeller Foundation and the Carnegie Foundation are household names, there is a new breed of foundation that has emerged, with the Bill and Melinda Gates Foundation (Gates Foundation) leading the pack. Foundations like Gates, Soros, Skoll and Hewlett, to name but a few, have become political players in the United States, Europe and further afield. They provide services that have been the domain of NGOs and governments, and they influence international development policy.

Because of its dominant role in global health, the Gates Foundation has received the most attention within the foundation world. Additionally, the sheer size of the Gates Foundation overshadows all other foundations, and this is even more the case since Warren Buffett's $30 billion donation. What is surprising, given the size and international involvement of foundations, is that there has been very little work done on how foundations as a sector are influencing international politics and international development. The American private foundation sector alone reached $6.2 billion in grants in 2008 (Spero 2010: ix), but the sector is under-explored. Those writing about foundations tend either to group them all together or to speak of one foundation (generally Gates), and they offer few explanations for the differences within the sector or for the sector's international influence. The foundation sector is becoming increasingly interesting, given that it has been changing over the past two decades with the rise of what have been called the 'new' foundations, 'philanthrocapitalists', or 'Billanthropists'. These 'new' foundations have emerged out of IT and finance company profits and have been operating in a different manner from their older foundation predecessors.

This chapter focuses on how the role of foundations has been changing, how their work is frequently an extension of the parent company's business values, and how foundations have been involved in philanthropy and human rights. The chapter first distinguishes between different types of foundation and the different ways in which these link to corporations. The second section explores how new foundations are actively engaged in development and politics, and the dilemmas that frequently arise as a result of a clash between philanthropic and business ethics. Historically, foundations have embraced and inhabited a liberal context, and the third section of the chapter explores the relationship that both the long-standing foundations and the newer foundations have to human rights.

Foundation types

The foundation sector is not homogeneous. There are various types of foundation and even if two foundations are of a similar type, their histories, contexts and missions might be completely different, affecting the ways in which they operate and the work that they do. Foundations have been, and increasingly are, extremely influential internationally, and the distinction between old and new, and private and corporate foundations is very important in the work they fund. Ostrower (2006: 510–11) states that it is necessary to distinguish between different types of foundation, and claims that:

> to capture broader elements of foundation approaches to philanthropy, we also need to develop ways of categorizing foundations that reflect differences in how they approach their work and the underlying philosophies that inform their philanthropy.

The foundation sector Foundations, as legal and organisational forms, emerged in the United States in the early twentieth century. Though the sector grew steadily thereafter, there has been a dramatic expansion in the number and types of foundations over the past twenty years. This expansion mirrors the growth of the IT and financial sectors, as well as the prominence of the idea of corporate social responsibility. Ostrower (ibid.: 510) claims that the most common categorisation of foundations is either by asset or by staff size. Another categorisation is by type of foundation, such as community foundations, corporate foundations or independent foundations.

The new foundations are undoubtedly having a quantifiable impact on the sector. For example, the OECD Development Assistance Committee (DAC) calculated that just the Gates Foundation's grant-giving alone, estimated at over $3 billion in 2008, exceeded the official development assistance of ten out of the twenty-two OECD member countries, and of all the non-DAC OECD states (DAC 2007; Moran 2008: 2).

It is hard to put a true value on the foundation sector internationally, since there is a wide spectrum of organisations that qualify as foundations, governed by different national frameworks. However, most foundations are based in North America and Europe, and even now American foundations dramatically outdo their European counterparts. For example, in 2003 the top fifty European foundations gave away 3.8 billion euro, while the biggest American foundations gave away the equivalent of 6.4 billion euro.[1] These figures pre-date the enormous Warren Buffett donation to the Gates Foundation of $30 billion. However, even prior to that donation, the Gates Foundation ranked as the largest foundation in the world, and it dominates the sector.

TABLE 7.1 US independent, corporate, community and grant-making foundations, 1992–2007

Year (circa)	Number of foundations	Total giving (in billions)	Total assets (in billions)
2007	75,187	44.40	682.20
2006	72,477	39.00	614.70
2005	71,095	36.40	550.60
2004	67,736	31.84	510.50
2003	66,398	30.31	476.71
2002	64,843	30.40	435.19
2001	61,810	30.50	467.34
2000	56,582	27.56	486.09
1999	50,201	23.32	448.61
1998	46,832	19.46	385.05
1997	44,146	15.98	329.91
1996	41,588	13.84	267.58
1995	40,140	12.26	226.74
1994	38,807	11.29	195.79
1993	37,571	11.11	189.21
1992	35,765	10.21	176.82

Source: Foundation Center, http://foundationcenter.org/

Legal definitions Foundations are organisations that are not for profit, and the legal framework allowing for their creation dates back over a century. Legally, in the United States, private foundations that have been set up and funded by an individual or a corporation differ from what are called 'community foundations', which are funded by donations from the public. The Internal Revenue Service in the United States distinguishes between community foundations and private foundations, with

TABLE 7.2 Top US foundations by total giving

Rank	Name/(state)	Total giving ($)	As of fiscal year end date
1.	Bill & Melinda Gates Foundation	2,805,251,969	12/31/2008
2.	AstraZeneca Foundation	796,600,000	12/31/2009
3.	The Ford Foundation	474,095,000	09/30/2009
4.	The Robert Wood Johnson Foundation	408,831,456	12/31/2008
5.	GlaxoSmithKline Patient Access Programs Foundation	386,079,449	12/31/2008
6.	The William and Flora Hewlett Foundation	379,599,742	12/31/2008
7.	The Susan Thompson Buffett Foundation	347,911,661	12/31/2008
8.	Lilly Endowment Inc.	336,551,359	12/31/2008
9.	The David and Lucile Packard Foundation	301,963,944	12/31/2008
10.	Silicon Valley Community Foundation	291,096,834	12/31/2008
11.	Janssen Ortho Patient Assistance Foundation, Inc.	280,784,371	12/31/2008
12.	The Andrew W. Mellon Foundation	267,479,576	12/31/2008
13.	Gordon and Betty Moore Foundation	261,740,279	12/31/2008
14.	sanofi-aventis Patient Assistance Foundation	260,740,827	12/31/2008
15.	Genentech Access To Care Foundation	256,821,547	12/31/2008
16.	John D. and Catherine T. MacArthur Foundation	252,254,918	12/31/2008
17.	W. K. Kellogg Foundation	244,511,126	08/31/2009
18.	The Bristol-Myers Squibb Patient Assistance Foundation, Inc.	227,622,788	12/31/2008
19.	Lilly Cares Foundation, Inc.	221,813,118	12/31/2008
20.	The Roche Patient Assistance Foundation	205,258,898	12/31/2008

Source: Foundation Center, http://foundationcenter.org/

private foundations having tighter restrictions and fewer tax benefits than community foundations. Generally, when the term 'foundation' is used, it refers to private foundations, such as Carnegie, Ford, Rockefeller or Gates.

The 1915 Commission on Industrial Relations was set up to examine the connections between concentrations of economic power and the emergence of large-scale philanthropies founded by wealthy industrialists like John D. Rockefeller and Andrew Carnegie. Arnove and Pinede (2007: 389–90) outline the process involving a congressionally created committee, which held hearings on a number of issues, such as the legal status of general-purpose foundations and their accountability to the public, their exemption from taxation, their impact on the institutions and research they funded, and the dangers of concentrating power in so few hands. The issues and criticisms examined by the 1915 commission remain relevant in contemporary debates on foundations.

Of the established foundations, the Carnegie and Rockefeller were both set up in the early 1900s. Andrew Carnegie, after amassing a large fortune in steel, wrote an influential essay entitled 'The Gospel of Wealth', in which he argued a case for the wealthy to share their riches through charity, provoking his fellow wealthy into action through ideas such as 'The man who dies thus rich dies disgraced'. Carnegie set up this first foundation – the Carnegie Corporation of New York – in 1911 and inspired other wealthy individuals to do the same. John D. Rockefeller was influenced by Carnegie's essay, and Frederick T. Gates, Rockefeller's business and philanthropic adviser, encouraged him to follow Carnegie's lead by setting up a 'permanent corporate philanthropy for the good of Mankind' (Chernow 1998: 563–6). He set up the Rockefeller Foundation to engage in the business of 'wholesale' and 'scientific' philanthropy (Arnove 1980; Sealander 2003). In the decades that followed, Henry Ford amassed his fortune in the automotive industry, and his son Edsel Ford set up the Ford Foundation in 1936, with the endowment being used 'for scientific, educational and charitable purposes, all for the public welfare'.

Private foundations By the 1960s, the Ford, the Rockefeller and the Carnegie Foundations had increased their presence and were referred to as 'the big three'. They were considered progressive, in the sense of being forward-looking and reform-minded organisations (Arnove and Pinede 2007: 391). All three foundations responded to the socially charged changes of the 1960s with new national and international programmatic initiatives. Arnove and Pinede (ibid.) argue that the rhetoric

Box 7.1 Corporate foundations – Reebok Human Rights Foundation

Standing up for human rights is a REEBOK hallmark – as much a part of our corporate culture and identity as our products. We believe that we all have a responsibility to UNDERSTAND HUMAN RIGHTS, to expose injustice, and to support efforts that ensure dignity and rights for all human beings. The BUSINESS PRACTICES we have developed and implemented around the world and OUR HISTORY are a reflection of our commitment ...

The MISSION of the REEBOK HUMAN RIGHTS FOUNDATION is to support human rights organizations, defending and extending human rights around the world, such as Physicians for Human Rights, Human Rights Watch, The Women's Commission for Refugee Women and Children, and the Carter Center. The Foundation also sponsors innovative programs targeted to address specific human rights issues. Two such programs include WITNESS, an organization that provides activists with technology tools to document human rights abuses, and the INDONESIAN WORKER HEALTH INITIATIVE, a program to improve the health of urban factory workers.

Source: www.reebok.com/Static/global/initiatives/rights/foundation/index.html

of their annual reports and presidential reviews became more radical, using terms like 'underclass' in highlighting issues of urban and rural poverty, and talking of the growing gap between the 'haves' and the 'have-nots' in access to education, health care, information technologies and other critical resources and services.

For example, Arnove and Pinede (ibid.) outline the Ford Foundation's activities during this time, which included support for voter registration drives; school decentralisation initiatives in New York, resulting in a teachers' strike; the creation of advocacy groups, such as the Mexican-American Legal Defense and Education Fund; and, most controversially, the political campaigns of former aides to Robert F. Kennedy. Additionally, the Ford Foundation was very active in the civil rights movement and the 1968 Poor People's Campaign. This political activity did not go unnoticed, and the result was that the United States Congress responded with the 1969 Tax Reform Act, which restricted the power of foundations.

Currently the Ford Foundation is the third largest American foundation, and the Rockefeller and Carnegie Foundations no longer remain at the top of the list. However, these foundations have retained their political ethos throughout the decades.

By 2003, the Carnegie Corporation assets had increased to $1.8 billion, but it had fallen to twenty-second in the ranking of the 100 largest foundations, thanks to the emergence of new giants in the field like the Bill and Melinda Gates Foundation (assets of $26.8 billion) and the Lilly Endowment (assets of $10.8 billion). While it would seem that the influence and status of the Carnegie Corporation is diminishing, other related Carnegie Foundations, such as the Carnegie Foundation for the Advancement of Education and the Carnegie Foundation for International Peace also hold sizeable endowments, and they influence public policy well beyond their assets (ibid.: 398).

The work and grant-making of Ford, Rockefeller and Carnegie revolved around institutional growth, innovation in research and 'risky areas' that other funding sources would not fund. Arnove and Pinede (ibid.: 392) claim that since they began, the 'big three' have funded nearly all social reform movements within the United States, as well as many reform movements abroad.

Corporate foundations Corporate foundations are entities that receive the bulk of their income from a company – either as an initial investment of assets, a regular donation from company income or as funding allocated from corporate marketing budgets. Companies donate money to their own corporate foundations for various reasons, ranging from the altruistic to the more corporate strategic and reputational. There are also tax reasons for setting up corporate foundations – in order to gain tax benefits for the parent corporation. Regardless of whether the motivation behind corporate foundations is driven by altruism or by corporate branding and marketing, they are a growing part of the foundation sector. However, their close relationship to the parent company means that they are frequently perceived as being public relations vehicles. The example of Reebok above (Box 7.1), with its focus on human rights, illustrates how far the company was affected by negative publicity surrounding the production of sporting goods using cheap labour in developing countries.

'New' foundations and philanthrocapitalism The newly formed foundations of the last few decades have marked a dramatic growth in the sector. Foundations such as Gates, Skoll and Google.org, to name but a

---

Box 7.2 New philanthropy

Adam Waldman, founder and president of the Endeavor Group, a Washington-based philanthropic consultancy, says the hallmarks of the new philanthropy are 'an entrepreneurial results-oriented framework, leverage, personal engagement, and impatience'. As befits an approach that emerged from the world of venture capital and Silicon Valley start-ups:

- 'Engaged' means direct intervention in, and a high measure of control over, the activities of the organisations that a foundation funds or supports in other ways, and a suspicion about receiving unsolicited proposals from outside (presumably because investors are the best judges of acceptable opportunities and risks). Venture philanthropists also support their partners with advice and capacity building help as well as money – though so do most other foundations too.
- 'Effectiveness' is measured using business metrics to monitor performance (expressed through ratios and numbers), often quantified in financial terms and supposedly with an emphasis on the long-term time horizon.
- 'Strategy' is dominated by aggressive revenue generation efforts to promote a certain vision of financial sustainability that releases managers from the torment of raising funds and an emphasis on rapid 'scaling-up' to meet potential demand.

Source: Edwards 2008: 20–1

---

few, illustrate a quantitative change in the size of the foundation sector. This quantifiable change can be seen in the now 68,000 foundations in the United States, with estimated assets of half a trillion dollars, with foundations making annual grants totalling $33.6 billion a year. There are estimates that future foundation and philanthropic funding in the United States will rise to $55 trillion over the next forty years.[2]

But what is new about these 'new' foundations? Are they qualitatively different from the more established ones? Legally speaking, very little is new about 'new' foundations, as they have the same status as the 'old' foundations. While the term 'new foundation' is used within the sector, there is little to formally distinguish them from other private foundations; however, the differences seem to be much more about the cultural and ideological approaches of 'new' foundations, as outlined in Box 7.2.

According to Bishop and Green (2008) (who coined the term 'philanthrocapitalists'), there is indeed a new type of foundation that has three distinguishing features. First, these foundations have vast resources, funds that are primarily derived from the IT and financial sectors. Second, the foundations are relatively new and are still highly connected (either institutionally or through their founder) to the parent organisation, and there is a strong connection to the business methods that worked to make the large corporate profits of the parent organisation. Third, they are highly results/outcome-based organisations, which see that these business methods can transform society and deal with the world's problems. While there are institutional and philosophical differences between these foundations, the 'new' foundations, or philanthrocapitalists, do differ (to varying degrees) from the likes of Ford, Rockefeller and Carnegie.

The largest, and by far the most influential, of the relatively newly formed foundations is the Gates Foundation. Bill Gates set up the Bill and Melinda Gates Foundation in 1994 and stepped down as CEO of Microsoft in 2009 to work full time at the Gates Foundation. One of his colleagues stated that Gates would run the Gates Foundation in the same way as he ran Microsoft, proclaiming that:

> If he [Gates] was going to put any money into philanthropy, he was going to do it in the same way he does business which is absolutely know what he was doing, have an impact, do it in a different way.[3]

Another foundation arising out of the IT sector was set up by Jeff Skoll, one of the founders of eBay, in 1999. Skoll set up the foundation to 'pursue his vision of a world where all people, regardless of geography, background or economic status, enjoy and employ the full range of their talents and abilities'.[4] The Skoll Foundation claims to drive large-scale change by investing in, connecting and celebrating social entrepreneurs and other innovators dedicated to solving the world's most pressing problems. The foundation has driven the idea of social entrepreneurship, and the Skoll Foundation identifies and funds social entrepreneurs, whom it sees as proven leaders whose approaches and solutions to social problems are helping to better the lives and circumstances of countless underserved or disadvantaged individuals. Thus, the foundation identifies the people and programmes that already bring positive changes to communities, and the Skoll Foundation states that it funds them and empowers them to extend their reach, deepen

Box 7.3 The Bill and Melinda Gates Foundation

During the last two centuries, there have been a huge number of innovations that have fundamentally changed the human condition – more than doubling our life span and giving us cheap energy and more food. Society underinvests in innovation in general but particularly in two important areas. One area is innovations that would mostly benefit poor people – there is too little investment here because the poor can't generate a market demand. The second area is sectors like education or preventative health services, where there isn't an agreed-upon measure of excellence to tell the market how to pick the best ideas...

I am optimistic that innovations will allow us to avoid these bleak outcomes...

Although innovation is unpredictable, there is a lot that governments, private companies, and foundations can do to accelerate it. Rich governments need to spend more on research and development, for instance, and we need better measurement systems in health and education to determine what works...

It is critical that we understand in advance what might prevent an innovation from succeeding at scale. For work in developing countries, the lack of skilled workers or electricity might be a key constraint. For work with teachers, we need an approach to measuring their effectiveness that they will welcome as a chance to improve rather than reject because they think it's more overhead or fear that it might be capricious. Even with the best efforts to make sure we understand the challenges, we need intermediate milestones so we can look at what we have learned about the technology or the delivery constraints and either adjust the design or decide that the project should end. We are focused on strong measurement systems and sharing our results where we have successes but also where we have failures. Innovation proceeds more rapidly when different parties can build on each other's work and avoid going down the same dead end that others have gone down.

Source: www.gatesfoundation.org/annual-letter/2010/Pages/investment-in-innovations.aspx

their impact and fundamentally improve society. The foundation has backed attempts to support 'the continuation, replication or extension of programs that have proved successful in addressing a broad array of critical social issues: tolerance and human rights, health, environmental sustainability, economic and social equity, institutional responsibility, and peace and security'.[5]

Another example of a 'new foundation' originating from the IT sector is Google.org. Google Corporation owns the range of Google search engines and is one of the most successful IT companies in the world. In 2004, Larry Page and Sergey Brin outlined their vision for the company to their shareholders, and detailed their commitment

> to contribute significant resources, including 1% of Google's equity and profits in some form, as well as employee time, to address some of the world's most urgent problems. That commitment became Google.org. Google.org is an integral part of Google Inc., and works closely with a broad range of 'Googlers' on projects that make the most of Google's strengths in technology and information.[6]

Google.org focuses on providing quality public services, such as clean water, health and education, particularly in the developing world. The foundation claims that:

> conventional approaches to tackling this challenge have focused on tracking money spent rather than results achieved. Accountability to citizens and communities has largely been absent. While there are no quick fixes, Google.org believes that providing meaningful, easily accessible information to citizens and communities, service providers, and policymakers is a key part of creating home-grown solutions to improve the quality of public services. Better information can help governments and other providers spend scarce resources wisely. And, empowered by information, citizens and communities can demand better services from providers or develop new solutions to meet their own needs.

Foundations as political actors

Foundations are, and always have been, both implicitly and explicitly political in the work they have done, given that their primary aims have been to alleviate social ills. They commonly step in where the state is not able to provide services, and they can be influential in local, national and international decision-making, through their involvement in issues and through their sheer wealth. Despite their frequent self-presentation as apolitical, they have historically taken political positions merely through the selection of their programmes and priorities, and they have worked within a particular liberal paradigm, which influences the nature of their work and their involvement in human rights.

Bell (1971: 466) argues that foundations are worthy of examination because of their financial grant-making capacities, but also because of 'their direct and indirect influence on other actors in world politics'. The budget of some of the older foundations is dwarfed by that of the newer ones, but they are still using their financial clout to frame, steer decision-making and change norms. Bull et al. (2004: 490) have described this as the power over the 'order of things' and the beliefs sustaining this 'order to things'. It is not a type of influence that involves an ability to make other actors do something they would not normally do; rather it is an influence that shapes and determines their wants. In a sense, foundations are able to set the agenda and influence others, the most obvious case being the influence of the Gates Foundation in determining the priorities of global health.

One view, as argued by Parmar (2002), is that foundations have been the vehicles of American hegemony and foreign policy. Clearly, it has been part of the general strategy of the American foundations to encourage 'Western-style' development through technocratic elites or 'competent' leadership groups trained in the necessary value-free social scientific ideology (Bodenheimer 1970). The hope was, according to Francis Sutton, a high official in the Ford Foundation's International Division, 'that successful and competent people will have a trusting view of this country and be understanding and forthcoming partners in new ventures' (Bell 1972: 121). That foundations are powerful in certain political arenas was captured by Bell (1971) when he wrote that the Ford Foundation had elements of a transnational political actor.

Political paradigms The powerful American foundations discussed here operate within a liberal framework, which has influenced their work and practices. Liberalism relies on some key tenets, such as cooperation between states and multilateral work; the utility of markets as a rational means of socio-economic change; incremental versus disruptive change; and the importance of rational individual agents and their human rights. Human rights and the market are pivotal to liberal thinking, and corporations and their resulting foundations are well embedded in this paradigm.

Liberal elements and practices of foundations are well described by Moran, with particular reference to global health-focused foundations. The following elements of foundation practices outlined by Moran (2010: 2–3) can be extrapolated more broadly to general approaches of foundations through:

- partnership brokerage – where foundations act as interlocutors between the public, private and third sectors;

- material influence through the provision of seed funding and philanthropic risk capital;
- technical development interventions;
- procedural influence through permanent representation on governing boards, secondment of employees; and
- ideational influence, which serves to advance what are termed 'quasi-market norms' and private sector approaches.

There have been two dominant forms of theoretical thinking and explanations for foundation practices in the academic literature. These may be broadly defined as the 'liberal pluralist' school (Scholte 2002) and the more critical Gramscian school (Moran 2008, 2010). Scholars using the Gramscian approach to foundations (Arnove 1980; Utting 2005) see foundations as an extension of corporate power, while other writers, such as Parmar (2002), argue that foundations are an extension of an American hegemonic project. Foundations are seen by this group of scholars as agents of elite classes; however, as Moran (2010: 3) points out, other scholars such as Arnove and Pinede (2007) argue that it is improbable that foundations consciously set out to maintain structural continuity in the international system.

Liberal thinkers such as Anheier and Daly (2004: 160) claim that:

it is no coincidence that the emergence of the modern foundation in the late nineteenth and early twentieth centuries … took place in the US, that is, the country mostly influenced by Protestantism and liberalism. Individual capitalists, guided by religious convictions as well as shrewd market thinking, turned personal fortunes into philanthropic funds.

Foundations seen in this light may be part of a broader set of interests that have a similar liberal world-view based on the above liberal principles, but as Moran (2010: 5–6) states, they 'cannot be characterised as intrinsically regressive – or equally should not be seen as benign'.

Human rights and social change The older foundations, like Ford, Carnegie and Rockefeller, were pivotal in carrying forward liberal democratic values, such as human rights. More often than not, these foundations (as their critics point out) were reinforcing American policies during the Cold War period. However, the foundations were also not averse to pushing agendas and funding programmes that did not align with US foreign policy. Spero argues that one of these agendas was human rights. During the American support for repressive Latin American regimes in the 1970s, foundations 'protected threatened scholars and intellectuals, supported individuals who challenged repressive practices, and funded human rights organisations that monitored, documented and publicised human rights abuses' (Spero 2010: 5). In the 1970s, Ford, Rockefeller and Carnegie also funded academia and civil society in apartheid South Africa, engaged in projects set up to challenge apartheid policies in South African courts and aided organisations that advocated basic human rights through the court system (ibid.). This approach went against official American foreign policy towards South Africa at the time. Additionally, during the height of the Cold War, the Ford Foundation launched an organisation to advance human rights in what was then the 'Eastern Bloc'. The Ford Foundation created and funded the group US Helsinki Watch, which made links with groups in the Soviet Union and Eastern Europe and which lobbied Western governments to speak out against human rights violations (ibid.: 6). US Helsinki Watch has since become Human Rights Watch, one of the most respected human rights organisations in the world.

The 'older' American foundations have historically promoted liberal democratic values abroad, and at the core of these are human rights. Specifically, foundations like the MacArthur Foundation have sponsored programmes that contribute to the International Criminal Court, have trained judges in human rights law, and have set up programmes and agencies to improve the protection of human rights (ibid.: 23). The older large foundations have always had a political agenda (albeit one that rarely differs from the American government) around liberal democratic values such as human rights.

New foundation culture One critic of these 'new' foundations is Michael Edwards. In his book, *Just Another Emperor*, he argues that the difference between 'old' and 'new' foundations is that the new foundations focus on quantifiable changes, which can depoliticise highly political issues. He argues that the depoliticisation comes from foundations constructing issues of poverty reduction as output-driven objectives. This, in turn, means that their work does not transform societies, which is what is needed, but merely offers short-term solutions. With this results-based approach to complex development issues, transformative change is written out of the picture, to be replaced by results-based metrics, which, in his eyes, do not make long-term differences to poor people's lives.

Edwards argues that history shows that systemic change has been achieved (in environment, civil rights, gender and disability) through the work of transformative social movements, rather than heroic wealthy individuals, and has involved politics and government, as well as civil society and business. However, not all new foundations have publicly stated that business methods are superior to those of other civil society actors. For example, Melinda Gates has said of the Bill and Melinda Gates Foundation:

> we may have more money to spend, but that doesn't make us different in kind, just in size ... We know we didn't invent philanthropy or a new way of doing it ... We have relied so much on those who came before us. (quoted in Edwards (2008))

Edwards also states that the methods of operation and focus of the new foundations are a response to the widespread dissatisfaction with the older foundations: that the older foundations are

> analog players in a digital world. Just as Microsoft wanted to avoid becoming IBM, the Gates Foundation – despite protests to the contrary – dreads turning into the Ford Foundation. West Coast foundations already hold 40 percent more assets than their cousins in the East. (ibid.: 21–2)

The underpinning principles of many of the new foundations and philanthrocapitalists are based on the idea that, by making foundations and other not-for-profits 'operate like businesses and expand the reach of markets, great things will be within our reach' (ibid.: 12). This view is captured in the words of the influential economist Jeffrey Sachs, when he claimed: 'Wealthy philanthropists have the potential to do more than the Group of Eight leading nations to lift Africa out of poverty' (ibid.). The argument against this view goes back to the principles of long-term change:

> Although these foundations claim to attack the root causes of the ills of humanity, they essentially engage in ameliorative practices to maintain social and economic systems that generate the very inequalities and injustices they wish to correct ... they continue to be optimistic about evolutionary social change occurring through rational planning by so-called 'politically neutral' experts. (Arnove and Pinede 2007: 393)

Conflicting values

With the increasing number of 'new' foundations, the values and strategies of the foundation sector are changing, particularly as the new foundations have been typically formed by exceptionally successful and competitive individuals.

Blended values Many foundations attempt to mix the values of charity and those of business, thus 'blending' these different values. The 'blended value approach', a concept led by Jed Emerson, refers to a way in which organisations can combine revenue generation with social value imperatives. The 'Blended Value Proposition' claims that both for-profit and not-for-profit organisations

> create value that consists of economic, social and environmental value components – and that investors (whether market-rate, charitable or some mix of the two) simultaneously generate all three forms of value through providing capital to organisations.[7]

Bonini and Emerson (2005: 17–18) argue that the foundation community must play a more proactive role in 'building the necessary infrastructure and mobilising more capital investment by creating alternative asset class offerings' and they go on to quote Eliot Jamison of the Origo think tank:

> We are in the process of researching what mechanisms (such as guarantees or the use of subordinated capital from philanthropic investors) could unlock new capital for expansion stage loans to social enterprises in developing countries. We see substantial opportunities for foundations, international development agencies and social investment funds to collaborate in this area despite a limited history of doing so in the past. (ibid.)

Profitability The primary aim and purpose of a corporation is to maximise its shareholders' value – to be profitable. Despite the aims of making corporations more fair, environmental, safe and equitable, the original bottom line is profitability. This is not to say that corporations cannot be any of these other things, but the primary responsibility of those running a corporation is to their shareholders.

Given that foundations have emerged out of corporate profits, it would be odd if we did not see these values coming into play in the foundation world. Michael Edwards (2008: 12–13) offers the following quotes from some of the largest and most influential foundations:

> The profit motive could be the best tool for solving the world's problems, more effective than any government or private philanthropy. (Larry Ellison, founder of Oracle)

> If you put a gun to my head and asked which one has done more good for the world, the Ford Foundation or Exxon ... I'd have no hesitation in saying Exxon. (Charles Munger, Vice-Chairman, Buffet and Berkshire)

The most pressing environmental issues of our time will be ... solved when desperate governments and nongovernmental organizations (NGOs) finally surrender their ideologies and tap the private sector for help... This is our time. (Jeff Skoll, co-creator of eBay)

Arnove and Pinede (2007: 417–18) discuss the role not only of the managers and leaders of organisations, but also of the foundation trustees. They state that, while these trustees are no longer exclusively an insular group of older, white, Anglo-Saxon men, they cannot be considered radical working outside of the global political economy. Colwell (1993) argues that:

The trustees still tend to be well-connected members of the establishment; a majority occupy powerful positions in business (e.g. Xerox Corporation, Alcoa Inc., the Coca-Cola Company, Goldman, Sachs & Co., J. P. Morgan, Boeing Company, and Rothschild, Inc.), government, education, and law.

While critics of new foundations (such as Edwards) admit that business methods can be part of the solution to global problems, the argument is that business is also the cause of many of these same social problems. Edwards quotes Jim Collins, the author of *Good to Great*, who argues that 'we must reject the idea – well intentioned, but dead wrong – that the primary path to greatness in the social sectors is to become more like a business' (quoted in Edwards 2008: 7).

Efficiency and sustainability Many of the new foundations have focused their work on the field of poverty and development, as they have identified a great and pressing need for change. They argue that, over the last fifty years, a lot of resources have been directed to issues of poverty by governments and NGOs, yet the problems of poverty have not been relieved. As illustrated by the comments of Larry Ellison, Charles Munger and Jeff Skoll, business practices need to be injected into the not-for-profit world, namely efficiency and sustainability. We can see these in play in terms of new foundations' internal governance. For example, the Gates Foundation uses models similar to those in business. In a recent interview about the Bill and Melinda Gates Foundation, Bill Gates stated: 'Corporations have a CEO. We have a CEO. Corporations have a board. We have a board...' (Jack 2009). It is this comparison with corporations that is indicative of the form of governance that the Gates Foundation aspires to – one akin to business (Chataway et al. 2010). The emphasis on efficiency and sustainability extends beyond new foundations' internal governance, and has become central to their means of operation.

Can this be a bad thing? Is efficiency and sustainability not what all organisations should aim to achieve? Key principles such as 'results based', 'evidence driven' and 'impact' are natural extensions of efficiency and sustainability, and are increasing in use in the non-profit sector. Chataway et al. (ibid.) suggest that this focus on performance is not necessarily new, as

> impact and efficiency in the not-for-profit sector has been there since Rockefeller and other older foundations such as Carnegie. Perhaps what is different is the standard to which foundations are currently being held to account and the use of diverse and creative models and methods such as systems dynamics commonly used in the business sector.

Bonini and Emerson (2005: 20) illustrate the increasing emphasis on efficiency and metrics:

> While we can hope that the advent of e-philanthropies and the focus on donor education will increase the efficiency and effectiveness of mainstream nonprofit funding, we should be realistic about the impact of such efforts and not expect the kinds of efficiencies we see in the for-profit capital market to evolve fully. With the creation of metrics, methods and regulatory frameworks that suit themselves more fully to nonprofit organizations, however, we have hope.

While the older foundations have not shied away from using and practising these terms, the newer foundations are now affecting (through their funding and influence) the aid industry through these principles. The Kellogg Foundation found that:

> the emphasis on sustainability, efficiency and market share has the potential to endanger the most basic value of the non-profit sector – the availability of 'free space' within society for people to invent solutions to social problems and serve the public good. (Edwards 2008: 49)

Edwards (ibid.) believes that the approach of the new foundations or philanthrocapitalists towards efficiency and competition will have a negative impact on the rest of the not-for-profit world of civil society. Edwards's primary criticism is that the new foundations' approach – what has worked for business should also work for citizen action – will lead to a 'social capital market', where the not-for-profit organisations compete for resources put up by investors, allocated using efficiency and impact metrics. One move in this direction, outlined by Edwards, is that technological advances in using and storing data have meant that those who want to give to charities, be they individuals or organisations, have information resources such as GuideStar, the Center for Effective Philanthropy and New Philanthropy Capital, which 'measures 54 indicators including the average years of experience of senior managers and the percentage increase in the budget from the previous year' (ibid.: 69). The problem with this is that these indicators and metrics have very little to do with social transformation.

Conclusion

The foundation sector will more than likely continue to increase in size and influence. With a projected $55 trillion dollars in philanthropic resources to be created in the United States alone in the next forty years, as Edwards (ibid.: 9) says, 'the stakes are very high'. While the foundation sector is extremely diverse, there are similarities between groups of organisations. The older, well-established foundations, such as Ford, Carnegie and Rockefeller, have a long history of working in the field of human rights in highly political contexts. In looking at 'new' foundations, such as the Gates Foundation, Skoll Foundation and Open Society, we find that their focus is quite different. They have emerged primarily from financial and IT companies, and the relationship and proximity of the key individuals (i.e. Bill Gates, Jeff Skoll and George Soros, respectively) to their 'new' foundations have meant that they arguably have a closer affinity to business ethics and practices, and are more sympathetic to the ideals of what has been termed 'philanthro-capitalism'.

The business ethics of profit, efficiency and sustainability have not only been imported into these 'new' foundations, but have also affected the ways in which other not-for-profit organisations operate. While business principles may have helped improve some people's lives, frequently economic development has contributed to large inequalities between groups. Edwards (ibid.: 77) argues that no great social changes have been mobilised through the market in the twentieth century. Societal change – such as the civil rights movement, the women's movement, the environmental movement, the New Deal and the Great Society – were pushed ahead by civil society and anchored in the power of government as a force for the public good.

Notes

1 See www.charitytimes. com/pages/ct_news/news%20 archive/February_05_news/Uk%20 Foundation%20tops%20Europe%20 giving%20list.htm

2 National Philanthropic Trust: Philanthropy Statistics, available at: www.nptrust.org/philanthropy

3 'Bill Gates: How a geek changed the world', Money

Programme Special Report, BBC2, 29 January 2009.

4 See www.skollfoundation. org/media/press_releases/ internal/092006.asp

5 See www.skollfoundation.org/ aboutskoll/index.asp

6 See www.google.com/ corporate/diversity/business.html

7 See www.blendedvalue.org/ about/

References

Anheier, H. and S. Daly (2004) 'Philanthropic foundations: A new global force', in H. Anheier, M. Glasius and M. Kaldor (eds), *Global Civil Society 2004/5*, London: Sage.

Arnove, R. F. (ed.) (1980) *Philanthropy and Cultural Imperialism: The foundations at home and abroad*, Boston, MA: G. K. Hall & Co.

Arnove, R. and N. Pinede (2007) 'Revisiting the "Big Three" foundations', *Critical Sociology*, 33(3): 389–425.

Bell, P. D. (1971) 'The Ford Foundation as a transnational actor', *International Organization*, 25(3): 465–78.

— (1972) 'The Ford Foundation as a transnational actor', in R. O. Keohane and J. S. Nye (eds) *Transnational Relations and World Politics*, Cambridge, MA: Harvard University Press.

Bishop, M. and M. Green (2008) *Philanthrocapitalism: How the rich can save the world*, New York: Bloomsbury Press.

Bodenheimer, S. J. (1970) 'The ideology of developmentalism: American political science's paradigm-surrogate for Latin American studies', *Berkeley Journal of Sociology*, 25: 95–137.

Bonini, S. and J. Emerson (2005)

'Maximizing blended value-building beyond the blended value map to sustainable investing, philanthropy and organizations', paper available at: www. blendedvalue.org

Bull, B., M. Boas and D. McNeill (2004) 'Private sector influence in the multilateral system: A changing structure of world governance?' *Global Governance*, 10: 481–98.

Chataway, J., J. Mugwagwa and L. Muraguri (2010) *Opening the Gates: Assessing the impact of 'new' foundations on health and development*, ESRC Innogen Centre working paper.

Chernow, R. (1998) *Titan: The life of John D. Rockefeller, Sr.*, New York: Warner Books.

Colwell, M. A. C. (1993) *Private Foundations and Public Policy: The political role of philanthropy*, New York and London: Garland Publishing.

DAC (Development Assistance Committee) (2007) *Final ODA Flows in 2006*, Paris: DAC, OECD.

Edwards, M. (2008) *Just Another Emperor: The myths and realities of philanthrocapitalism*, Demos/ Young Foundation.

Jack, A. (2009) 'A profitable view of philanthropy', *Financial Times*, 1 December.

Moran, M. (2008) '"The 800 pound gorilla": The Bill & Melinda Gates Foundation, the GAVI Alliance and philanthropy in international public policy', paper prepared for the International Studies Association 49th Annual Convention, San Francisco, March 26–29.

— (2010) 'The private foundations of global health partnerships', paper presented to the International Studies Association 51st Annual

Convention, New Orleans, February 17–20.

Ostrower, F. (2006) 'Foundation approaches to effectiveness: A typology', *Nonprofit and Voluntary Sector Quarterly*, 35: 510.

Parmar, I. (2002) 'American foundations and the development of international knowledge networks', *Global Networks: A Journal of Transnational Affairs*, 2(1): 13–30.

Scholte, J. A. (2002) 'Civil society and democracy in global governance', *Global Governance*, 8: 281–304.

Sealander, J. (2003) 'Curing evils at their source: The arrival of scientific giving', in Lawrence J. Friedman and Mark D. McGarvie (eds), *Charity, Philanthropy, and Civility in American History*, Cambridge: Cambridge University Press.

Spero, J. (2010) *The Global Role of US Foundations*, New York: Foundation Center.

Utting, P. (2005) 'Corporate responsibility and the movement of business', *Development in Practice*, 15(3/4): 375–88.

8 | Combating transnational corporate corruption: enhancing human rights and good governance

JOHN HATCHARD

Introduction

The devastating effect of corruption on human rights and good governance is encapsulated in the words of former UK Lord Chancellor Lord Falconer, in his Foreword to the Draft Corruption Bill: 'Corruption worldwide weakens democracies, harms economies, impedes sustainable development and can undermine respect for human rights by supporting corrupt governments with widespread destabilising consequences' (Home Office 2003). The scale of the problem was highlighted in July 2009 by the Joint Committee of the House of Lords and House of Commons on the Draft Bribery Bill, which noted with concern the World Bank's estimate that around a trillion dollars' worth of bribes are paid each year, which adds 10 per cent to the cost of doing business globally and as much as 25 per cent to the cost of procurement contracts in developing countries (though it is not at all clear how such 'estimates' are arrived at) (Joint Committee 2009).

For many, corruption is perceived as a problem that essentially affects developing countries. This view is perpetuated by the Transparency International (TI) Corruption Perception Index (CPI), in which developing countries consistently account for the vast majority of those in the bottom half of the index.[1] Such indices must be viewed with considerable caution;[2] in any event, it is not enough to focus attention on the developing world. Rather we must recognise that, particularly as regards grand corruption,[3] the problem often has a transnational dimension. As member of the Commission for Africa Anna Tibaijuka has argued: 'It is not enough to say that people in [the developing world] are corrupt, but to ask *who is corrupting them* and *how do we deal with them.*'[4]

Some indication of 'who is corrupting them' comes from Transparency International's Bribe Payers Index (BPI), which evaluates the supply side of corruption (TI 2008). The findings of the 2008 BPI reveal that 'a number of companies from major exporting countries still use bribery to win business abroad, despite awareness of its damaging impact on corporate reputations and ordinary communities'.[5] Of particular concern is the fact that enterprises based in emerging economies – in particular China, India, Mexico and Russia – are perceived as routinely engaging in bribery when doing business abroad. The BPI also suggests that public works and construction companies are the most corruption prone when dealing with the public sector, and are most likely to exert undue influence on the policies, decisions and practices of governments. This point is emphasised in the report of the Commission for Africa, *Our Common Interest*:

> Procurement, the way that governments buy in goods and services, suffers particularly severely from corruption. Abuse of this system takes many forms. Though public sector contracts are widely put out to sealed tender, bribes [often paid by international corporations, particularly through the use of agents], known by euphemisms such as a 'signature bonus' can be requested or offered which result in the accepted bid not being the best available. It is not only the politicians and public officials who create the problem: it is also the corporations, bankers, the lawyers and the accountants, and the engineers working on public contracts.
> (Commission for Africa 2005: 150)

It is against this background that this chapter explores the key issue raised by Tibaijuka of how to tackle the supply side of transnational corruption. In particular, it examines some of the key international and national efforts designed to combat the bribery of foreign public officials through the use of the criminal law, and questions whether focusing attention on this approach offers the most effective way of combating the problem. It is divided into five sections. The first section explores the link between human rights, corruption and business. The second and third sections examine international and national efforts designed to break this link through the use of the criminal law. The next section then considers the development of two promising alternative approaches towards breaking the link, while the final section provides some conclusions.

Making the link: human rights, corruption and business

One can readily define the concept of human rights – i.e. 'the rights and freedoms to which every human being is entitled' (*Oxford Dictionary of Law* 1997). National constitutions and a range of international and regional instruments then identify specific 'human rights'. In the case of 'corruption', the matter is more complex. A widely cited definition is that developed by Transparency International: 'the misuse of entrusted power for private gain' (TI 2009b). While this has the advantage of brevity, it does not assist in identifying what, from a legal point of view, constitutes 'corruption'. This chapter adopts the approach taken in several international and regional anti-corruption instruments that 'corruption' encompasses a range of acts and omissions, including bribery, abuse of functions, misappropriation of state funds, illicit enrichment and trading in influence.[6] Yet even here some grey areas remain. For example, facilitation payments – i.e. payments to foreign public officials to facilitate or expedite performance of a 'routine governmental action' – are not prohibited by two of the most influential attempts to combat transnational corruption, the USA Foreign Corrupt Practices Act (FCPA) and the OECD anti-bribery convention.[7]

Although 'grey areas' remain, there is a widespread recognition both that 'corruption' is morally and ethically wrong and that it has a negative effect on the promotion and protection of human rights and good governance. As Chaskalsen P noted in the Constitutional Court of South Africa in *South African Association of Personal Injury Lawyers* v. *Heath*:[8]

> Corruption and maladministration are inconsistent with the rule of law and the fundamental values of our Constitution. They undermine the constitutional commitment to human dignity, the achievement of equality and the advancement of human rights and freedom. They are the antithesis of the open, accountable, democratic government required by the Constitution. If allowed to go unchecked and unpunished they will pose a serious threat to our democratic state.

The International Council on Human Rights Policy (ICHRP), in its 2009 seminal publication *Corruption and Human Rights: Making the connection*, also points out that UN treaty bodies and UN special procedures have concluded that, where corruption is widespread, states cannot comply with their human rights obligations (ICHRP 2009).[9]

It is perhaps useful to explore the link between corruption, human rights/good governance and business diagrammatically.

Good governance

Promotion and protection
of human rights

Figure 8.1 The link between human rights and good governance

Figure 8.1 emphasises the importance of establishing and maintaining a strong link between integrity and good governance (or the more helpful formulation 'just and honest governance' developed by the Commonwealth) and the protection and promotion of human rights. Good governance/just and honest government leads to respect for human rights and vice versa. The importance of this link is encapsulated in the Harare Commonwealth Declaration of 1991, when Commonwealth heads of government pledged to work for:

> the protection and promotion of the fundamental political values of the Commonwealth:
> - democracy, democratic processes and institutions which reflect national circumstances, the rule of law and independence of the judiciary, just and honest government; [and]
> - fundamental human rights, including equal rights and opportunities for all citizens regardless of race, colour, creed or political belief.

Figure 8.2 demonstrates the link between corruption, bad governance/unjust and dishonest governance and abuses of human rights. Here corruption can lead to bad governance and bad governance can lead to human rights violations. For example, the bribery of election officials to manipulate electoral results in favour of certain political leaders undermines the right to free and fair elections.[10] Furthermore, corruption itself can lead directly to human rights abuses, for example through the bribing of judges by a litigant.[11]

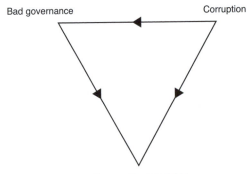

Figure 8.2 The link between corruption, bad governance and abuses of human rights

These linkages are recognised in the UN Convention against Corruption, Chapter 1 of which sets out a good governance agenda as a key strategy through which state parties can combat corruption. This includes requiring a state party to 'take the necessary steps to establish appropriate systems of procurement', to promote 'integrity, honesty and responsibility among its public officials' and to 'take measures to strengthen integrity and to prevent opportunities for corruption among members of the judiciary'.[12]

Increasing attention is now being paid to the link between human rights, governance, corruption and business. One of the key drivers of grand corruption is the role of transnational corporations in paying bribes to foreign public officials in order to obtain or retain business.[13] This point is also recognised in the UN Convention against Corruption, which requires state parties to take measures to prevent corruption involving the private sector and to criminalise the bribery of foreign public officials.[14] The challenge is to break the undesirable links demonstrated in Figure 8.2. This is considered in the following sections.

Breaking the link: combating transnational corporate bribery at the international level

This section mainly concentrates on the operation of the major international instrument designed to combat transnational corporate bribery – the Organisation for Economic Co-operation and Development (OECD) Convention on Combating Bribery of Foreign Public Officials in International Business Transactions (the OECD Convention). This is illustrated by a short case study of the Al Yamamah/BAE affair, involving the sale of arms to Saudi Arabia. The impact of the UN Convention against Corruption will then be considered.

The OECD Convention on Combating Bribery of Foreign Public Officials in International Business Transactions (the OECD Convention) The OECD Convention came into force on 15 February 1999 and has been ratified by all thirty OECD members (including the United Kingdom), as well as by eight non-member states: Argentina, Brazil, Bulgaria, Chile, Estonia, Israel, Slovenia and South Africa.

The Convention is concerned with 'active corruption', i.e. corruption on the supply side.[15] Among other things, Article 1 requires state parties to establish in their domestic law the criminal offence of bribery of a foreign public official.[16] The issue of enforcement is the key to the operation of the whole Convention. Article 5 provides that investigations and prosecutions 'shall not be influenced by considerations of national economic interest, the potential effect upon relations with another state or the identity of the national or legal person involved'.

Article 5 is supported by paragraph 6 of the Annex to the 1997 *Revised Recommendations of the OECD Ministerial Council* (the Annex), which stresses that 'public prosecutors should exercise their discretion independently, based on professional motives', while Commentary 27 to the Convention makes it clear that the prosecutorial decision must not be subject to improper influence by concerns of a political nature.

A major feature of the Convention is Article 12, which requires participating states to 'cooperate in carrying out a programme of systematic follow-up to monitor and promote the full implementation of this Convention'. Responsibility for this programme lies with the OECD Working Group on Bribery in International Business Transactions (WGB).[17] The effectiveness of this process in the context of the United Kingdom can now be considered.

The OECD Convention in practice The OECD Convention represents a major commitment on the part of participating states to tackling transnational corruption. However, there remains a mixed picture within these countries as regards the prosecution of transnational corruption. While some countries are particularly active in this respect (for example, the USA under the Foreign Corrupt Practices Act), in 2008 there was significant enforcement in sixteen countries but little or no enforcement in the others (Dell and Heimann 2009: 7). The UK has been criticised on more than one occasion by the WGB, which, in its 2005 monitoring report on the UK, noted that: 'It is surprising that no company or individual has been indicted or tried for the offence of bribing a foreign public official since the ratification of the convention by the UK.'[18]

However, it is the Al Yamamah case in the United Kingdom that promises to test the effectiveness of the Convention in practice. The case arose as a result of a criminal investigation launched in 2004 by the Serious Fraud Office (SFO) into allegations that a major UK-based defence contractor, BAE Systems, had paid large bribes to a senior Saudi prince in order to obtain a multi-billion-dollar defence contract from Saudi Arabia. In December 2006, the director of the SFO announced that he had decided to discontinue the investigation. The SFO statement read, in part:

This decision has been taken following representations that have been made both to the Attorney General and the Director [of the SFO] concerning the need to safeguard national and international security.

It has been necessary to balance the need to maintain the rule of law against the wider public interest.

No weight has been given to commercial interests or to the national economic interest.

Not surprisingly, the decision provoked a political and legal storm.[19] For present purposes, three issues are relevant.

THE SECURITY IMPLICATIONS ARGUMENT The decision to discontinue the investigation was defended by the Attorney General as follows:

> It should be stressed that commercial considerations played no part in the SFO decision. Rather it was based on potential damage to the UK's counter-terrorism strategy, and ultimately on the risk to the lives of our citizens and service people if the case had gone ahead. The judgment was that UK cooperation with Saudi Arabia in the counter-terrorism field is of crucial importance ... and that if Saudi Arabia were to withdraw that cooperation, the UK would be deprived of a key partner in our global counter-terrorist strategy.[20]

The issue of non-prosecution of foreign bribery cases on the grounds of national security represents a serious challenge to the effectiveness of the OECD Convention. The Convention does not specifically address the issue, and the reality is that this may be seen as a loophole for other states to utilise in order to avoid their Convention obligations. If so, this means that the international arms trade will be effectively excluded from the scope of the Convention, and this can only seriously damage its credibility and integrity. In fact, since Article 5 provides that investigations and prosecutions shall not be influenced by 'the potential effect upon relations with another State',[21] it might be argued that this means there is no basis for an implicit national security exception. However, the issue certainly requires clarification (Cullen 2007; Rose-Ackerman and Billa 2007).

THE DECISION TO PROSECUTE As noted above, the Annex provides that public prosecutors should 'exercise their discretion independently, based on professional motives'. The WGB has stressed the importance of this principle and, during country visits, examiners have sought assurances that participating states will adhere to it. For example, the Phase 2 Review of France states that: 'the lead examiners noted the assurances given by the Ministry of Justice that, in accordance with the law, no instruction not to prosecute is given in specific cases'.[22] This makes the intervention of the UK government while the BAE criminal investigation was ongoing a particular matter of concern, and again raises doubts as to the effectiveness of the Convention.[23]

RESPONSE OF THE WGB Given the potentially deleterious consequences of the Al Yamamah case for the Convention, the response of the OECD was swift. In January 2007, the OECD secretary-general noted that the 'Working Group has serious concerns as to whether the decision was consistent with the OECD Anti-Bribery Convention'. Then, at its March 2007 meeting, the Working Group reaffirmed its serious concerns about the United Kingdom's discontinuance of the BAE/Al Yamamah investigation. In 2008, the WGB undertook a supplementary review of the United Kingdom ('Phase Two bis'). Its report found that the unsatisfactory treatment of certain cases since the 2005 Phase 2 report had revealed systemic deficiencies, including uncertainty over the application of Article 5 to all stages of the investigation and prosecution of foreign bribery cases, and the hurdle created by the special Attorney General consent requirement for foreign bribery prosecutions. The report also urged that these issues should be addressed, and that the independence of the Serious Fraud Office should be strengthened. The Working Group also recommended that the UK ensure that the SFO attributes a high priority to foreign bribery cases and has sufficient resources to address such cases effectively (OECD 2008).

What is of particular interest here is the manner in which the WGB is mandated to publicly make a detailed assessment of both the implementation of, and compliance with, convention obligations by individual states. At the very least, this ensures that the issue of state compliance (or otherwise) with convention obligations is kept under constant review and is widely publicised. The UK response to the WGB reports is noted below.

The United Nations Convention against Corruption The impact of the OECD Convention is also limited by the fact that several major exporting countries that fare poorly in the TI Bribe Payers Index (including India, China, Mexico and Russia) are not parties to the Convention. This emphasises the fact that, unless there is a concerted international effort and political willingness to combat the issue, taking effective action against the bribery of foreign public officials will remain elusive. This is recognised in an OECD Policy Statement on Bribery in International Business Transactions of 19 June 2009, in which the OECD calls 'on major exporting countries that are not Parties to the Convention to criminalise the bribery of foreign public officials and to join the Parties to the Convention in their fight against transnational bribery as soon as possible' (OECD 2009).

Here the United Nations Convention against Corruption (UNCAC) has a potentially key role to play. It came into force on 14 December 2005 and is the first global instrument designed to tackle corruption in both the public and the private sectors. As of 15 September 2010, it had 140 signatories and 146 ratifications/accessions, including Russia, China, Mexico and the majority of the OECD members.[24] Article 16 of UNCAC requires state parties to criminalise the bribery of foreign public officials in their domestic law, and uses similar terms to Article 1(1) of the OECD Convention. Thus the hope is that a combination of the two conventions will cause states worldwide to take effective steps to criminalise and prosecute such conduct.

Yet, as the OECD Convention has demonstrated, requiring states to criminalise the bribery of foreign public officials is one thing; putting the provisions into practice is quite another. In this respect, UNCAC is faced with two key problems. First, it does not include a similar provision to Article 5 of the OECD Convention. Second, the monitoring arrangements remain a divisive issue. Article 63(1) of UNCAC establishes a Conference of the State Parties (COSP) whose function is 'to improve the capacity of, and cooperation between, State Parties ... to achieve the objectives [of the Convention] and to promote and review its implementation'. Article 63(7) then requires the COSP to establish 'any appropriate mechanism or body to assist in the effective implementation of the Convention'. Efforts continue to develop a meaningful process along the lines of the WGB.[25]

Breaking the link: combating transnational corporate corruption at the national level by prosecuting the corporation in the victim state

Ongoing events in Lesotho illustrate the manner in which 'victim' states can tackle transnational corruption by utilising their own criminal law. Lesotho is one of the smallest and most impoverished nations in the world. A land-locked country that is entirely surrounded by South Africa, its one major natural resource is water. This led to the establishment in 1986 of the Lesotho Highlands Water Project (LHWP), which was, and remains, one of the world's largest dam construction projects. Part funded by the World Bank, many major Western companies (the contractors) were awarded construction contracts.[26] These were awarded by the Lesotho Highlands Development Authority (LHDA), while a Joint Permanent Technical Commission (the Commission) was established to oversee the project. The first chief executive of the LHDA was a local state official, Masupha Sole, who had considerable influence over which of the companies obtained the dam construction contracts.

Concern over the running of the LHDA led to an audit in 1994, which uncovered serious financial irregularities on the part of Sole, and he was dismissed the following year. The Swiss authorities actively assisted the local investigators, who discovered that Sole had several bank accounts in Switzerland totalling well over US$1 million. Furthermore, while the payments had been received via so-called intermediaries, the payments originated with some of the contractors (or their agents) working on the LHWP. Sole was convicted of bribery and fraud.[27] However, for present purposes, the most significant aspect of the affair was the decision by the Lesotho authorities also to prosecute those construction companies allegedly involved in paying the bribes.[28] Not surprisingly, this led to a plethora of preliminary issues being raised by the companies, each anxious to avoid any prosecutions and the resultant bad publicity. In the event, over a hundred such applications were made before the first trial even began. To their enormous credit, this did not dissuade the prosecutors in Lesotho from pursuing the case.

In 2001, Acres International Ltd, a Canadian construction company, was convicted in the High Court of Lesotho of paying bribes to Sole. Thereafter a German company, Lahmeyer International GmbH (Lahmeyer) was also convicted of bribing Sole, and a French company, Spie Batignolles and an Italian construction company, Impregilo, both pleaded guilty to bribery.[29]

Even then, there remained the suspicion that other local state officials had also taken bribes from the construction companies, and in 2008 Reatile Mochebelele (who was, at all relevant times, Lesotho's chief delegate to the Joint Permanent Technical Commission) and Letlafuoa Molapo (who was one of Lesotho's three permanent delegates to the Commission) were convicted of bribery. The key to these successful prosecutions lay in the cooperation given to the Crown by Lahmeyer, which supplied detailed documentation of the bribe arrangements. The cooperation of Lahmeyer was all the more remarkable, given its earlier strenuous efforts (together with the other construction companies involved in the LHWP) to prevent any prosecutions taking place.

The change of policy seemingly stemmed from the fact that Lahmeyer was originally charged alongside Mochebelele and Molapo. With Lahmeyer anxious to avoid more bad publicity (and a possible further period of debarment from World Bank-funded and other multilateral development bank-funded projects), it reached an agreement with the prosecution whereby the charge against it was dropped in return for the company assisting the prosecution. In the circumstances, such a bargain was understandable, and the subsequent convictions of Mochebelele and Molapo highlight the positive results that can stem from such an agreement.[30]

The Lesotho experience is important, in that the decision to prosecute the corporations and their agents should encourage other victim states to follow suit. Here the political will to address the problem was crucial. As the Attorney General of Lesotho has put it:

Lesotho is committed to completing these prosecutions, primarily to eradicate corruption in the country, but also to set an example for other countries. Here the hope is expressed that other developing countries will realise that corruption can be combated successfully, provided the necessary will is there and also that the countries involved give each other the necessary support. (Maema 2003)

This approach is supported by Article 16(1) of UNCAC, which requires state parties to criminalise the bribery of foreign public officials.

However it must also be recognised that, on occasions, the political will to prosecute 'corruption' may take on a more sinister motive – for instance, to discredit political and other opponents or to 'punish' a company that has refused to pay a bribe. It follows that, in undertaking corruption prosecutions, the prosecution service must enjoy independence, and that the decision to prosecute must be based on clear and objective criteria.[31]

Breaking the link: changing the method of enforcement?

Combating transnational corporate corruption by the use of the criminal law remains a considerable challenge. While the need for the political will to prosecute is fundamental, other practical hurdles to prosecuting bribery successfully remain, including the potential length, complexity and cost of the trial, and the challenge of obtaining sufficient admissible evidence in circumstances where, by its very nature, the corrupt agreement is made and carried out secretly by willing parties.

It follows that there is scope to develop alternative methods of combating transnational corporate corruption. Two can usefully be considered here.

'Encouraging' corporations to cooperate with investigations This is one of the most promising recent approaches, and is the model employed in the United States Foreign Corrupt Practices Act (Colares 2006). Under the Act, it is unlawful for United States nationals and companies to make a corrupt payment to a foreign official for the purpose of obtaining or retaining business for or with, or directing business to, any person. What makes the FCPA so powerful is that it extends to acts that establish a connection with US territory, for example using a US bank account

through which to pay bribe monies, even if the person or company doing so is not resident in the US and does no business there. In addition to bringing criminal proceedings, the FCPA allows the US Department of Justice (DOJ) to make use of a Deferred Prosecution Agreement with a corporation, under which criminal charges are withdrawn if certain conditions are met, or a Non-Prosecution Agreement, under which the DOJ agrees not to prosecute the corporation. In exchange, the corporation agrees to enhance its compliance regime (often overseen by a government-approved monitor) and to pay a monetary penalty.

Perhaps the most high-profile case to date under the FCPA is that of the German firm Siemens AG (Siemens). In December 2008, Siemens, Europe's largest engineering company, while not formally entering a guilty plea to bribery allegations, agreed to pay a record $800 million in fines in the United States and to be monitored to ensure future compliance with anti-bribery laws. This was in order to settle corporate corruption investigations in the USA involving alleged payments of more than $1 billion to government officials around the world in order to win infrastructure projects.[32] A key factor in reaching the agreement between Siemens and the US Department of Justice (later endorsed by the US District Court for the District of Columbia) was the cooperation of Siemens in the investigation. As the DOJ Sentencing Memorandum noted, Siemens

> provided extraordinary cooperation in connection with the investigation of its past corporate conduct, and has undertaken uncommonly sweeping remedial action in response to the discovery of its prior misconduct. In addition, Siemens has provided substantial and timely assistance in the investigation of other persons and entities.[33]

In the UK, a somewhat similar approach was first adopted in a case involving Balfour Beatty plc. In April 2005, following an internal company investigation, Balfour Beatty 'self-reported' to the SFO certain 'payment irregularities' within one of its subsidiaries involved in a US$130 million UNESCO project to rebuild the Alexandria Library in Egypt. Rather than pursue a criminal trial, in 2008 the SFO (with the consent of Balfour Beatty) obtained a Civil Recovery Order (CRO) in the High Court, made under section 240 of the Proceeds of Crime Act. The CRO enabled the SFO to recover the proceeds of any 'unlawful conduct' through the recovery of property 'which is, or represents, property obtained through unlawful conduct'. Under the terms of the CRO, Balfour Beatty agreed to pay £2.25 million and to contribute to the cost of the proceedings. It also agreed to put in place compliance mechanisms to prevent any repetition of the irregularities, and to submit these processes to supervision for a specified period. As the director of the SFO commented:

> This is a highly significant development in our efforts to reform British corporate behaviour. We now have a range of enforcement tools at our disposal, and a major factor in determining which of those tools is deployed will be the responsibility demonstrated by the company concerned.[34]

In July 2009, the Serious Fraud Office in England then announced a new policy for dealing with overseas corruption through a system of self-reporting cases of overseas corruption to the SFO (SFO 2009). In essence, the 'negotiated settlement' approach means that a 'corporate' (ibid.: 2) is encouraged to report instances of bribery and corruption within the organisation to the SFO. In return, the SFO will settle such cases civilly 'wherever possible'. As with the FCPA approach, the importance of the negotiated settlement is that, in appropriate cases, it avoids the uncertainty of a criminal trial. From the point of view of the company, it has a number of potential benefits. Perhaps the most important is that it avoids the prospect of debarment (also known as 'blacklisting' or 'exclusion'). This is the mechanism by which a company or individual is prevented from tendering for, or participating in, a project (or projects) for a specific reason, such as previous involvement in corrupt practices. In some cases, debarment is discretionary (for example, the World Bank); in others (for example, under the European Union Procurement Directives), a purchasing body must exclude from tendering any company that has been convicted of corruption.[35]

In addition, the hope is that the new system will contribute to, as the SFO puts it:

> crafting effective and proportionate sanctions for this type of case and of helping to produce a new corporate culture. This will bring about behavioural change within businesses themselves and will create corporate cultures in which no form of corruption is tolerated.[36]

Of course, the use of the criminal law remains an option, and, as former UK Lord Chancellor and Secretary of State for Justice Jack Straw has emphasised: 'there needs to be a credible threat of successful investigations and prosecutions'.[37] There is now some progress here. In September 2008, Niels Tobiasen, the managing director of CBRN Team Ltd, a UK security consulting firm, and a Ugandan government official, Ananais Tumukunde, both pleaded guilty in Southwark Crown Court to bribery in connection with a contract in Uganda.[38] Then, in July 2009, the first prosecution was brought in the UK against a company for overseas corruption. The case arose from the voluntary disclosure to the SFO by the management of the holding company of Mabey & Johnson Ltd of evidence indicating that it had sought to influence decision-makers in obtaining public contracts in Jamaica, Ghana and Iraq. In July 2009, in Southwark Crown Court, the company pleaded guilty to a conspiracy to corrupt and to one charge of breaching UN sanctions in Iraq. It was fined £3.5 million, ordered to pay a £1.1 million confiscation order and £350,000 in prosecution costs. It was also ordered to make reparation payments of £1,413,611 to Ghana, Jamaica and Iraq.[39] The case has wider implications. First, the prosecution of any company official implicated in an affair is not precluded.[40] Second, twelve government ministers and senior public officials from Ghana, Angola, Madagascar, Bangladesh, Jamaica and Mozambique were named as recipients of bribes from the company. This may well assist and encourage 'victim' countries to take action against individuals.

The prosecutions demonstrate a seemingly new-found willingness on the part of the UK to fulfil its commitments under the OECD Convention, and represent a positive response to the criticism from the WGB noted earlier. Certainly the SFO has asserted that more criminal investigations and prosecutions are expected in 'appropriate cases'. Yet it is not clear why the SFO decided to prosecute Mabey & Johnson, while adopting a civil recovery solution in the case of Balfour Beatty.[41] This uncertainty of outcome might well make a company reluctant to self-report if, after doing so, the SFO still has the option of launching a criminal prosecution and of using the information supplied by the company to help build its case. Thus it is clearly vital to develop a process that is credible to companies, and the SFO has rightly indicated that it expects to revise its approach, where necessary, in the light of experience and feedback.[42]

Encouraging the ethical corporation Prosecution (or at least the threat of prosecution) and the development of a self-reporting approach are key strategies in seeking to combat transnational corporate corruption. Yet in recent years, much attention has also been focused on bringing about behavioural change within corporations by encouraging them to develop and maintain robust ethics and compliance policies.[43] This has led to a plethora of initiatives. These include the *TI Business Principles for Countering Bribery*, which aim to 'provide a framework for good business practices and risk management strategies for countering bribery' (TI 2009a),[44] the World Economic Forum's Partnering against Corruption Initiative (PACI),[45] the Extractive Industries Transparency Initiative (EITI) which is a multi-stakeholder anti-corruption initiative involving mining and oil companies[46] and the *ICGN Statement and Guidance on Anti-Corruption Practices*, developed by the International Corporate Governance Network (ICGN 2009).

While the need to act ethically and to respect human rights as enshrined in these initiatives has received considerable corporate support, arguably the greatest incentive for corporations to refrain from transnational bribery is the economic one. This is found in a 2008 report by PriceWaterhouseCoopers entitled *Confronting Corruption: The business case for an effective anti-corruption programme*. This sets out a strong business case for having an anti-corruption strategy that goes beyond avoiding potential enforcement penalties and is based on the following findings:

- Almost 45 per cent of respondents say they have not entered a specific market or pursued a particular opportunity because of corruption risks, 39 per cent say their company has lost a bid because of corrupt officials and 42 per cent say their competitors pay bribes.
- If corruption was discovered, 55 per cent say the most severe impact would be to corporate reputation. This is greater than the combined total of those who say legal, financial and regulatory impacts would be the most severe.
- More than 70 per cent believe that a better understanding of corruption will help them compete more effectively, make better decisions, improve corporate social responsibility and enter new markets.
- Some 65 per cent of respondents believe a level playing field is crucial to their company's future business activities. (PriceWaterhouse Coopers 2008: 2)

This argument is supported by the ICGN, which takes the view that 'corruption matters to investors',[47] and this approach forms the basis for ICGN (2009). Yet it remains to be seen how far one can take this point. For example, despite the enormous fine levied on Siemens its share price was little affected. Arguably, it is the economic impact on the individual firm that is the key here. In the case of Siemens, it was 'business as usual' with its announcement, shortly after the fine, that it had won a billion-dollar contract for a power plant in Iraq. Crucially, it was not banned from bidding for US public sector projects.[48]

Some conclusions

Effective international and national action is needed to break the link between corruption, bad governance and abuses of human rights. A major contribution towards doing so is by tackling the bribery of foreign public officials by corporations. In this respect, several conclusions can be drawn from the discussion.

The need for a global response: encouraging states to become parties to the UN Convention against Corruption Many of the initiatives discussed in this chapter emanate from Western countries. Yet today South–South cooperation is becoming increasingly important, with China's economic power, in particular, giving it increased prominence and influence. As the South African Institute of International Affairs (SAIIA) has noted: 'When engaging in Africa, China has emphasised its non-colonialist credentials and its policy of non-interference into the internal affairs of the countries with which it cooperates.'[49] Brautigam has argued that, as regards China's relationship with African states, Beijing is hesitant to hobble its companies with Western-style restraints before they have become world-class competitors. As she puts it: 'The Chinese are kind of starting out where everyone else was years ago, and they see themselves as being at a disadvantage.' In other words a case of 'Thinking Business, Not Ethics' (Brautigam 2009).

In some ways, this view has similarities with the position in the United States following the passing of the Foreign Corrupt Practices Act in 1977. This statute was widely seen by the business community as placing it at a competitive trade disadvantage compared with other Western countries. This led the US government to spearhead a move towards an international agreement to combat transnational bribery. The result was the OECD Convention (Nicholls et al. 2006). To what extent history is repeating itself must remain a matter for debate; but the possibility remains that the countries that are particularly keen to push 'anti-corruption' strategies are those that fear the erosion of their traditional dominance in the developing world by China and other emerging economies.[50]

Whatever the motives, combating transnational corporate corruption requires global support, and this highlights the significance of the UN Convention against Corruption. As a global anti-corruption initiative, the Convention offers states worldwide the opportunity to take effective steps to tackle the bribery of foreign public officials. In view of the earlier discussion, it is interesting to note that China, Russia and Mexico have all ratified the Convention, while prominent OECD member states such as Germany and New Zealand have failed to do so. This means that continued efforts are needed to encourage all UN member states to ratify the Convention.

The need to encourage states to comply with their convention obligations The challenge remains of ensuring that states comply with their obligations under the anti-corruption conventions. Certainly some progress is being made as regards the OECD Convention, and much of this is due to the rigorous monitoring role of the Working Group on Bribery. Yet there remain a significant number of states in which insufficient action is seemingly being taken. This makes it all the more important for all OECD participating states to adhere to their recent pledge to 'comprehensively implement their obligations under the Convention, particularly their obligations in relation to enforcement' (OECD 2009).

The impact of the OECD Convention is further limited, in that it does not apply to a number of countries which, according to Transparency International's BPI, are perceived as routinely engaging in bribery when doing business abroad. The need to address this situation is emphasised by the OECD participating states themselves, which have called on 'major exporting countries that are not Parties to the Convention to criminalise the bribery of foreign public officials and to join the Parties to the Convention in their fight against transnational bribery as soon as possible' (ibid.).

This highlights the importance of UNCAC. As a global convention, it has the potential to unite states in their efforts to combat transnational corporate bribery. This makes the current impasse on the development of an effective review mechanism a matter of considerable concern and one which threatens the effectiveness of the Convention.

The need to develop effective methods of enforcement Developing effective mechanisms to investigate and, where appropriate, to prosecute successfully transnational corporate corruption remains a key strategy for all states. Yet the use of the 'negotiated settlement' approach in the United States under the Foreign Corrupt Practices Act and its influence on the development of a similar policy by the Serious Fraud Office in England and Wales should not be underestimated. In appropriate cases, this approach is mutually beneficial to both prosecutors and corporations, and should lead to long-term benefits, such as the establishment and monitoring of more effective corporate compliance programmes.

In this respect, we are arguably at something of a watershed, for the negotiated settlement approach may well lead to the use of criminal law against corporations being viewed as a last resort. So long as there is a 'credible threat of successful investigations and prosecutions', this is no bad thing, and it usefully complements the aims of the OECD Convention and UNCAC in combating transnational bribery.

Adopting the negotiated settlement approach can also benefit those 'victim' states struggling to combat the problem of the bribery of their own public officials. While the plea bargain reached between the Crown and Lahmeyer in the *Mochebelele* case ensured that two corrupt local public officials were convicted, it also enabled the company to avoid any criminal or other liability for its criminal activities over many years. The negotiated settlement approach would have ensured that Lahmeyer also took responsibility for its actions.

Overall, finding answers to the questions posed by Anna Tibaijuka in her statement 'It is not enough to say that people in [the developing world] are corrupt, but to ask who is corrupting them and how do we deal with them' remains a considerable challenge. However, ongoing national and international developments provide a justifiable hope that there is now a sustainable movement towards enhancing human rights, integrity and good governance through effectively combating transnational corporate corruption.

Notes

1 See www.transparency.org/policy_research/surveys_indices/cpi

2 For a convincing critique of the CPI, see van Hulten (2007). For an in-depth assessment of the issue, see UNDP/Global Integrity (2008).

3 This describes cases where 'massive personal wealth is acquired from States by senior public officials using corrupt means. It often arises where such officials have power over the granting of large public contracts and receive bribes either as a direct payment in return for showing favour or payment of part of the proceeds of a contract granted as a result of the bribe' (Society for Advanced Legal Studies 2002: paragraph 2).

4 Speaking at the launch of the Commission's report, *Our Common Interest*, February 2005 (my italics).

5 Huguette Labelle, TI chair, in a TI press release at the launch of the report, 8 December 2008.

6 For example, the United Nations Convention against Corruption does not define 'corruption'. Rather it includes a range of conduct which state parties are required (or in some cases merely recommended) to criminalise 'in order to prevent and combat corruption more efficiently' (Article 1(a)).

7 For details of the instruments, see below. The FCPA lists the following examples as constituting lawful facilitation payments to foreign public officials: obtaining permits, licences or other official documents; processing governmental papers, such as visas and work orders; providing police protection, mail pick-up and delivery; providing phone service, power and water supply, loading and unloading cargo, or protecting perishable products; and scheduling inspections associated with contract performance or transit of goods across country. See the US Department of Justice commentary on the FCPA, available at www.justice.gov/criminal/fraud/fcpa/. For a full analysis, see Nicholls et al. (2011), ch. 15.

8 [2000] ZACC 22; 2001 (1) BCLR 77 at paragraph 4.

9 See, for example, the statements by the Committee on Economic, Social and Cultural Rights on the position in Moldova that 'the state faces serious problems of corruption, which have negative effects on the full exercise of rights covered by the Covenant [ICESCR]' E/C.12/1/ADD.91 (CESCR 2003: paragraph 12); and by the Committee on the Rights of the Child on the position in the Philippines that it 'remains concerned at the negative impact corruption may have on the allocation of already limited resources to effectively improve the promotion and protection of children's rights, including their right to education and health' CRC/C/PHL/CO/3-4, paragraph 19.

10 As Anastasio Somoza, a former president of Nicaragua, reportedly put it: 'You won the elections. But I won the count!'

11 For a range of helpful illustrations of corrupt practices and their impact on human rights, see ICHRP (2009: Appendix 1).

12 Articles 9, 8(1) and 11(1), respectively.

13 In addition, corporate entities are frequently used to launder the proceeds of corruption through the international financial system. However, that is beyond the scope of this chapter.

14 Articles 12(1) and 16(1), respectively.

15 For a full discussion of the OECD Convention, see Nicholls et al. (2006: chapter 10) and Pieth et al. (2007).

16 Article 1(1) states: 'Each Party shall take such measures as may be necessary to establish that it is a criminal offence under its law for any person intentionally to offer, promise or give any undue pecuniary or other advantage, whether directly or through intermediaries, to a foreign public official, for that official or for a third party, in order that the official act or refrain from acting in relation to the performance of official duties, in order to obtain or retain business or other improper advantage in the conduct of international business.' Article 1(4) provides a wide-ranging definition of 'foreign public official'.

17 The WGB is made up of government experts from the thirty-eight participating countries.

18 See www.oecd.org/dataoecd/62/32/34599062.pdf paragraph 16. See below for recent developments. The WGB report on the United Kingdom also recommended (as did an earlier 2003 Working Group report) that the UK enact modern foreign bribery legislation at the earliest possible date. A Bribery Bill is due to be presented to the UK parliament in 2010.

19 For instance, the order by the UK government to the Serious Fraud Office to drop its investigations into the arms deal was described as 'the triumph of realpolitik over principle' (*Guardian*, 18 December 2006, p. 24).

20 Letter from the Attorney General's Office dated 25 January 2007 (reference B/O6/52) to the non-governmental organisation The Corner House. Copy in the possession of the author.

21 See also Commentary 27, noted earlier.

22 See *Phase 2 Report of France*, page 31, available at: www.oecd.org/dataoecd/36/36/26242055.pdf

23 It is also significant that the BAE investigation was halted just as the Swiss authorities had agreed to provide the SFO with banking details

of those being investigated, which can often be a turning point in investigating transnational corruption.

24 The United Kingdom ratified UNCAC on 9 February 2006.

25 In November 2009, the latest attempt to develop an effective monitoring process by COSP met with limited success. See Transparency International press release of 13 November 2009, available at: www.transparency. org/ news_room/latest_news/press_ releases/ 2009/2009_11_13_review_ mechanism_f lawed

26 Those awarded contracts were Sogreah, Spie Batignolles, Asea Brown Boveri Schaltanlagen GmbH, Asea Brown Boveri Generation AG, Sweden, Lahmeyer International GmbH, Acres International Ltd, Dumez International, Sir Alexander Gibb & Partners Ltd, Cegelec and Coyne et Bellier.

27 In addition, the Swiss authorities returned the proceeds of corruption to the government of Lesotho, thus depriving Sole of any financial gain from his misdeeds.

28 For a detailed analysis of the affair, see Darroch (2003).

29 As one lawyer close to the case has suggested to the author: 'Perhaps Impregilo's desire to settle stems from the fact that they have been given the contract to build a bridge linking Sicily and the rest of Italy and may not have been all that forthright in their tender about the little hiccup they are having at present in Southern Africa.'

30 Even so, the fact is that it enabled Lahmeyer to avoid any criminal or other liability for its apparent bribery of these officials over so many years. This is further considered below.

31 While regrettably only an optional provision, Article 11(2) of UNCAC provides that state parties may take measures to ensure that the prosecution service enjoys independence similar to that of the judicial service.

32 Siemens is listed on the New York Stock Exchange and accordingly it is subject to the FCPA.

33 The memorandum is available at: www.siemens.com/press/pool/de/ events/2008-12-PK/DOJ2.pdf

34 SFO press release, 6 October 2008.

35 See Directives 2004/17/EC and 2004/18/EC of the European Parliament and of the Council of 31 March 2004. See also Hatchard (2007: 23–8).

36 This approach was criticised by Thomas LJ in *R* v. *Innospec Ltd* [2010] EW Misc 7 (EWCC) where the issue of whether the SFO had the power to strike plea bargain-type deals with companies and individuals was questioned.

37 Speech at the 5th European Forum on Anti-Corruption, 23 June 2009. He added: 'To that end we have devoted £6 million to two anti-corruption teams in the Metropolitan Police, and have nearly doubled the size of the dedicated unit in the Serious Fraud Office.'

38 Unlike the FCPA, the English legislation also permits the prosecution of those who receive the bribes. Tobiasen received a suspended prison sentence, while Tumukunde was sentenced to twelve months' imprisonment. He also signed a disclaimer releasing £52,800 from his bank account into the custody of the City of London police for restitution.

39 The company also agreed to submit its internal compliance programme to an SFO-approved independent monitor at a cost of up to £250,000 in the first year.

40 See, for example, the case of *R v. Dougall* [2010] EWCA 1048.

41 The SFO has indicated that an exception to a civil settlement would be if board members of the corporate had engaged personally in the corrupt activities, particularly if they had derived personal benefit from this.

42 In addition, the negotiated settlement approach does not prevent the prosecution of those company officials and employees who were involved in the unlawful conduct itself.

43 See, in particular, Woolf Committee (2008), which was compiled for BAE Systems following the Al Yamamah affair. Another incentive for the corporate sector to develop such policies lies in section 7 of the Bribery Act 2010, which makes it an offence for a commercial organisation to fail to prevent bribery by a person associated with it, i.e. an employee, agent or subsidiary. This is subject to the defence that the organisation had 'adequate procedures' in place to prevent bribery: see further Nicholls et al. (2011), ch. 4.

44 See also the FTSE4Good criteria for countering bribery and corruption, available at: www.ftse.com/ Indices/FTSE4Good_Index_Series/ index.jsp and the work of the International Chamber of Commerce.

45 See www.weforum.org/en/ initiatives/paci/index.htm

46 See http://eitransparency.org/

47 ICGN letter to the Secretariat of the Conference of State Parties to UNCAC, 27 October 2009.

48 By way of contrast, in January 2009 the share price of a major Indian IT company, Satyam Computers, plummeted following disclosure of its involvement in bribery and fraud. In this case, the company itself was a 'fraud', in that it displayed 'Ponzi-like' features behind a façade of legitimate business activity.

49 World Bank Group 'Knowledge sharing and best experiences for improving coordination among non-executive agencies of control and civil society in their fight against corruption' (2007), referenced in 'South–South cooperation in the fight against corruption', a background paper prepared by the UNODC Secretariat for the Conference of State Parties to UNCAC (2009), available at: www.unodc.org/ documents/treaties/UNCAC/COSP/ session3/V0987479e.pdf

50 I am grateful to my colleague, Phil Bates, for suggesting this important and interesting perspective.

References

Brautigam, Deborah (2009) *The Dragon's Gift: The real story of China in Africa*, Oxford: OUP.

Colares, J. (2006) 'The evolving domestic and international law against foreign corruption: Some new and old dilemmas facing the international lawyer', *Washington University Global Studies Review*, 5(1).

Commission for Africa (2005) *Our Common Interest*, Harmondsworth: Penguin.

Cullen, P. (2007) 'Article 5: Enforcement', in M. Pieth, L. A. Lowe and P. J. Cullen (eds), *The OECD Bribery Convention: A commentary*, Cambridge: Cambridge University Press.

Darroch, F. (2003) 'The Lesotho corruption trials – A case study', *Commonwealth Law Bulletin*, 29.

Dell, G. and F. Heimann (2009) *TI Progress Report 2008: Enforcement* of the OECD Convention on Combating Bribery of Foreign Public Officials, Berlin: Transparency International.

Hatchard, J. (2007) 'Recent developments in combating the bribery of foreign public officials: A cause for optimism?', University of Detroit Mercy Law Review, 85(1).

Home Office (2003) Corruption: Draft Legislation, Cm5777, available at: http://www.archive2.official-documents.co.uk/document/cm57/5777/5777.pdf

ICGN (International Corporate Governance Network) (2009) ICGN Statement and Guidance on Anti-Corruption Practices, available at: www.icgn.org/files/icgn_main/pdfs/best_practice/guidance_on_anti-corruption_practices/2009_anti-corruption_practices_(march).pdf

ICHRP (International Council on Human Rights Policy) (2009) Corruption and Human Rights: Making the connection, Geneva: ICHRP.

Joint Committee (2009) of House of Lords and House of Commons, Draft Bribery Bill, First Report of Session 2008–09, available at: www.publications.parliament.uk/pa/jt200809/jtselect/jtbribe/115/115i.pdf

Maema, L. F. (2003) 'Prosecuting bribery in Lesotho', paper delivered at the 11th International Anti-Corruption Conference, Seoul, May, available at: www.odiousdebts.org

Nicholls, C., T. Daniel, M. Polaine and J. Hatchard (2006) Corruption and Misuse of Public Office, Oxford: Oxford University Press.

— (2011) Corruption and Misuse of Public Office, 2nd edn, Oxford: Oxford University Press.

OECD (2008) United Kingdom: Phase

2bis Report on the application of the Convention on Combating Bribery of Foreign Public Officials in International Business Transactions, available at: www.oecd.org/dataoecd/23/20/41515077.pdf

— (2009) Working Group on Bribery in International Business Transactions Policy Statement on Bribery in International Business Transactions, available at: www.oecd.org/dataoecd/36/36/43117861.pdf

Oxford Dictionary of Law (1997) (4th edition), Oxford: OUP.

Pieth, M., L. A. Lowe and P. J. Cullen (eds) (2007) The OECD Bribery Convention: A commentary, Cambridge: Cambridge University Press.

PriceWaterhouseCoopers (2008) Confronting Corruption: The business case for an effective anti-corruption programme, available at: www.pwc.com/en_GX/gx/forensic-accounting-dispute-consulting-services/pdf/pwc-confronting-corruption.pdf

Rose-Ackerman, S. and B. Billa (2007) Treaties and National Security Exceptions, Yale Law & Economics Research Paper No. 351.

SFO (Serious Fraud Office) (2009) Approach of the Serious Fraud Office to Dealing with Overseas Corruption, London: SFO.

Society for Advanced Legal Studies (2002) Banking on Corruption: The legal responsibilities of those who handle the proceeds of corruption, London: Society for Advanced Legal Studies.

TI (Transparency International) (2008) 2008 Bribe Payers Index, available at: www.transparency.org/news_room/latest_news/press_releases/2008/bpi_2008_en

— (2009a) Business Principles for Countering Bribery, available at: www.transparency.org/

publications/publications/other/business_principles_for_countering_bribery

— (2009b) *The Anti-Corruption Plain Language Guide*, available at: www.transparency.am/misc_docs/TI_Plain_Language_Guide_280709.pdf

UNDP/Global Integrity (2008) *A User's Guide to Measuring Corruption*, Oslo: Global Integrity.

van Hulten, M. (2007) 'Ten years of corruption (perceptions) indices', available at www.corruptie.org

Woolf Committee (2008) *Business Ethics, Global Companies and the Defence Industry: Ethical business conduct in BAE Systems plc – The way forward*, available at: www.dorsey.com/files/upload/Fraud/5WoolfExecutiveSummary-Burkill.pdf

9 | Business in zones of conflict: an emergent corporate security responsibility?

NICOLE DEITELHOFF AND KLAUS DIETER WOLF

Introduction

Economic globalisation has challenged the political steering capacities of individual states and of intergovernmental governance systems that exist at the international level. This chapter argues that economic globalisation has thus increased the need to make use of the problem-solving potential of non-state actors to address regulatory problems, and has raised expectations of the business sector's participation in providing collective goods in the transnational sphere. The ongoing debate about new modes of governance portrays the general increase and heightened importance of business actors in global governance as a shift in the public–private divide so intimately connected to the Westphalian order.

Norm setting and norm implementation by private self-regulation or co-regulation seem to promise more effective solutions to all kinds of collective problems at the global level. The commitments and practices of business companies under what is generally referred to as corporate social responsibility (CSR) arose in the late 1980s and 1990s. There is a growing belief that companies, no matter where they operate or where they sell their products or services, should at least comply with, if not go beyond, existing international social, environmental and labour standards – and indeed human rights more broadly. Governance initiatives, such as the Global Compact or the Extractive Industries Transparency Initiative (EITI), are examples of a general willingness within the business sector to share responsibility for global governance (Ottaway 2001). With the private sector thus changing its role from one in which it is seen as the cause of problems requiring legally binding state or interstate regulation to one in which it is treated as a co-performer of governance functions (Schuppert 2008), a great number of transnational corporations (TNCs) – if we take business participation in the UN Global Compact as a reliable indicator, almost 6,000 of them – seem to have accepted responsibilities that go far beyond Milton Friedman's doctrine that 'the social responsibility of business is to increase its profits' (Friedman 1970). This extreme position speaks to the traditional notion of a neat separation between the public and the private sector within the confines of the state, whereby the state is responsible for providing public goods and for fulfilling citizens' human rights, while the business sector supports this provision by generating wealth and economic development within society. However, the general increase in public–private partnerships and multi-stakeholder initiatives in global governance witnessed over the last couple of decades raises doubts about this neat separation. Increasingly, the state is overburdened with the task of providing collective goods and has come to share this responsibility with private actors, civil society and business, thus giving rise to a seemingly new phenomenon: the co-production of governance, which blurs the line between the public and the private spheres. Business today has to operate within a richly textured environment crowded with public actors, such as states and international organisations, civil society movements, customers, shareholders and (last but not least) other companies. All these actors bring with them particular challenges, role conceptions and normative standards for the conduct of business operations that can alter a company's cost–benefit calculations to a remarkable degree.

Even if it is safe to assume that the provision of collective goods might never become the primary goal of business, under these altered circumstances the voluntary self-commitments made by private corporations in such fields as the environment, health, education and human rights become a business case. Indeed, examples such as EITI or the Global Compact clearly signal that the self-perception of having beyond-profit responsibilities is 'being incorporated into the mainstream of business practice' (Waddock 2008: 52).

In this chapter we explore such general expectations against empirical evidence, by focusing on a hard case for corporate governance contributions: contributions to peace and security in zones of violent conflict. Drawing on findings from a recently completed comparative research project on corporate governance contributions in zones of conflict (Wolf et al. 2007; Deitelhoff and Wolf 2010a),[1] we assess direct and indirect corporate governance contributions to peace and security in zones of conflict, in order to show the types of governance contributions that can realistically be expected of TNCs where the state fails to provide fundamental collective goods or to protect human rights and basic normative standards. By assessing the range of corporate governance contributions, we seek in the next section to qualify the widespread assumption that there actually is something like a nascent new understanding of responsible engagement observable in the business sector. From our findings, in the following section, we draw general conclusions as to what we learn about the factors conditioning the role shift of corporations to co-performers of governance functions. We also look at the effectiveness and desirability of business contributions to global governance. For while we have come to expect companies to take on responsibilities in general, there are also concerns about how far such private contributions to the provision of collective goods should go.

If we want to assess the potential and limits of corporations acting as co-performers of governance functions by filling governance gaps that are the result of states' unwillingness or inability to provide basic public goods (or even by attempting to change the governance situation in their host states), zones of conflict offer a particularly 'hard case'. Zones of conflict are usually characterised by varying degrees of state failure to provide collective goods in general, and particularly in a field that is so closely connected to the very idea of the modern state: peace and security. Security is obviously a hard case for private self-regulation as a meaningful complement, or even substitute, for public governance. Therefore, if corporate governance contributions to peace and security could be systematically observed in zones of conflict and under conditions of state failure, this would offer particularly strong support for the expectations raised above. To be sure, these expectations are more than a merely academic construct: the general spread of zones of conflict and violence has also increased political pressure, from the international community and transnational civil society alike, on TNCs operating in zones of conflict to contribute to peace and security.

Corporate governance contributions to peace and security in zones of conflict

By focusing on the security-related governance contributions of TNCs, we do not intend to paint a bright picture of the involvement of TNCs in zones of conflict, but rather to analyse an empirical phenomenon and a widespread political expectation that has not yet been systematically investigated. TNCs operate in areas where they are increasingly confronted by violent conflict environments and by the withdrawal of the state from the provision of security, either because the state lacks the resources or because it profits from insecurity (as in the case of the so-called 'shadow' or 'over-extended' states). Certainly many companies, not just those in the extractive industry, have been involved in conflicts in many ways – whether by financing conflict parties (often in an attempt to appease all potential future authorities in a country), by trading conflict-related goods (for instance 'blood diamonds') or by simply exploiting the regulatory gaps left by weak or failing state authorities.

Operating in zones of conflict, TNCs have the opportunity to realise profits, but also run the risk of incurring substantial war damages and rising security costs and of being publicly associated with bloodshed and human rights violations. But it is precisely this obvious tension between corporations' undisputed contributions to destabilisation – to fuelling, prolonging and taking commercial advantage of violent conflicts – on the one hand, and high-flying expectations of their potential contributions to security on the other that renders the search for circumstances under which private actors can make meaningful contributions to peace and security all the more important.

Companies' operations in zones of conflict have become the target for a whole range of campaigns and protests over the past decade. The best known among them are the 'blood diamond' campaign, focusing on the business sector's fuelling of the conflicts in Angola, Sierra Leone and the Democratic Republic of Congo (DR Congo) by purchasing diamonds from, and trading them with, conflict parties (Bone 2004; Smillie et al. 2000) and the Publish What You Pay campaign, which challenges extractive companies to disclose their payments to host governments in an attempt to counter the lack of transparency in money flows (Fort and Schipani 2004: 17; Deitelhoff and Wolf 2010b).

Additionally, the political sphere has started to reach out to the business sector for a contribution to peace and security in zones of violent conflict. The very first policy dialogue of the UN Global Compact was on 'The Role of the Private Sector in Zones of Conflict'. It offered a forum for companies to discuss the risks and negative impacts associated with their operations in zones of conflict, to promote the principles of the Global Compact in these zones, and to proactively counter corruption and bribery, which are regarded as drivers in many conflicts. In 2004, even the UN Security Council took up the issue and established a working group on the 'role of business in conflict prevention, peacekeeping and post-conflict peace-building' (UN 2004). In 2006, the OECD published guidelines for companies operating in weak zones of governance. Finally, there is also empirical evidence that companies are able or willing to contribute to peace and security in zones of conflict, such as the Kimberley Process Certification Scheme to combat the trade in conflict diamonds or the Voluntary Principles on Security and Human Rights, developed by the US and British governments in partnership with the biggest oil companies, such as Shell and BP.[2]

Companies operating in zones of conflict have several behavioural options. At the onset of conflict they might (a) simply go on doing business; (b) take advantage of regulatory gaps or of the turmoil of a conflict; or (c) withdraw. Against these alternative options, governance contributions would involve sustained and intentional unilateral or collective policies and activities that work towards the creation and implementation of collectively binding rules and norms related to the provision of collective goods. Even within this focus, the security relevance of corporate governance contributions in zones of conflict may differ: they may *directly* address the level of violence in conflict zones. In this narrow sense, security governance refers to issues such as security sector reform, as well as disarmament, demobilisation and reintegration efforts. It might also include corporate involvement in peace negotiations and the handling of public and private security forces where this affects a broader public or communities.

But corporate governance contributions can also be intended as *indirect* contributions to peace and security, by addressing underlying causes of violent conflict in neighbouring policy areas that are identified as relevant for peace and security: political order, socio-economic governance and the socio-cultural sphere. In the dimension of *political order*, governance contributions aimed at promoting democratic structures and the rule of law, the protection of human rights, the promotion of civil society, and anti-corruption and transparency provide the focus. In the *socio-economic dimension*, contributions to transforming war economies, combating poverty and bridging social divides are of interest. This dimension may also encompass management of the environment and natural resources. In the *socio-cultural dimension*, corporate engagement that deals with the legacy of violent conflict and that aims at establishing a culture of peace is addressed. This might include free and independent media, reconciliation initiatives and peace education.

In an effort to gain a comprehensive understanding of the range of direct and indirect corporate governance contributions to peace and security in zones of conflict, our comparative research project included cases from various industries and branches, operating in different zones of conflict and with several home-state origins. Cases covered included the food and beverage industry operating in Rwanda and the eastern part of DR Congo (Feil 2010), the oil industry in Nigeria (Zimmer 2010), the information and communications technology (ICT) sector in DR Congo (Wallbott 2010), the activities of aviation and logistics companies in Northern Ireland (Haidvogl 2010), the tourism industry in the Israel/Palestine conflict (Fischer 2010), the role of the early modern chartered companies in East Asia (Wolf 2010), and the contracting out by states to private security and military companies (Deitelhoff 2010).

The systematic comparison of corporate governance contributions in these diverse cases results in a surprisingly clear picture of the extent and kind of governance contributions to peace and security that can be expected from business companies in zones of conflict. The most striking general empirical finding is the virtual lack of any direct contributions to security by corporations in the case studies, with the notable exceptions of the early modern chartered companies, the private security companies and the oil industry in Nigeria (with some reservations). Still, in all the case studies we observed a remarkable amount of indirect contribution to peace and security, as well as general governance contributions not related to peace and security. Companies have taken up issues closely related to conflict drivers and causes by addressing the livelihood of rural communities in Rwanda, fair employment issues in deeply segregated societies such as Northern Ireland and anti-corruption measures in societies that suffer chronically from corruption and patronage, such as Nigeria.

Obviously, corporations shy away from interfering in the core of public security – that is, the organisation and use of force, which they perceive to be core responsibilities of the state. While they may contradict Friedman's image of businesses as non-political actors and may possess a social responsibility that goes beyond 'doing good' in general, contributing to security in a narrow sense appears to remain a taboo for companies. This conclusion finds support in another general trend that is apparent across the case studies: even when corporations provide indirect contributions to peace and security, they frame their activities as CSR, rather than as a form of 'security' responsibility. By doing so, they reflect the functional division of labour between the public and the private sectors that was evident in the (now fading) golden age of the nation state and at the same time fall dramatically short of taking on a form of CSR proposed by representatives of states and international organisations in the political debate. The prevailing corporate notion of the public–private functional divide demonstrates that the outsourcing of security-related governance functions to private actors finds far less favour now than in the early modern period, when chartered companies took on the complete range of state functions in overseas areas. Even the outsourcing to private security companies reinforces this trend, as is signalled by the speedy demise of private security and military companies involved in direct combat, such as Executive Outcomes and Sandline International, and the latest public outcries over scandals such as the killing of civilians by the US company Blackwater (now Xe) in Iraq in September 2007. Although this overall pattern of governance contributions to peace and security frustrates political expectations of corporate problem solving, it does not rule them out. This becomes clear once explanatory factors are examined to account for this pattern.

Explaining corporate governance contributions to peace and security

In comparative studies within a common analytical framework, the role of company, production and conflict characteristics, as well as the characteristics of the political, social and market environments in which a corporation operates, were investigated as potentially relevant factors.

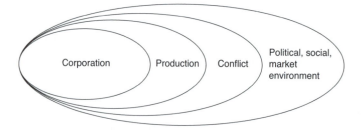

Figure 9.1 Embedding of factors examined to explain corporate governance contributions to peace and security (*source*: Deitelhoff and Wolf 2010a)

The comparison revealed the particular significance of a factor or background condition embedded in the social and political environment cluster that was observed to be at work in all case studies: nearly all report the similar influence of an altered transnational normative environment on companies. With the spread of multi-stakeholder initiatives and public–private partnerships, in particular, and the almost ten-year-long public debate on responsibility, the idea of corporate social responsibility beyond company core business seems to have diffused into the business sector (Waddock 2008: 52). Companies, states and civil society organisations take part in the discourse about company obligations and responsibilities. Within this global public discourse, companies are increasingly acknowledged to be political actors (Ruggie 2004). CSR has become a nascent general standard of appropriateness no longer disputed by companies. One important push factor for this development, as the case studies on the oil and telecommunications industries particularly highlight, was the NGO campaigns that shamed or litigated companies for their misbehaviour. The transnational public observes business and company operations critically. Within the business sector, investors have begun to rate company receptiveness to CSR and to build sustainability profiles, thus creating market incentives to further CSR activities.

A company representative in the case study on Northern Ireland makes the point most bluntly: 'You can't hide anymore' (Haidvogl 2010: 124). Even companies that operate from home states where civil society and critical media reports are negligible, such as China, find it increasingly difficult to ignore this normative environment, as the case study on oil companies and the telecommunications industry reveals, and have started to develop their own CSR programmes, albeit only recently. This normative context pushes companies to more governance contributions over time. This is instrumental in understanding the observed pattern of governance contributions. The dominance of indirect contributions to peace and security, as well as the way they are perceived by companies as part of their CSR activities, pays tribute to the socialising effects on the business sector of this altered normative context.

The case studies indicate that this normative context affects all companies and all business sectors, but not uniformly. Its effects are mediated, for instance, by a company's visibility (related to its size or the kind of product it sells – its location in the production chain), which determines the probability of its becoming the target of public campaigns. Moreover, the effects are directed by the political and legal environment in host and home states, the existence of regulatory schemes unfavourable to governance contributions, and a company's vulnerability to violent conflict in the first place: the proximity of its operation, facilities and staff to violent conflicts, or its potential to withdraw from the scene. This is where further important conditions should be added to the so far clear-cut overall picture. These additional factors are often interrelated and are, at times, interacting, resulting in multi-causal paths to corporate governance contributions. There is no single route to corporate governance contributions to peace and security: a mix of encouraging and inhibiting factors works at different levels.

Company characteristics The companies we investigated vary in size, corporate culture, product visibility, dependence on reputation, and the institutionalisation of corporate interfaces. The size of a company should make a difference to the level of corporate governance contributions, since larger companies with more financial and human resources have a greater capacity to engage than do small companies with a smaller turnover and only a few employees. This assumption is confirmed by the case study on Northern Ireland, which highlighted the importance of company size (and relates to the visibility of the company). That and institutionalised corporate interfaces both promote corporate governance contributions. Still, our findings on the causal status of size are inconclusive. Regarding the tourism industry, for example, the smallest company proved to be the best performer, thanks to its corporate culture and product characteristics. This suggests that corporate culture might trump size.

Indeed, corporate culture figured prominently in the majority of case studies. Corporate culture is the pattern of collectively shared norms, beliefs and attitudes within a company. The pattern is socialised within the organisation to solve problems that emerge inside and outside the company (see Steinmann and Schreyögg 2000: 621–2). The corporate identity and culture of the business group under investigation in the case study on food and beverage companies in Rwanda and the DR Congo clearly influenced the kind of policies and activities adopted by the subsidiaries. The group's policy forbidding political involvement was one of the main reasons why the companies that were investigated did not engage in direct security governance. Similarly, the case study on Northern Ireland underlines this relationship: the best performer, Bombardier Aerospace, had an extensive and institutionalised corporate citizenship culture that encouraged the adoption of the global corporate citizenship norm in corporate daily routines.

Reputation sensitivity was identified as another relevant factor in several case studies. Organisational research has shown that the question of legitimacy has become very important to private companies (DiMaggio and Powell 1983; Walgenbach 2002: 353). The general assumption here is that the more the market success of a company depends on its image and reputation, the more the company will engage. This played out in the case study on the food and beverage industry in Rwanda and DR Congo. The influence of image and reputation may be – but is not necessarily – linked to a company's size. It seems clear that large companies are more visible to the public than are smaller ones, and therefore need to take more care of their image and reputation.

In line with that, product characteristics played an important role in our cases. For the food and beverage industry in Rwanda and DR Congo, the fact that the food and the beverages were household names and end-consumer products clearly influenced the extent and type of governance contributions. It created expectations of integrity and exemplary behaviour in core business, as well as broader social engagement, including governance contributions. Similar influences were observed in the oil industry in Nigeria and the tourism sector generally. Globally visible and end-consumer-oriented oil companies, such as Shell, regularly attract the attention of a critical public. Companies that cause detriment to the environment easily become the target of campaigns. Tourism requires an intact ecological and social environment. Such factors as operating in a market segment where customers possess awareness or being ranked as market leader thus promote the necessary conditions for corporate engagement.

Finally, the organisational interfaces of a corporation also influence how companies respond to their environment (Rosenstiel and Koch 2003: 198). Through, for example, departments for public relations and environmental performance, organisations become aware of changes in their environment to which they must respond (Carroll and Buchholtz 2003: 113). This played a significant role in the study on the telecommunications industry (where most of those companies that engaged had such a department) and affected the performance of the companies in Northern Ireland, where the best performer likewise had a well-established PR department to manage its CSR activities. Obviously, this factor is related to size and corporate culture.

Production characteristics Solid evidence could also be found of the importance of production characteristics. If we compare the case studies, we see that company facilities and production location make a difference. The more companies have to maintain facilities and production sites and the more they are dependent on local supply and distribution chains, the more they seem inclined to engage (Wolf et al. 2007: 306; Wenger and Möckli 2003: 108). In the case of the oil industry in Nigeria, onshore production makes companies more vulnerable to sabotage, kidnappings and violent protests, and thus makes security a more precarious issue than for offshore production. In the case of telecommunications companies and coltan (a vital ingredient in mobile phones) in DR Congo, the companies are not on the ground in the conflict zone. They do not support any facilities and their sunk costs are negligible. This might explain why companies have issued policy statements (at best), but have displayed no activities to promote peace and security, even though the coltan issue was the focus for a transnational public campaign. Similarly, tour operators with no important facilities on the ground can withdraw from a conflict zone as soon as a security crisis emerges, which goes to explain the tourism industry's generally low level of engagement (Fischer 2010).

Thus, susceptibility to conflict and flexibility come into play when we consider the roles of sunk costs, supply chain position and the existence of facilities and human resources on the ground. The important role of sunk costs in a corporation's decision on how to engage in a conflict zone (Rittberger 2004: 23) is generally supported by our empirical findings. Concerning the influence of supply-chain position on a company's engagement, the findings from the case study on the telecommunications industry are instructive: companies directly in touch with the end-consumer tend to shy away from taking responsibility for individual supplier wrongdoing. It seems important to investigate the mechanism that might then enhance corporate engagement in peace and stability by the whole supply chain – for example, regulation or voluntary standards.

The empirical findings suggest that the maintenance of facilities, production sites and local supply and distribution chains in conflict zones should be treated as an important factor in explaining corporate engagement. Companies become more easily embroiled in the political dynamics of the respective host state if they have to maintain facilities (such as office buildings, production and storage facilities or pipelines) that can be targeted by conflict parties (see Haufler 2001a: 661). Against this background, many companies cooperate with public security forces, private security companies, or sometimes even with local paramilitary groups. This is particularly visible in the case study on the oil industry in Nigeria, which also highlights the often detrimental effects of this engagement, ranging from complicity in human rights violations by security forces to a perception by the local population that the companies are party to the conflict (Zimmer 2010: 65).

Similarly, human resources influence company behaviour. When it comes to managing staff, especially expatriates, company engagement strongly resembles the reaction to facility management. They make a big effort to ensure the security of their staff, and therefore request public security forces (or hire private ones). Company staff often live in sheltered areas and receive special transportation (Wenger and Möckli 2003: 108). However, an even more interesting aspect of human resources is the treatment by companies of local staff. The case study on the food and beverage industry in Rwanda and DR Congo points to the dependence on the local workforce: this might have a significant influence on systematic corporate engagement (for example, support of local livelihoods).

Conflict characteristics Corporations that operate in conflict zones function in extreme conditions, and this sets them apart from companies that operate in peaceful environments. Whether a company is operating in an atmosphere of fierce tension, during the escalation to outright war or in a post-conflict, traumatised and unstable society makes a difference to the governance contributions it is willing to engage in. Overall, the empirical findings strengthen the hypothesis that large-scale violence in a company's environment obstructs governance contributions. If companies do not withdraw outright from the scene, they are mainly concerned with protecting their staff and facilities, leaving scarcely any scope for voluntary governance contributions. This pattern could be observed in our case studies. During manifest conflict phases, corporations focused on securing staff and operations, while governance contributions emerged in post-conflict phases. However, the comparison highlights the fact that the differentiation between these phases is not clear cut, as it pays little heed to the actual levels of violence or to its location in relation to companies.

Conflict characteristics affect corporate governance contributions indirectly through companies' core business. *Proximity* concerns the question of how close the violent conflict comes to company operations and assets. Only once violence presents a real risk to staff and facilities does it become a genuine threat that may affect how (and whether) a company makes governance contributions to peace and security (Berman 2000: 28–9). According to our findings, however, proximity appears mainly as a threshold for governance contributions. Rather than triggering any kind of engagement, proximity of violence may lead to an interruption in production. The case study on the food and beverage industry in Rwanda and DR Congo confirmed this. It also matters in the tourism industry, where companies simply cancel their tours in response to security risks and violent attacks, but do not take direct issue with the situation.

Operating in tandem with proximity, conflict *intensity* – that is, the level of violence – influences corporate engagement. Outright war, with high levels of insecurity, appears to have a different conflict influence from lower-level, sporadic clashes between individuals or isolated groups. Within a conflict zone, the level of violence often demarcates conflict phases and escalations (or de-escalations) of violence during each phase. The case of the oil industry in Nigeria reflects the importance of, and interrelatedness between, conflict proximity and intensity. Only when a conflict is close to a company's operations and facilities for any length of time does it begin to affect corporate behaviour, particularly in the method (rather than the level) of engagement – in this case, the involvement in security governance by oil companies.

Short-term conflicts are handled by crisis management and do not entail sufficient motivation to engage in governance contributions. However, in post-conflict phases the intensity of violence heavily influences the level of engagement. Again, this can be shown in the food and beverage companies in Rwanda and DR Congo, as they belong to the same corporate group. While both companies displayed corporate governance contributions in the post-conflict phase, the company in Rwanda had stronger policies and activities than the one in DR Congo, which was still enduring the effects of the recurring violence between rival militias in its immediate surroundings.

While our case studies broadly confirm the prevailing notion that large-scale violence inhibits corporate governance contributions, the relationship between the intensity and proximity of violence and corporate governance contributions needs further examination. At the same time, conflict characteristics clearly demonstrate their impact through other influences, such as production characteristics. If a company has few employees and no substantial facilities on the ground, the mechanism of proximity discussed above does not apply in the same way, but instead leads to a temporary retreat or closure.

Societal and political environment in home and host state The impact of the political, societal and market environments in the home and host states of companies figured prominently in our case studies. Regarding the *political and regulatory environment* in the home and host states, it is often assumed that companies engage in self-regulation because they want to avoid legally binding regulation (Haufler 2001a, b).

Home states do not seem to be keen to restrict the behaviour of their corporations in operations abroad. However, they have other strategies and instruments at their disposal that can raise companies' awareness of, and sensitivity to, their operations in conflict zones, and so encourage corporate governance contributions. Examples are dialogue processes, public–private partnerships and the requirements of export credit agencies. Empirical findings confirm the influence of legal regulation and socialisation of the norms, values and practices of home state contexts. Blurring the much overrated distinction between the rationalist logic of consequences and the constructivist logic of appropriateness, companies are driven by a mixture of 'complex market rationalism' that includes the normative expectations of consumers and the need to manage reputation risks in cost–benefit calculations, and intrinsic motivations based on corporate identity and self-perception.

The comparison of oil companies in Nigeria highlighted the fact that

CSR policies and general normative attitudes in home states encourage company voluntary commitments. The policies and activities of the Norwegian company Statoil were clearly influenced by the Norwegian government's attitude (being a 'good international citizen' and demonstrating a successful oil history), while the negligible engagement by Chinese companies is similarly framed by the conservative stance of the Chinese government.

Regulating company conduct, by contrast, discourages voluntary contributions. Companies contribute to governance in order to avoid binding regulations. Thus, the longer the regulatory shadow of their home state, the more they shy away from governance contributions. This pattern could be most clearly observed for the companies in Northern Ireland, operating as they do in a densely regulated environment, but also for US telecommunications companies in relation to the coltan issue. In a dense regulatory setting, companies see neither the opportunity nor the need to engage. By contrast, in their host states companies are quite often confronted by varying degrees of state failure and the under-provision of collective goods. While legal frameworks often exist, states lack the willingness or capacity to implement them or to provide certain public goods. There is a clear link between state willingness and capacity and the likelihood of company engagement. The stronger policies and activities of the food and beverage company in Rwanda, compared to the one in DR Congo, were partly a result of the differences between capacity and willingness of the host states: the one had a strong government that was willing and (partly) capable of setting and implementing a legal governance framework, while the other was characterised by a weak political will and capacity in both the central state and its operational environment, with changing ruling authorities and hardly any long-term political willingness (Feil 2010: 53). While companies need to cooperate with these authorities to continue their operations, the lack of perspective reduces voluntary governance contributions.

The case highlights the fact that companies need a capable and, above all, reliable partner in the public sector to contribute to governance. In contrast, an unwilling state and persisting governance gaps serve to inhibit any meaningful engagement. This point was reinforced by the study on the oil industry in Nigeria. The regulatory framework for companies was insufficient, and consecutive governments reinforced their disregard for environmental and human rights concerns, obstructing companies' motivation to contribute to governance. Only after transnational civil society campaigns and the turn to a democratic government in 1999 did systematic governance contributions begin to emerge (Zimmer 2010: 75). Finally, in the Northern Ireland case, the comparatively low level of activities across the board was obviously the result of the strong capacity and willingness of the host state. Proactive legislation by the government, which has set up highly demanding fair employment legislation to address the persistent segregation in Northern Ireland society, leaves little scope for companies to make voluntary contributions.

With regard to the role of the political environment of the home and host states, it can thus plausibly be assumed that if the home state has a proactive and cooperative attitude, the likelihood of corporate governance contributions increases, while strict legal (hierarchical) settings discourage such contributions. In the host state environment, the most favourable conditions for governance contribution seems to be a mixture of strong political willingness and low capacity. Companies do not feel capable of 'going it alone' and need a reliable partner in the public sector. However, the case studies do not conclusively demonstrate anything about the interplay between different home and host state contexts: demands might reinforce one another and promote company engagement, but they can also be contradictory. More and more TNCs have their home state outside the OECD world – for example in China or Latin America. How these companies position themselves in discourses about their political role has rarely been examined. In two of our case studies (the ICT companies and the oil industry), Chinese companies were included. Although they did display the lowest level of engagement across the board, both case studies reported some movement in that direction. The Chinese government has taken up the CSR issue and tried to localise it as part of fostering 'harmonious society'. Thus, there may be a diffusion of common standards of appropriateness in progress.

As highlighted above, *civil society* organisations have an instrumental role in bringing CSR- related issues and standards on to the agenda and in holding corporations accountable. However, they target certain industries (such as extractives and textile) more than others (the service sector, such as logistics or tourism). In fact, the direct influence of civil society actors via immediate targeting figured prominently in only two of the cases – the ICT industry over the coltan issue, and the oil industry in Nigeria. There are two main reasons for this. First, the influence of civil society activities depends on the reputational sensitivity of companies. Second, to attract public support for its campaigns, civil society needs to be able to frame its issues as moral wrongs or scandals (Zald 1996: 266). Thus, they focus their campaigns on companies that grossly violate well-established norms (wrongdoers), rather than on mere non-performers. Local protests and global civil society activities have certainly influenced the emergence of CSR in the oil industry, increasing governance contributions. Similarly, the transnational media campaign on company involvement in the illegal coltan trade spurred the development of policy statements by ICT companies. After all, these actors played a major role in what was initially identified as a crucial background condition for the readiness of corporations to perform governance functions: the emergence of a new transnational normative environment. The effectiveness of transnational campaigns and pressure is strongly connected to company and production characteristics, such as product type and company visibility. Companies that produce goods that are highly visible to end-consumers, or that can be easily replaced, are more sensitive to reputational damage and are thus keener on maintaining a positive image.

Finally, the *market environment* also plays a role in company engagement. As initial findings from the tourism sector suggest, a highly competitive market, with intense price competition, a high number of company takeovers and horizontal and vertical integration, seems to have a restricting influence on corporate engagement. It may be assumed that most participants decide to concentrate on economic performance, and only the market leaders and corporations that operate in specific sub-segments of the market will engage. However, further research is needed to substantiate such conjectures, as the case studies could not systematically cover these variables.

In sum, the empirical case studies outline push and pull factors for corporate governance contributions.

Push factors affect the *reputational* and *material* vulnerability of companies. Reputational vulnerability covers company characteristics such as size, product and image, and it is enhanced by transnational public pressure that addresses corporations as market actors interested in avoiding reputational costs. Material vulnerability bundles together factors such as conflict characteristics and the locations of facilities and staff: in other words, a company's exposure to violence.

Pull factors concern reliability and predictability, and bundle together the political-legal environment in home and host states, as perceived by the acting corporations. As a further pull factor, appeals to their sense of beyond-profit responsibility, mainly from political and societal realms, challenge corporations to rethink their roles as social entities. The emergence and sustainability of corporate governance contribution is thus a function of several aspects of a company's vulnerability.

Conclusions

After an optimistic decade of public–private partnering in such areas as the environment, social and labour standards and human rights more broadly, the field of business addressing conflict in weak state environments appears rather bleak. However, as is clear once the question of the normative desirability of corporate governance contributions to peace and security is examined, matters could be even worse. After all, corporations cannot refer to any kind of legal authority when they are expected to take on political functions as co-performers of governance functions along with (or even without) the state. In particular, they are not accountable to the people targeted by their potential contributions to security governance in zones of violent conflict. Corporate governance contributions are usually voluntary, informal and self-authorised. There seems to be a particular necessity to link them back to standards of appropriateness that are generally accepted as serving the public interest, and to some kind of democratically legitimised public monitoring.

Our finding that companies need a capable and reliable partner in the public sector as a pre-condition for their willingness to contribute to governance in zones of conflict leads us into broader considerations of the institutional and public embedding of corporate governance activities to meet basic demands of responsiveness, participation and accountability.

Responsiveness means ensuring that private self-regulation is mindful of people's demands or context specificities (for example, in conflict zones) and that action deemed necessary by the public is taken. A traditional approach to meeting accountability demands is formal delegation: corporate governance contributions could be legally authorised by a public agency that has the legitimate legal authority to do so. However, delegation of governance competencies does not automatically confer legitimacy: authorisation by the home state government would clearly violate the congruence demand. Host state governments are not usually reliable conferrers of legitimacy on private security governance contributions, either because they are (often) unwilling or because they are unable to respect their own people's right to self-determination in zones of violent conflict. Even though international organisations such as the United Nations may be advocates that are more credible and trustees for those who cannot speak for themselves, they can be biased in the sense of representing the global North, thus perpetuating the paternalism problem (albeit in a more subtle form) when establishing and monitoring rules for private governance contributions.

Given the shortcomings of these ways of making traditional political institutions ensure that private governance contributions to peace and security respect basic normative demands, one alternative could be to reduce legitimacy demands by confining corporate governance contributions to peace and security to soft modes of governance – such as voluntary self-regulation or best practice – which do not involve formal or informal coercion. Private corporate governance contributions could claim legitimacy in their own right in contexts of horizontal, consensus-seeking and learning-oriented governance processes. Feeding this argument back into the case studies, the soft mode of indirect governance contributions to peace and security inherent in the 'best practice' approach of the tourism industry, for example, raises next to no objections in terms of legitimacy, whereas the community-development activities of the oil industry in Nigeria already imply a more significant use of private authority.

Finally, the question of the likely consequences of more and more substantial contributions to peace and security by business companies also needs to be discussed from the perspective of desirability. Direct contributions to security remain a taboo for business companies. In the few cases where companies address security issues direct (for example, in the case study on private military and security companies and, to some extent, the oil industry), some troubling features were observed. The more companies take on responsibility for public goods in non-consolidated state settings, the more they are perceived as an extended arm of the state and, consequently, the more the local population expects and demands of them. Instead of addressing their concerns to their state, they begin to focus on the companies to satisfy their needs. Companies are perceived as a 'shadow' section of the government. This was seen in oil companies in the Niger Delta, and the situation is akin to what happens when private security and military companies (PSMCs) operate in weak states or are part of military interventions and post-conflict reconstruction. Even though companies are able to increase the level of security within these settings, they are drawn into the political conflicts that gave rise to violence in the first place, becoming a conflict party in the eyes of the local population (Deitelhoff 2010: 197).

From the perspective of the host state in conflict-ridden and weak-governance zones, the outsourcing of security to PSMCs and the voluntary contributions by companies to the provision of basic collective goods have the potential to diminish the need to invest in state consolidation in the first place. Developing their economy and nationwide public institutions (such as schools, hospitals, the police) and establishing tax revenues become less important the more companies take over such tasks. Again, the Nigerian government's practice of dispatching police troops to oil companies and the latter paying for them is a telling example. These substitutions undermine the very conditions required for sustainable state consolidation (Leander 2005: 617–18; Singer 2008: 56–7).

Thus, in the end the reluctance of the business sector to engage in security might be good news, since it reminds the academic and political debates that sustainable peace-building is essentially an exercise in state-building, in which the private sector can – and is willing to – complement efforts, but in which the states remain the principal actors. On the subject of the much-quoted blurring of the public–private divide in global governance, the search for business contributions to security governance in zones of violent conflict leads to a somewhat peculiar picture. Apparently (and in a way that is quite different from the age of the chartered companies), today's TNCs seem to insist on maintaining this divide, at least so far as direct security governance is concerned. In most of the conflict zones analysed, the divide has never been solidly established by an effectively functioning nation state. This reluctance coincides with the normative expectations of local populations of establishing the traditional divide. The fact that the demand for the public–private divide to be blurred by turning corporations into co-performers of governance functions has its origins in the OECD world would seem to be indicative of a profound lack of synchronicity between regions of the world, where modern statehood is in transition in some areas but is regarded as something still worth achieving in others.

For the time being, expectations are more likely to be on the sceptical rather than the optimistic side, at least so far as un-embedded corporate contributions to governance in general, and to security-related governance in particular, are concerned.

Notes

1 This chapter draws on the research of the Business in Conflict research group at PRIF and is based on Deitelhoff and Wolf (2010a). We wish to thank our co-authors Moira Feil, Susanne Fischer, Andreas Haidvogl, Linda Wallbott and Melanie Zimmer for allowing us to sum up the results of our joint research.

2 See www.voluntaryprinciples. org.

References

Berman, J. (2000) 'Boardrooms and bombs. Strategies of multinational corporations in conflict areas', *Harvard International Review*, 22(3): 28–32.

Bone, A. (2004) 'Conflict diamonds: The De Beers Group and the Kimberley Process', in A. J. K. Bailes and I. Frommelt (eds), *Business and Security. Public–private sector relationships in a new security environment*, Oxford: Oxford University Press.

Carroll, A. B. and A. K. Buchholtz (2003) *Business & Society. Ethics and stakeholder management*, Cincinnati, OH: South-Western.

Deitelhoff, N. (2010) 'Private security and military companies: The other side of business and conflict', in N. Deitelhoff and K. D. Wolf, *Corporate Security Responsibility? Corporate governance contributions to peace and security in zones of conflict*, Houndmills: Palgrave Macmillan.

Deitelhoff, N. and K. D. Wolf (2010a) *Corporate Security Responsibility? Corporate governance contributions to peace and security in zones of conflict*, Houndmills: Palgrave Macmillan.

— (2010b) 'Gesellschaftliche Politisierung privater Sicherheitsleistungen: Wirtschaftsunternehmen in Konflikten', in M. Zürn and M. Ecker-Ehrhardt (eds), *Gesellschaftliche Politisierung internationaler Institutionen*, Frankfurt a. M.: Suhrkamp (forthcoming).

DiMaggio, P. J. and W. W. Powell (1983) 'The iron cage revisited: Institutional isomorphism and collective rationality in organizational fields', *American Sociological Review*, 48(2): 147–60.

Feil, M. (2010) 'Here's to peace! Governance contributions by companies in Rwanda and the Democratic Republic of Congo', in N. Deitelhoff and K. D. Wolf (eds), *Corporate Security Responsibility: Corporate governance contributions to peace and security in zones of conflict*, Houndmills: Palgrave Macmillan.

Fischer, S. (2010) 'Travelling for peace: The role of tourism in the Israeli–Palestinian conflict', in N. Deitelhoff and K. D. Wolf (eds), *Corporate Security Responsibility? Corporate governance contributions to peace and security in zones of conflict*, Houndmills: Palgrave Macmillan.

Fort, T. L. and C. A. Schipani (2004) *The Role of Business in Fostering Peaceful Societies*, Cambridge: Cambridge University Press.

Friedman, M. (1970) 'The social responsibility of business is to increase its profits', *New York Times Magazine*, 13 September.

Haidvogl, A. (2010) 'Walking the extra mile: Corporate contributions to the peace process in Northern Ireland', in N. Deitelhoff and K. D. Wolf (eds), *Corporate Security Responsibility? Corporate governance contributions to peace and security in zones of conflict*, Houndmills: Palgrave Macmillan.

Haufler, V. (2001a) 'Is there a role for business in conflict management?', in C. A. Crocker, F. Hampson and P. Aall (eds), *Turbulent Peace. The challenge of managing international conflict*, Washington, DC: United States Institute of Peace Press.

— (2001b) *A Public Role for the Private Sector: Industry self-regulation in a global economy*, Washington, DC: Carnegie Endowment for International Peace.

Leander, A. (2005) 'The market for force and public security: The destabilizing consequences of private military companies', *Journal of Peace Research*, 42(5): 605–22.

Leibfried, S. and M. Zürn (2005) 'Reconfiguring the national constellation', in S. Leibfried and M. Zürn (eds), *Transformations of the State?*, Cambridge: Cambridge University Press.

Ottaway, M. (2001) 'Reluctant missionaries', *Foreign Policy*, 125: 45–54.

Palestine Investment Conference (2008) *Palestine Investment Conference*, available at: www.pic-palestine.ps/download/brochure.pdf

Rittberger, V. (2004) 'Transnationale Unternehmen in Gewaltkonflikten', *Die Friedenswarte*, 79.

Rosenstiel, L. von and S. Koch (2003) 'Change in socioeconomic values as a trigger of organizational learning', in M. Dierkes, A. B. Antal, J. Child and I. Nonaka (eds), *Handbook of Organizational Learning and Knowledge*, Oxford: Oxford University Press.

Ruggie, J. G. (2004) 'Corporate social responsibility and the Global Compact', *Journal of Corporate Citizenship*, 5: 27–36.

Schuppert, G. F. (2008) *Von Ko-Produktion von Staatlichkeit zur Co-Performance of Governance. Eine Skizze zu kooperativen Governance-Strukturen von den Condottieri bis zu Public Private Partnerships*, SFB-Governance Working Paper Series No. 12, Berlin: SFB.

Singer, P. W. (2008) *Corporate Warriors: The rise of the privatized military industry*, Ithaca, NY: Cornell University Press.

Smillie, I., L. Gberie and R. Hazleton (2000) *The Heart of the Matter. Sierra Leone, diamonds and human security*, Ottawa: Partnership Africa Canada.

Steinmann, H. and G. Schreyögg (2000) *Management. Grundlagen der Unternehmensführung. Konzepte – Funktionen – Fallstudien*, Wiesbaden: Gabler.

UN (2004) 'Security Council discusses role of business in conflict prevention, peacekeeping, post-conflict peace-building', press release SC/8058, available at: www.un.org/News/Press/docs/2004/sc8058.doc.htm

Waddock, S. (2008) 'Corporate responsibility/corporate citizenship: The development of a construct', in A. G. Scherer and G. Palazzo (eds), *Handbook of Research on Global Corporate Citizenship*, Cheltenham: Edward Elgar.

Walgenbach, P. (2002) 'Institutionalistische Ansätze in der Organisationstheorie', in A. Kieser and M. Ebers (eds), *Organisationstheorien*, Stuttgart: Kohlhammer.

Wallbott, L. (2010) 'Calling for peace: The international ICT sector and the conflict in the Democratic Republic of Congo', in N. Deitelhoff and K. D. Wolf (eds), *Corporate Security Responsibility? Private governance contributions to peace and security in zones of conflict*, Houndmills: Palgrave Macmillan.

Wenger, A. and D. Möckli (2003) *Conflict Prevention: The untapped potential of the business sector*, Boulder, CO: Lynne Rienner.

Wolf, K. D. (2010) 'Chartered companies: Linking private security governance in early and post modernity', in N. Deitelhoff and K. D. Wolf (eds), *Corporate Security Responsibility? Private governance contributions to peace and security in zones of conflict*, Houndmills: Palgrave Macmillan.

Wolf, K. D., N. Deitelhoff and S. Engert (2007) 'Corporate security responsibility: Towards a conceptual framework for a comparative research agenda', *Cooperation and Conflict*, 42(3): 294–320.

Zald, M. N. (1996) 'Culture, ideology, and strategic framing', in D. McAdam, J. D. McCarthy and Z. N. Mayer (eds), *Comparative Perspectives on Social Movements. Political opportunities, mobilizing structures, and cultural framings*, Cambridge: Cambridge University Press.

Zimmer, M. (2010) 'Oil companies in Nigeria: Emerging good practice or still fuelling conflict?', in N. Deitelhoff and K. D. Wolf (eds), *Corporate Security Responsibility? Private governance contributions to peace and security in zones of conflict*, Houndmills: Palgrave Macmillan.

10 | Human rights, ethics and international business: the case of Nigeria

OLUFEMI AMAO

Our Business Principles include support for fundamental human rights. We review the human rights risks faced by our projects and operations in high-risk countries. Where we identify risks, we systematically develop action plans so that we avoid violating the rights highlighted. Our Shell-wide security standards define how we protect our people and assets, while respecting the rights of others, including local communities.Shell, *Living by Our Principles* (2008a)

Introduction

In recent times, global companies have been paying more attention to issues of human rights and ethics. As the above quote from Shell International shows, businesses are actively seeking to internalise human rights principles in their governance structure and are working to mainstream the principles in their practices. It is therefore pertinent to understand the way in which these practices are evolving and the issues that are driving them.

The main goals of this chapter are, first, to explore the interface between business (especially in the international context), ethics and human rights from a developing country's perspective. In this sense, the chapter will use Nigeria as a case study. Second, the chapter examines corporate social responsibility (CSR) practice and its relationship to ethics and human rights (principles and law), and considers the theoretical underpinnings of the CSR concept. In its final part, the chapter makes suggestions on how business should respond to ethics and human rights challenges: in other words, how to weigh profit considerations against the social and environmental impacts of corporate decisions.

There are thousands of global corporations or multinational corporations (MNCs)[1] operating around the world today. According to UNCTAD (2007), in 2006 there were 78,411 parent corporations and 777,647 affiliates worldwide. The increase in global business has raised important issues in the areas of human rights and ethics – issues that cut across national boundaries. These issues also span various spheres of corporate activity, including employment, security, socio-economic impact, environment and community/societal responsibilities. The issues are of significance not only to the host states[2] of MNCs, but also to businesses, since they impact on corporate image and profitability. Appropriate ethical decisions are, therefore, becoming more important for business profitability. As Shell International acknowledges:

> What are human rights and why are they important for the Royal Dutch/ Shell Group of companies? The answers to these questions can be found in the responsibilities and dilemmas that Shell companies have to face each and every day. These include day-to-day 'human rights' responsibilities such as human resource management issues (equal opportunities, non-discrimination and working conditions), the maintenance of health and safety standards, environmental protection and security. They also include the more complex issues linked to some of our operations, and those with whom we do business, in different parts of the world. Western investments in developing countries, in particular, are increasingly the focus of human rights concerns. (Shell 1998b)

The situation in Nigeria provides a classic example of human rights and ethical issues that can arise from international business activities in developing countries. This is because Nigeria is host to major MNCs from around the world, including the UK, the US, France, Italy and China. The activities of these MNCs and their operations have raised ethical and human rights issues, which have dominated academic research in human rights and business ethics over the past three decades. This chapter critically analyses these issues and the way in which companies are responding to them. In dealing with these issues, the chapter seeks to explore the balance between corporate interest and changing social expectations. It further considers emerging issues in the discourse, including corporate strategies, the widening scope of business stakeholders, the increasing role of pressure groups and potential exposure to international human rights litigation for violations of human rights. The chapter also examines the theoretical justifications underpinning changes in corporate practice in these areas, and goes on to assess the efficacy of corporate strategies and to suggest ways of improving them. It focuses on the extractive industries and Royal Dutch Shell's (Shell) operations in Nigeria. The choice of Nigeria and Shell is apposite because of the strategic importance of the oil industry to the Nigerian state and the pivotal role of Shell in the industry.[3]

It must be noted, however, that the issues discussed in this chapter are not only relevant in the Nigerian context, but are of global

Box 10.1 The Ivory Coast toxic waste scandal (2006)

In 2006, a Panamanian-registered tanker was chartered by a Dutch firm Trafigura to transport a mixture of petrochemical waste to West Africa. The waste was transported from Amsterdam to Nigeria, but was not discharged in Nigeria because of disagreement with local contractors. It was then moved to Ivory Coast. A local contractor eventually disposed of the waste illegally at the dead of night and in open-air spaces across Ivory Coast. More than a dozen people died from exposure to the waste, and thousands fell sick. (Amao 2007: 67–79)

significance. Similar issues have arisen in other countries, such as Guatemala, Chile, South Africa, Sudan and Ivory Coast, to mention but a few;[4] the Ivory Coast incident is described in Box 10.1.

CSR and MNCs

CSR has emerged as the voluntary way in which companies respond to issues for which (it is generally assumed) they have no legal responsibility, such as the promotion and protection of human rights and social welfare (Zerk 2006: 42). Corporations argue that, as private actors, they are not designed to take on such responsibilities (ibid.; Idoho 2008). Furthermore, corporations generally argue against any notion of moral duty to act otherwise than in the interests of shareholders, as provided under company law. However, because of the constant pressure from civil societies, activists, media and consumers, corporations have found it advantageous to adopt the concept of CSR. This approach gives the leaders of the corporate domain the ability to determine what CSR should be and the scope of such voluntary responsibility (Dickerson 2001: 1431). The widespread acceptance of moral obligation can be inferred from the widespread adoption of voluntary initiatives, such as statements of principles, codes of ethics, codes of conduct and social reporting (McBarnet 2007: 10).

Considering such trends, Jackson (1993: 547) opines that corporations clearly assume significant non-economic (i.e. political, legal and moral) roles, as well as economic ones. Additionally, globalisation has made corporate decisions around CSR subject to pressures from other sources, such as home-market consumers, and complex problems from less developed countries (Dickerson 2001: 1431). According to Muchlinski, this trend shows that MNCs appear to be rejecting a purely non-social role through the adoption of codes of conduct, and the trends appear to indicate an increasing social dimension to the role of MNCs (Muchlinski 2001: 37–8). This poses the question of how to justify or account for this shift in a coherent and logical way. Academics have proffered theoretical justification for the CSR concept. The next section considers the major theories on the underpinnings of CSR.

Theoretical justification for CSR

Moir (2001: 16) correctly identified three theories, which may help in the analysis and explanation of the theoretical underpinnings of CSR. These theories are the stakeholder theory, the social contract theory and the legitimacy theory.

Stakeholder theory According to Freeman, a stakeholder is 'any group or individual who can affect or is affected by the achievement of the firm's objectives' (quoted in Roberts 1992: 595). Across disciplines, it is generally agreed that stakeholders in this sense include shareholders, creditors, employees, customers, suppliers, public interest groups and government. Stakeholder theories address the question of which group in society corporations should be responsible to (Matten and Crane 2005: 166; Moon et al. 2005: 429). Stakeholders are typically analysed into primary and secondary stakeholders (Clarkson 1995: 92). Primary stakeholders are those whose participation directly ensures the continuity of the corporation as a going concern. This group includes shareholders, employees and customers, as well as the government, which provides the necessary infrastructure, market and enabling legal framework (ibid.). The secondary groups are described as those that influence or affect (or are influenced or affected by) the corporation, but that are not involved in transactions with the company and are not necessary for its survival (Moir 2001). Inquiries that have shaped the debate on CSR theories in this area include determining whether stakeholder theory is part of the motivation for business to be responsible, and identification of relevant stakeholders to be taken into consideration by business managers.

Legitimacy theory Legitimacy theory has been defined as a generalised perception that the actions of the organisation are proper or appropriate within a given social system (Schuman 1995: 571). Schuman identifies three key challenges to legitimacy management: gaining, maintaining and repairing legitimacy. He posits that legitimacy management is dependent on communication.[5] Moir therefore suggested that, in the debate on CSR, it is necessary to examine corporate communications (Moir 2001). The primary argument of legitimacy theory is that external factors influence corporate management to seek to legitimise the firm's activities. Legitimacy may not necessarily be a benign process through which organisations obtain legitimacy from society (ibid.). An organisation may employ different strategies when faced with the legitimacy threat: it may choose to educate its stakeholders about its intention of improving the organisation's performance; it may seek to change the organisation's perception of the event without changing performance; it may divert attention from the event; or it may choose to change external expectations of its performance (ibid). It therefore stands to reason that, while legitimacy might be an important reason for corporations to undertake CSR, it may not be the only reason. It has also been argued, as an alternative view, that since society grants power to business, society expects that power to be used responsibly. According to Moir, this would amount to a restatement of the social contract between the firm and society (ibid.).

The social contract theory The social contract concept has been very influential in the political context. The original understanding of the social contract postulates that society decides to move from a situation of undefined rights and incessant conflict over resources to one with a social contract, whereby individuals agree to honour the rights of others in return for guarantees that their own rights will be respected and protected. The state is the repository in which individuals vest authority, in order to ensure that the terms of the contract are complied with. The state thus mediates between individuals themselves and between individuals and society. It has been suggested that the idea of a corporate social contract underlies the CSR concept (Lantos 2001: 595). The idea is that the corporate social contract concerns 'a firm's indirect societal obligations and resembles the "social contract" between citizens and government traditionally discussed by philosophers who identified the reciprocal obligations of citizen and state' (ibid.: 599). Thus business should act in a responsible manner because it is part of society, and should also enter into a social contract with society. From this perspective, CSR is described as 'the obligation stemming from the implicit "social contract" between business and society for firms to be responsive to society's long-run needs and wants, optimising the positive effects and minimising the negative effects of its actions on society' (ibid.).[6] Despite their differences, the three theories underscore a wider role for corporations within society.

The Nigerian case: historical and contextual background

The modern history of Nigeria – and indeed of the whole of Africa – would be incomplete without an examination of the role of foreign MNCs in the emergence of the continent. Foreign MNCs played a pivotal role in opening up this part of the world and in uncovering the wealth of the region. Corporations were instrumental in the development and advancement of nation states in Africa, and it is therefore not surprising that they have emerged as the driver of globalisation in the modern era (Wallace 2002: 9; Braithwaite and Drahos 2000: 147). For example, in the case of Nigeria, a British company, the Royal Niger Company, facilitated the effective colonisation of the country by the British government (Mockler-Ferryman 1902).

In 1879, an official of the British Royal Engineers, George Goldie Taubman, amalgamated all the British traders interested in trade in parts of the area now known as Nigeria to form a new venture, which was initially called the United African Company (then later the National African Company and eventually the Royal Niger Company). The company had a monopoly of trade in the area but had no power of administration. Goldie sought political authority for the company. In order to receive a Royal Charter for that purpose, Goldie made illiterate traditional rulers sign treaties, which ceded their 'sovereignty', their land and their natural resources to the company (ibid.). The company received its Royal Charter in 1886. According to Staley, it was the only one of the British chartered companies of that era to prove a paying investment for its stockholders, as it declared a regular yearly dividend of 6–6.5 per cent (Staley 1935). Though the company eventually lost its Charter in 1899, it paved the way for effective colonial administration in the country.

Nigeria gained independence in 1960, and this changed ownership interest in the oil industry. However, this has not changed the dominance of MNCs in the sector. MNCs continue to dominate major sectors of the Nigerian economy, including manufacturing, construction, telecommunications and the oil and gas sector.[7] Their impact is, however, most felt in the oil production and extraction industry, for Nigeria is the tenth-largest oil producer in the world and the Nigerian economy is heavily dependent on its oil: the country earns over 95 per cent of its export revenue from the oil and gas sector, which accounts for over 40 per cent of GDP and 80 per cent of government revenue (Shell 2008b: 20).

All the foreign MNCs in the oil and gas sector operate in joint-venture partnership with the Nigerian National Petroleum Corporation (NNPC), a state-owned corporation. The joint-venture partnership is typically in a ratio of 55–60 per cent to the government and 40–5 per cent to the corporation. The shareholders of the parent company are predominantly in the countries of the North, usually the United States and Europe.[8] The MNCs maintain managerial control of the enterprise. The government contributes proportionately to the cost of carrying out the oil operations, and receives a share of the production in the same proportion. The fact that, by agreement, the MNCs maintain managerial control implies that the MNCs not only dictate the pace and pattern of the industry according to their objective of ensuring maximum production for profit (Hassan et al. 2002), but also make the government heavily dependent on their operations (Watts 2005: 373).

Shell in Nigeria Oil prospecting started in Nigeria in 1906. Under the Oil Ordinance No. 17 of 1914, oil exploration and exploitation was limited to British citizens and British companies.[9] Therefore, in 1937, an exploration licence covering the entire mainland of Nigeria was granted to Shell D'Arcy by the British colonial government (Manby 1999: 27). (The company originally commenced operation in Nigeria in the period following the First World War as the Shell D'Arcy Company. In 1956 it was renamed Shell-BP. The company became Royal Dutch Shell in February 1957, when it merged its operation with the Royal Dutch Petroleum Company in order to maintain a global competitive edge.) The area covered by the licence was 357,000 square miles. The company was able to explore and select 15,000 square miles of the original concession without competition, thus securing a first-mover advantage over later entrants to the market (Frynas et al. 2000: 407–9).[10] In 1958, the company discovered oil in commercial quantities in Oloibiri in the present Rivers State (ibid.).

Figure 10.1 Main oil-producing areas of Nigeria

By 1959, on the brink of Nigeria's independence, the sole-concessionary right granted to Shell-BP had been reviewed, and companies of other nationalities from Europe and the USA were brought into the field (ibid.). Today, the Shell/NNPC joint venture is the largest oil and gas joint venture in the country and is the leading producer of crude oil in the country (Figure 10.2). It accounts for more than 40 per cent of total production, and represents about 14 per cent of Shell's global production. Shell's sister company, Shell Nigeria Exploration and Production Company Ltd (SNEPCO) has substantial interest in two major oilfields in Nigeria. Shell also has a 26 per cent interest in Nigerian Liquefied Natural Gas Limited, which accounted for over 10 per cent of the world's liquefied natural gas capacity in 2008 (Shell 2008b: 20).

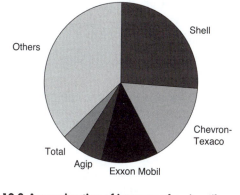

Figure 10.2 Approximation of interests of major oil companies in Nigeria

Human rights impact of MNC operations   MNCs are mostly concentrated in the Niger Delta area of Nigeria, where more than 80 per cent of oil exploration activities are carried out (see Figure 10.1). In recent times, the activities of MNCs in this area have raised issues that have engaged the attention of business ethics and human rights scholars. The issues have also engendered the question as to whether, as participants in society with significant impacts on people, MNCs have entered into a 'social contract' with those affected by their operations. The people in the Niger Delta have had to contend with the burden of environmental degradation, including oil spills from pipelines polluting land and waterways, gas flaring polluting the air, and destruction of fishing and farming opportunities leading to damage to the livelihood of farmers and fishermen (Amnesty International 2009: 10; Meredith 2005: 576). The situation led to antagonism towards the oil companies and the government on the part of the host communities. The companies' original position was that they owed no direct obligation to communities, apart from paying royalties and taxes to the government. The Nigerian government's attempt to deal with the problem by clamping down on agitations among host communities has served to exacerbate the problem. There have been extrajudicial executions, brutal repressions and violent confrontations. The situation has become a public-relations nightmare for Shell and has led to massive cuts in its operations and consequent loss of profit. In normal times, the company has the capacity to produce an average of 1 million barrels of oil equivalent a day. In 2003, the company was producing 990,000 barrels per day. At the time of writing, the company's production has dropped to 140,000 barrels per day (Alike 2009). The Nigerian situation is further complicated by the blame trading between oil companies and the government as to who bears responsibility for the problems in the oil-producing area (Okoronkwo 2009; Ugeh and James 2009).

Hassan et al. (2002) carried out research into the impact of MNCs in the oil and gas sector on women in one of the oil-producing states of Nigeria (see also Etiebet 1994). Their findings encapsulate the far-reaching impact of the corporations on local communities. The writers found that, prior to the discovery of oil in the Niger Delta of Nigeria, the people of the area made their living from the exploitation of the resources of the land, water and forestry, as farmers, fishermen and hunters. However, the effects of the operation of MNCs have changed the situation in the area. According to the authors:

> the people cannot farm or fish because of oil spillage and pollution, they can hardly obtain potable water and their health is in severe jeopardy. The ecological problem in the Niger Delta is that multi-national companies and the government are exploiting the ecosystems for resources beyond the level of sustainability. The environment has been exploited and damaged to such an extent as to be unable to continue providing the resources that people of the oil communities depended upon prior to the commencement of oil exploration and production activities ... The activities of the oil companies have seriously affected local livelihoods due to water pollution, take-over of fishing grounds by equipment and installation and damage to fishing nets ... Health problems were generally reported due to the heat and air pollution resulting from gas flaring as well as water pollution due to oil spoilage. (ibid.)

The findings of the researchers were corroborated by a 2009 Amnesty International report, which concluded that the oil industry in the Niger

Box 10.2 Oil spill at Bodo (2008)

On 28 August 2008 a fault in the trans-Niger pipeline resulted in a significant oil spill into Bodo Creek in Ogoniland. The oil poured into the swamp and creek for weeks, covering the area in a thick slick of oil and killing the fish that people depend on for food and for their livelihood. A local NGO, the Centre for Environment, Human Rights and Development (CEHRD), which investigated the case (including by taking video footage of the leak), reported that the oil spill has resulted in death or damage to a number of species of fish that provide the protein needs of the local community. Video footage of the site shows widespread damage, including to mangroves which are an important fish breeding ground ... Although the oil spill has seriously undermined the local community's right to food, at the time of writing (May 2009) no adequate action had yet been taken to address the food insecurity. On 2 May 2009, eight months after the spill, SPDC [Shell Petroleum Development Corporation] staff reportedly brought food relief to the community, which they rejected as wholly inadequate.

Source: Amnesty International 2009: 7–8

Delta had brought human rights abuses, conflict, impoverishment and despair to a majority of people in the oil-producing area. According to the report, decades of pollution and environmental damage caused by MNCs in the oil sector have led to violations of rights to adequate standards of living, rights to food and water, rights to gain a living through work and rights to health (Amnesty International 2009: 79).

Hassan et al. further highlight the conflict situation that has been one of the prominent consequences of the activities of MNCs. They classified the conflict into three types: conflict between corporations and youths in the community; conflict between leaders of the community and youths; and conflict between oil companies and women of the community. According to the researchers, the sources of the conflict include expectations of employment and contracts by young people whose means of livelihood have been wiped out by the corporations, and the sharing of largesse that MNCs or their contractors usually give to community leaders to gain support for their activities. Another source of conflict is the failure of corporations to fulfil the promises made to communities. Hassan et al. cite the example of Mobil, which failed to fulfil a promise to instal a gas turbine to give uninterrupted electricity supply to one community. Though the above empirical research centred on a particular part of the country and on women, it can nevertheless be used as a guide to understanding the many ways in which MNCs have affected the day-to-day lives of a large number of people. The enormous impact of the operations of the corporations on people's lives make relevant the question of whether the people should be recognised as legitimate stakeholders, based on an implicit social contract between MNCs and the people thus affected.

CSR in the Nigerian context CSR became a prominent issue in Nigeria in the 1990s, following a series of human rights and environmental law infringements involving Shell. Shell has been a focal point in Nigeria 'not only because the company is the largest oil producer and polluter in Nigeria, but also because unlike other major oil producers, Shell's operations are predominantly onshore and as such involve greater inter- actions with human settlements' (Omeje 2006: 58). Indeed, Shell's CSR activities have been described as 'a classic business school case study' because of the peculiar challenges faced by the company and the various ways it has attempted to deal with the challenges (McBarnet 2007: 14). The concept has since taken root in the oil and gas industry in Nigeria (Idemudia and Ite 2006: 194–5).

This shift in approach shows a willingness on the part of corporations to accept some responsibility based on the impact of their operations (in the manner suggested by the social contract theorists) and on rec- ognition of other stakeholders aside from shareholders (as suggested by stakeholder theorists).

Generally, companies individually devise their CSR policies. However, norms of legal character – especially in the areas of international law on human rights, labour and environmental protection, national and supranational legislation – are widely used to inform or guide corporate actions and reporting within the sphere of CSR (Buhmann 2006). The business principles of most corporations draw on these instruments. A recent trend (which is still embryonic) is for some governments to legislate on aspects of CSR especially in the areas of social reporting and directors' duties.[11] Recently Indonesia has gone further by moving towards a broader legislative framework for CSR.[12]

Questions have been raised as to whether there is any difference be- tween the practices of CSR in developed countries and in less developed countries. It has been suggested that the concept differs 'according to national social economic priorities – which are themselves influenced by historical and cultural factors – and according to the different types of social actors that are demanding action on these priorities' (IISD 2004). In the case of South Africa, for example, it was noted that the earlier practice of CSR was rooted in philanthropy. During the apartheid era, it was common for businesses to make charitable donations to, and to seek patronage from, local chiefs (ibid.). However, after the 1994 elections, the business community took a more holistic approach to CSR, and the government also embarked on a series of legislative drives to back up the CSR agenda. The CSR agenda in South Africa is presently influenced by the need to respond to the legacies of apartheid and to address local priorities. Prominent CSR initiatives in South Africa include the Black Economic Empowerment programme and the current heavy corporate involvement in the struggle against HIV/AIDS. Research in many other parts of Africa has suggested that CSR is largely associated with philanthropy (Kivuitu et al. 2005; Amaeshi 2006).

The Ogonis and the evolution of Shell CSR policies[13] The Ogonis are an agricultural and fishing community in the Niger Delta area of Nigeria. The community consists of about half a million people, occupying a land area of about 1,000 square kilometres. They are believed to have lived in the area for more than 2,000 years (Boele et al. 2001). The area that they occupy is one of the most important wetlands in the world, and contains a unique, rare and delicate biodiversity. Wetlands are essential wildlife habitat, providing natural basins and helping to prevent flooding. The area has a very fragile ecosystem, containing mangroves, freshwater swamp forests, lowland rain forests and coastal barrier islands (ibid.). Shell started operating in the Ogoni area in 1958. Complaints about the company's operation in the area began right from the early days (ibid.). Describing the impact of Shell activities in Ogoniland, Boele et al. (ibid.) state:

> Oil impacted upon the lives of the Ogoni people with both environmental and social costs. The Communities were confronted first with seismic surveys and building works, and then with the effects of oil extraction such as leaks, oil spills and gas flaring. Apart from the environmental pollution, the communities saw oil exploration as aggravating already heavy pressure on land in one of Africa's most populated regions … The advent of oil, oil workers and oil installations brought important societal changes such as oil workers migrating into an area, the increasing importance of money economy and rising food prices. Temporary employment was particularly destructive. As young men were relatively

highly paid for short periods of time, their spending habits changed and they imitated mainstream culture, which caused division separating them from their communities. As the main farm workers, women reported being especially hard hit by the environmental and social consequences of the oil exploration. They saw their lands appropriated for oil extraction, and received neither adequate compensation nor secure jobs in return.

These observations were reaffirmed in a recent report (Amnesty International 2009).

It must be noted that the community was not only complaining about the activities of the corporation, but also about the government for not effectively protecting their interests as stakeholders and not controlling the MNC. The situation led to significant agitation against the company and the government in the 1990s. The Ogonis published what they called the 'Ogoni Bill of Rights', which was a statement of what they considered to be their rights and that were being violated by the oil company and the government. An organisation was set up to champion their cause – the Movement for the Survival of the Ogoni People (MOSOP). It sought to engage in non-violent struggle against the government and all oil companies operating in the area.

By 1992, Ken Saro-Wiwa had become the organisation's main spokesperson. In December 1992, MOSOP demanded of Shell, the NNPC and Chevron that they should (among other things) pay compensation for the impact of oil exploration on the Ogoni land and community. A deadline of thirty days was set. The companies did not respond. On 4 January 1993 a day that was declared Ogoni Day, a peaceful protest involving about 300,000 people (about 60 per cent of the Ogoni population) took place in Ogoniland calling for the foreign oil companies – and in particular Shell – to leave the area. The tension led to Shell suspending operations in the Ogoni area. Nigerian military forces were subsequently deployed to protect Shell infrastructure and personnel. But this did not stop the agitation, and in subsequent clashes the military personnel violently suppressed the agitators and, in the process, killed many people.

There was evidence of collusion between Shell and the government in the suppression in Ogoniland, and also evidence that Shell was supplying arms to the Nigerian security operatives for their operations and making special payments to them (Manby 1999b; Owolabi 2007; Frynas 2000; Pegg 1999). In a desperate bid to stop the agitation, the Nigerian government arrested Ken Saro-Wiwa and other Ogoni leaders, accused them of murdering some pro-government individuals, and brought them before a military tribunal, which sentenced nine of them, including Saro-Wiwa, to death in a trial that is widely regarded as unfair. It was alleged that, at a meeting with Shell's then managing director, Brian Anderson, Anderson suggested to a sibling of Saro-Wiwa that he could get the latter released if he agreed to call off the MOSOP campaign against Shell. Shell agreed that the meeting had taken place, but disputed the facts (Okonta and Douglas 2003). The nine men were subsequently executed.

This incident led to international outrage against Shell and its operations in Nigeria. Strident criticism came from the media, academics, NGOs and even some company shareholders (Boele et al. 2001; Weinraub 1998). Activists in the US and Europe picketed the company's petrol stations. As a consequence of boycott campaigns against Shell, the market value of the company fluctuated dramatically in the wake of negative reaction from shareholders (Schultz 2000: 78). The backlash dogged Shell International's activities for a long time to come and forced the company to reassess its operation policies.

Shell's response: a 'social contract' or a public relations strategy? With the sustained campaign against Shell's operations, the company found that it had to actively deal with the problem. Its first step was to initiate a project called Society's Changing Expectation which was an elaborate audit of the company's 'stakeholders' (Clutterbuck et al. 2003: 74). Shell also started engaging in regular dialogues with human rights NGOs, such as Amnesty International and Pax Christi. It is reputed to have been the first major energy company to declare publicly its support for the Universal Declaration of Human Rights (Pegg 1999: 473).

Another major step taken by Shell was the revision of its 1976 Statement of General Business Principles. Shell's revised Statement of General Business Principles recognises five areas of responsibility: to shareholders, customers, employees, business partners and society at large. This goes beyond the requirement of the law. It further states *inter alia* that it respects the human rights of its employees and that it will

> conduct business as responsible corporate members of society, comply with applicable laws and regulations ... support fundamental human rights in line with the legitimate role of business, and ... give proper regard to health, safety, security and the environment.[14]

This development may be taken as recognition of an implicit social contract with the community and an acknowledgement of responsibility to a wider set of stakeholders.

This was followed in 1998 by the company's first ever corporate statement of social and environmental performance, entitled *Profit and Principles: Does there have to be a choice?* (Shell 1998a). This was an attempt to give a detailed assessment of the company's progress in living up to the values expressed in its revised Statement of General Business Principles. In it, Shell recognised the damage done to its reputation by the Saro-Wiwa affair and claimed that this incident represented an important turning point for the company. It also introduced a 'management primer' on human rights (Shell 1998b). The document is a guideline for Shell personnel, and it discusses the implementation of human rights policies in the business context, underscoring the wider role of business in society. Shell has engaged in various forms of CSR activities, including voluntary social reporting, community-development and assistance projects and other philanthropic measures.

Shell's CSR initiatives include building roads, clinics and schools, providing scholarships, supplying transport, promoting arts and culture, and other initiatives. Since 2002, it is claimed that Shell has spent an average of $50 million dollars annually on community development (Omeje 2006: 87; *Guardian* (Nigeria) 2006). In Foster and Ball's opinion:

> Shell Nigeria act in some ways like a government, spending over $50 million per year in infrastructure projects, consulting those affected by its activity in order to ensure, if not its popularity, its acceptance. (Foster and Ball 2006: 93)

While Shell has been more prominent in the Nigerian context, other multinationals in the oil industry have had similar problems and are responding in similar ways (Manby 1999b: 281). Faced with continued hostility from host communities that feel deprived by the exploitation of their land and environment in the Niger Delta area of Nigeria, the MNCs have begun meeting among themselves to work out a common strategy to address the concerns of the people of the region (Lawal 2007).

CSR strategy: effective response? However, rather than improving, the situation in Ogoniland and the whole of the Niger Delta area of Nigeria appears to be worsening. Discontent with the oil companies has led to the emergence of militias in the Delta. There is a high frequency of attacks against oil companies' facilities and their employees. Incidents of kidnapping of both expatriate and local company employees are on the increase. The situation in the Niger Delta at the time of writing shows that the CSR strategies of these corporations may be deficient. While companies in the region tout their CSR policies as their way of meeting other stakeholders' demands, it is obvious that the host communities are not satisfied by the approach.

There is little independent evaluation of the CSR policies of the company. Christian Aid, an NGO, carried out research in which it focused on the compliance of Shell with its environmental commitment, as stipulated in its code (Christian Aid 2004; Frynas 2005: 581). Its finding was that, despite the company's claim to be observing CSR standards, the reality was rather different. It found that, though Shell claims to have turned over a new leaf in Nigeria and to be striving to be a 'good neighbour', it still fails to quickly clean up oil spills that ruin villages and runs 'community development' projects that are frequently ineffective and that sometimes divide communities living around oilfields. Amnesty International recently described the situation in the area as a 'human rights tragedy' (Amnesty International 2009: 79). The situation raises the question as to the effectiveness of Shell's strategies in addressing these issues.

There is an emerging recourse to litigation based on human rights law at the international and domestic levels. The downside of litigation is that not only may companies be ordered to pay compensation, but – and far more important – they may suffer damage to their reputation. Appropriate corporate strategies are therefore needed to avoid such litigation. Two recent cases involving Shell illustrate this point.

THE SARO-WIWA CASE IN THE UNITED STATES The *Wiwa* v. *Royal Dutch Petroleum Co.*[15] cases arose from the Ogoni situation discussed earlier. Three cases were brought against Royal Dutch Shell and Shell Transport and Trading Corporation, the parent companies of Royal Dutch Shell Group. These cases were instituted in 1996 in the USA. The cases were brought under the Alien Tort Claims Act 1789 and the Torture Victim Protection Act 1991. The plaintiffs' actions were based *inter alia* on violations of the United Nations Charter, Universal Declaration of Human Rights, International Covenant on Civil and Political Rights, UN Convention against Torture and Other Cruel, Inhuman or Degrading Treatment or Punishment and customary international law. The plaintiffs alleged that the company had participated in grave human rights abuses against them and/or their relations in Nigeria. It was alleged that the company was complicit in human rights abuses against the Ogoni people, including summary execution, crimes against humanity, torture, inhuman treatment, arbitrary arrest, wrongful death, assault and battery, and infliction of emotional distress.

The complainants alleged that the company conducted its operations in Ogoniland and the Niger Delta negligently and with reckless disregard for the effect of these operations on the population, wildlife and Ogoniland. The actions included the many incidents of oil spillage and gas flaring by the company; it also included the alleged collusion between the company and the Nigerian state's military, police and other personnel assigned by the government to the company in orchestrating raids and terror campaigns in the area, leading to the arrest, detention, torture and death of some Ogoni activists and hundreds of residents of the area. The legal tussle went on for thirteen years. The negative publicity created serious reputational damage to the corporate image of Shell globally. Shell eventually settled the lawsuits in June 2009 by paying US$15.5 million in compensation and legal costs.[16]

THE GBEMRE CASE IN NIGERIA[17] The second case was brought by Jonah Gbemre on behalf of himself and the Iwhereken community in Delta State in the Niger Delta area of Nigeria against Shell Petroleum Development Company Nigeria Ltd, the NNPC and the Attorney General of the Federation. The case was brought under the fundamental rights enforcement procedure in the Nigerian Constitution, alleging violations of both constitutional provisions and the African Charter. The plaintiffs claimed that the oil exploration and production activities of Shell, which led to incessant gas flaring, had violated their right to life and the dignity of the human person under sections 33(1) and 34(1) of the Nigerian Constitution and Articles 4, 16 and 24 of the African Charter. The plaintiffs alleged that the continuous gas flaring by the company had led to poisoning and pollution of the environment, which exposed the community to the risk of premature death, respiratory illnesses, asthma and cancer. They also alleged that the pollution had affected their crop production, thereby adversely affecting their food security.

They claimed that many of the indigenes had died and many more were suffering from various illnesses. The community was therefore left in a state of gross underdevelopment. In its judgment, the Federal High Court held that constitutionally protected rights include rights to a clean, poison-free, pollution-free environment, and that the actions of Shell in continuing to flare gas in the course of its oil exploration and production activities in the community violated the people's right to life and/or the dignity of the human person under the Constitution and the African Charter. The decision's explicit recognition of the duties of non-state actors (i.e. corporations) vis-à-vis human rights signals the possibility of a horizontal application of human rights provision to corporations in Nigeria. However, no monetary compensation was awarded in that case, which makes the Nigerian forum less attractive than the US was in the case in *Wiwa* v. *Royal Dutch Petroleum Co.*

Shell's strategies going forward Shell has over the years striven to successfully map out human rights-related issues emanating from its operations and has attempted to address those issues. The question, however, is whether the responses are adequate and appropriate. For example, a strategy of philanthropy – such as promoting art and culture – cannot offer redress for pollution and environmental degradation affecting people's livelihood. The task therefore is to develop strategies that appropriately address relevant issues.

According to Shell Nigeria, its commitment to human rights is guided by the Shell General Business Principles.[18] As stated earlier, in its 1997 revision of the Shell General Business Principles (SGBP), Shell for the first time included direct references to human rights (Shell 2002). Principle 2 provides *inter alia* that the company commits:

To employees

To respect the human rights of their employees ...

To society

To conduct business as responsible corporate members of society, to observe the laws of the countries in which they operate, to express support for fundamental human rights in line with the legitimate role of business and to give proper regard to health, safety and the environment consistent with their commitment to contribute to sustainable development.

In its 1999 Report, the company presented a visual map of its human rights responsibility. The map was restated in its 2001 Report (Shell 2001: 10). It includes five layers of responsibilities, represented by concentric circles. The inner circles identify the responsibilities of the company to staff, in relation to security matters, and to local communities. The outer layers are human rights issues connected to investments and promotion of human rights. Shell developed this map to inform a better understanding of the company's human rights responsibilities. According to the company, the three inner circles identify its clear responsibilities, while the outer circles represent responsibilities that are mainly in the province of government. The company drew a distinction between these two sets of responsibilities. It acknowledges a direct responsibility in respect of the inner-circles issues, while its responsibility in respect of the outer-circles issues are more diffused and include 'contributing to public policy debate and supporting international codes' (ibid.). In the SGBP, the company gives a clear indication of its recognition of stakeholders other than its shareholders. These include customers, employees, business partners and society. This recognition is not a matter of law but of ethics and good corporate practice. Shell's recognition of an expanding class of stakeholders underscores an important change in its corporate strategy.

However, it is not enough merely to recognise other stakeholders; contact and dialogue need to be established with them. In the case of local communities in the Niger Delta, engagement has proved problematic for Shell. The situation has been made more difficult at the time of writing by the recourse to violence on the part of aggrieved communities. Had the company had an effective stakeholder-engagement policy in the early days of its operations in Nigeria, today's precarious situation may have been avoided (Wheeler et al. 2002: 302). It is thus important for the company to overhaul its community-engagement and consultation process. This was also the view of Amnesty International in its report advocating robust oversight of the community-engagement process and an enhancement of women's access to the engagement process (Amnesty International 2009: 85). Such a process will be further enhanced by a mechanism that allows the community access to top-level management in the company to raise concerns.

The SGBP and the *Shell Code of Conduct* are to be applied by all the companies in the group. They also apply to contractors, consultants and partners. According to the company:

> Every employee, director or officer in every wholly-owned Shell company and in every joint venture company under Shell control must follow the Code of Conduct. Contract staff must also follow the Code. Contractors or consultants who are our agents or working on our behalf or in our name, through outsourcing of services, processes or any business activity, will be required to act consistently with the Code when acting on our behalf. Independent contractors or consultants will be made aware of the Code as it applies to our staff in their dealings with them. We apply the Code in all joint operations where Shell is the lead operator. When participating in a joint venture company not under Shell control we encourage the company to adopt similar principles and standards. (Shell 2006)

Furthermore, the SGBP and the Code are adapted to each local situation by supplementary documents that address in detail issues such as bribery and corruption, environmental standards and human rights.

However, as Holzer (2007) rightly noted, Shell has not been able to effectively translate its ethical policies into action at the local level.

Shell has taken steps to address human rights issues arising from its security arrangements, and in 2000 signed up to the Voluntary Principles on Security and Human Rights (VPSHR). These principles are designed to guide companies in the maintenance of safety and security of their operations in a way that ensures respect for human rights. The company claims that it has since been organising human rights awareness workshops, based on the principles, for senior government security officers, its staff and other stakeholders. In 2007, Shell also included the principles in its Group Security Standards, and it states, as part of its standard risk assessment, that it requires all its operators to undertake background security checks on their personnel, to ensure that they have no previous record of human rights abuse. It further claims that it now refers to the principle in its contract with private security companies and when using government security forces. Nonetheless, the VPSHR has no monitoring mechanism, which makes it difficult to evaluate adherence to its principles (Amnesty International 2005).

Apart from designing an appropriate corporate response, the company also faces the challenge of operationalising its strategies in a transparent and effective way. The Statement of General Business Principles of Shell International provides for a good-faith commitment, which is at the discretion of the corporation and its subsidiaries to implement and enforce. The company requires its entire staff to complete training that explains what its Code of Conduct requires of them. It also provides staff with online and face-to-face training in specific areas, including human rights. A global helpline and supporting website allows staff and business partners to report concerns confidentially and to get advice on suspected infringements of the law, the Code of Conduct or the SGBP. However, there is no independent evaluation of how effective these internal processes have been. A commitment to independent oversight and monitoring will go a long way in courting other stakeholders' confidence (Amnesty International 2009: 85). This will have a positive effect on the profitability of the company.

Conclusions

The major theorists that have proffered insights into the underpinnings of CSR have underscored the emerging wider role for corporations in society. This role requires the recognition of a wider stakeholder base for the corporation than the traditional stakeholders – shareholders. Furthermore, the social contract theorists postulate that the modern corporation is a new entrant into the social contract underlining societal order, which imposes new responsibilities – beyond legal obligations – on corporations. Even where corporations act for public relations reasons, the legitimacy theorists may explain this as part of corporate strategy to gain legitimacy from society. Whichever way one looks at it, there is no doubt that corporate approaches in this area have undergone a dramatic change.

In Nigeria, from a position in which corporations argue that they owe no moral or legal duty to act in the interest of anyone other than shareholders, corporations like Shell appear to have shifted to a position where they recognise responsibility towards other stakeholders. The implications of this are twofold: first, a stakeholder approach to management as expressed by the stakeholder theorists; and second, an increasing recognition of an implicit social contract between corporations and society. Consequently, corporations like Shell are increasingly accepting non-legal, ethical responsibilities, but the challenge for them is how to define these responsibilities and respond to them in a way that is acceptable to all stakeholders.

To define these responsibilities, corporations have resorted to selectively adopting norms with legal character, especially in the area of international law on human rights, labour and environmental protection. Many corporations are also involved in the practice of voluntary reporting on social and environmental issues. The problem with the present approach, however, is that corporations pick and choose their responsibilities and the manner of meeting these responsibilities, with little or no independent oversight or involvement on the part of other stakeholders. The lack of independent oversight makes stakeholders suspicious of the sincerity of the corporations. The challenge for corporations, therefore, is to design effective stakeholder-engagement policy that is committed to independent oversight and monitoring. Transparency and better information-disclosure systems on human rights and social issues will significantly improve corporate practice in this area.

Notes

1 The term multinational corporation (MNC) is used to describe a company with foreign origin/ seat that operates in one or more other countries through affiliates or subsidiaries and has production or marketing facilities in those other countries.

2 Host countries are countries in which MNCs from other countries operate; home countries are the foreign origin/seat of the MNCs.

3 The conflicts arising out of Shell's operations in Ogoni, Nigeria, have been described as 'the quintessential case that put the intercon-

nectedness of business, the natural environment and human rights on the corporate agenda' (Wheeler et al. 2002).

4 On Guatemala and MNCs, see Schlesinger and Kinzer (1990: 65), Gibney (1997–98) and Streeter (2000). On Chile and MNCs, see Winston (1999) and Barnet and Muller (1974). On South Africa and MNCs, see Seidman (2003), Goldstein (2000) and Meznar et al. (1994). On Ivory Coast and MNCs, see Amao (2007). On Sudan and MNCs, see Abusharaf (1999).

5 For a fuller discussion of Schuman's idea in this regard, see Moir (2001: 16–22).

6 Lantos has, however, criticised the social theory for being vague, as it is not in writing, varies from place to place and does not indicate to what extent the corporation should be conceived as a public (rather than private) enterprise and the relevance of a firm's size to the equation.

7 According to available statistics MNCs' investment in the mining and quarrying sector is about 30 per cent and in manufacturing 32 per cent. There is increasing interest in the telecommunications sector. But investment in that sector accounts for below 2 per cent. See UNCTAD (2007); Ayanwale (2007).

8 For example, Exxon Mobil is owned by NNPC (60 per cent) and Mobil Oil (40 per cent). Shell Petroleum Development Corporation shareholding structure comprises NNPC (55 per cent), Shell International (30 per cent), Elf Petroleum (10 per cent), Agip Oil (5 per cent). Chevron Nigeria Limited is owned by NNPC (60 per cent) and Chevron Texaco (40 per cent). Nigeria Agip Oil Company is owned by NNPC (60 per cent), Agip Oil (20 per cent) and

Phillips Petroleum (20 per cent). Elf Nigeria Ltd is owned by NNPC (60 per cent) and TotalElfFina (40 per cent). And Texaco Overseas (Nigeria) Petroleum Company is owned by NNPC (60 per cent), Chevron (20 per cent) and Texaco (20 per cent). See www.nnpcgroup.com/jv-operations

9 It has, however, been noted that this provision resulted in a paradox, because the first company ever to undertake oil exploration in Nigeria (albeit unsuccessfully due to the First World War) was the German Bitumen Company. See Okonmah (1997); Manby (1999: 27); Omoregbe (1987: 273–4).

10 Simply put, first-mover advantage suggests that pioneering businesses are able to obtain positive economic advantages as a result of their early entry into the market.

11 The UK, France, Germany, Belgium and Sweden. See McBarnet (2007: 32–5); Amao (2008: 75–95).

12 See Limited Liability Company Law 2007, Articles 1 and 27; Investment Law No. 25, 2007 Article 15(b).

13 See generally Omeje (2006: 61–95).

14 The Shell General Business Principles are incorporated in the Shell Code of Conduct (Shell 2006: 6). The Code of Conduct is complementary to the Shell General Business Principles, which the Code elaborates upon.

15 United States District Court Southern District of New York, 96 Civ. 8386 (KMW) (HBP); 01 Civ.1909 (KMW)(HBP); 04 Civ. 2665 (KMW) (HPB). See also Fellmeth (2002).

16 For all settlement agreements and orders, see http://wiwavshell. org/wiwa-v-shell-victory-settlement/

17 *Jonah Gbemre* v. *Shell Petroleum Development Corporation of Nigeria Ltd and Others* (Suit No.

FHC/B/CS/53/05, Federal High Court, Benin Judicial Division, 14/11/05).

18 Shell's website at: www.shell.com/home/content/environment_society/society/human_rights/respecting/

References

Abusharaf, A. (1999) 'The legal relationship between multinational oil companies and the Sudan: Problem and Prospects', *Journal of African Law*, 43.

Alike, E. (2009) 'Shell's output drops to 140,000 bpd', *Thisday* (Nigeria), 1 July.

Amaeshi, K. (2006) 'Corporate social responsibility in Nigeria: Western mimicry or indigenous influences?', *Journal of Corporate Citizenship*, 24.

Amao, O. (2007) 'Controlling corporate cowboys: Extraterritorial application of home countries' jurisdiction to EU corporations abroad', in *UCD Law Review (Symposium Edition)*.

— (2008) 'Mandating corporate social responsibility: Emerging trends in Nigeria', *Journal of Commonwealth Law and Legal Education*, 6(1).

Amnesty International (2005) *Nigeria: Ten Years on: Injustice and Violence Haunt the Oil Delta*, London: Amnesty International.

— (2009) *Nigeria: Petroleum, Pollution and Poverty in the Niger Delta*, London: Amnesty International Publication.

Ayanwale, A. B. (2007) *FDI and Economic Growth: Evidence from Nigeria*, African Economic Research Consortium.

Barnet, R. J. and R. E. Muller (1974) *Global Reach: The power of multinational corporations*, New York: Simon and Schuster.

Boele, R., H. Fabig and D. Wheeler (2001) 'Shell, Nigeria and the Ogoni. A study in unsustainable development: I. The story of Shell, Nigeria and the Ogoni People – Environment, economy, relationships: conflict and prospects for resolution', *Sustainable Development*, 9.

Braithwaite, J. and P. Drahos (2000) *Global Business Regulation*, Cambridge: Cambridge University Press.

Buhmann, K. (2006) 'Corporate social responsibility: What role for law? Some aspects of law and CSR', *Corporate Governance*, 6.

Christian Aid (2004) *Behind the Mask: The real face of corporate social responsibility*, London: Christian Aid.

Clarkson, M. B. E. (1995) 'A stakeholder framework for analysing and evaluating corporate social performance', *Academy of Management Review*, 20.

Clutterbuck, D., S. Hirst and S. Cage (2003) *Talking Business*, Oxford: Butterworth-Heinemann.

Dickerson, C. M. (2001) 'How do norms and empathy affect corporation law and corporate behaviour? Human rights: The emerging norm of corporate social responsibility', *Tulane Law Review*, 76.

Etiebet, D. (1994) *Report of the Ministerial Fact-finding Team to Oil Producing Communities in Nigeria – Don E Etiebet Report*, Nigeria.

Fellmeth, A. X. (2002) 'Wiwa v. Royal Dutch Petroleum Co.: A New Standard for the Enforcement of International Law in US courts?', *Yale Human Rights and Development Law Journal*, 5.

Foster, N. H. D. and J. Ball (2006) 'Imperialism and accountability in corporate law: The limitations of incorporation as a regulatory mechanism', in S. Macleod (ed.), *Global Governance and the Quest for Justice: Corporate governance*, Oxford: Hart Publishing.

Frynas, J. G. (2000) 'Shell in Nigeria: A further contribution', *Third World Quarterly*, 21(1).

— (2005) 'The false developmental promise of corporate social responsibility: Evidence from multinational companies', *International Affairs*, 81(3).

Frynas, J. G., M. P. Beck and K. Mellahi (2000) 'Maintaining corporate dominance after decolonization: The "first mover advantage" of Shell-BP in Nigeria', *Review of African Political Economy*, 27(85).

Gibney, M. (1997–98) 'United States responsibility for gross levels of human rights violations in Guatemala from 1954 to 1996', *Journal of Transnational Law and Policy*, 7: 77–80.

Goldstein, A. E. (2000) *Big Business and the Wealth of South Africa: Policy issues in the transition from Apartheid*, Christopher H. Browne Center for International Politics, University of Pennsylvania Working Paper Series No. 00-01.

Guardian (Nigeria) (2006) 'MOU with EA neighbouring communities: Putting the record straight', *Guardian* (Nigeria), 7 June.

Hassan, C., D. Ihedioha and J. Olawoye (2002) 'Impact of international trade and multinational corporations on the environment and sustainable livelihoods of rural women in Akwa-Ibom State, Niger Delta Region Nigeria', available at: www.gdnet.org/cms.php?id=research_paper_abstract&research_paper_id=4833

Holzer, B. (2007) 'Framing the Corporation: Royal Dutch/Shell and human rights woes in Nigeria', *Journal of Consumer Policy*, 30.

Idemudia, U. and U. E Ite (2006) 'Corporate–community relations in Nigeria's oil industry: Challenges and imperatives', *Corporate Social Responsibility and Environmental Management*, 13.

Idoho, F. M. (2008) 'Oil transnational corporations: Corporate social responsibility and environmental sustainability', *Corporate Social Responsibility and Environmental Management*, 15(4).

IISD (International Institute for Sustainable Development) (2004) *Perceptions and Definitions of Social Responsibility*, Canada.

Jackson, K. T. (1993) 'Global distributive justice and the corporate duty to aid', *Journal of Business Ethics*, 12.

Kivuitu, M., K. Yambayamba and T. Fox (2005) 'How can corporate social responsibility deliver in Africa? Insights from Kenya and Zambia', *Perspectives on Corporate Responsibility for Environment and Development*, 3.

Lantos, G. P. (2001) 'The boundaries of strategic corporate social responsibility', *Journal of Consumer Marketing*, 18.

Lawal, Y. (2007) 'Oil firms plan joint solutions to Niger Delta Problem', *Guardian* (Nigeria), 10 July.

Manby, B. (1999a) 'The role and responsibility of oil multinationals in Nigeria', *Journal of International Affairs*, 53(1).

— (1999b) *The Price of Oil: Corporate responsibility and human rights violations in Nigeria's oil producing communities*, New York: Human Rights Watch.

Matten, D. and A. Crane (2005)

'Corporate citizenship: Toward an extended theoretical conceptualization', *Academy of Management Review*, 30(1).

McBarnet, D. (2007) 'Corporate social responsibility beyond law, through law, for law: The new corporate accountability', in D. McBarnet, A. Voiculescu and T. Campbell (eds), *The New Corporate Accountability: Corporate social responsibility and the law*, Cambridge: Cambridge University Press.

Meredith, M. (2005) *The State of Africa: A history of fifty years of independence*, London: Free Press.

Meznar, M. B., D. Nigh and C. Kwok (1994) 'Effects of announcements of withdrawal from South Africa on stockholder wealth', *Academy of Management Journal*, 37(6).

Mockler-Ferryman, A. F. (1902) 'British Nigeria', *Journal of Royal African Society*, 1.

Moir, L. (2001) 'What do we mean by corporate social responsibility?', *Corporate Governance*, 1.

Moon, J., A. Crane and D. Matten (2005) 'Can corporations be citizens? Corporate citizenship as a metaphor for business participation in society', *Business Ethics Quarterly*, 15(3).

Muchlinski, P. T. (2001) 'Human rights and multinationals: Is there a problem?', *International Affairs*, 77.

Okonmah, P. D. (1997) 'Right to clean environment: The case for the people of oil-producing communities in Nigerian Delta', *Journal of African Law*, 41(1).

Okonta, I. and O. Douglas (2003) *Where Vultures Feast: Shell, human rights, and oil*, London and New York: Verso.

Okoronkwo, K. (2009) 'Govt blames oil firms for Niger Delta Crisis', *Guardian* (Nigeria), 23 June.

Omeje, K. (2006) *High Stakes and Stakeholders: Oil conflict and security in Nigeria*, Farnham: Ashgate.

Omoregbe, Y. (1987) 'The legal framework for the production of petroleum in Nigeria', *Journal of Energy and Natural Resources Law*, 15.

Owolabi, O. (2007) 'Oil and security in Nigeria: The Niger Delta crises', *Africa Development*, 1.

Pegg, S. (1999) 'The cost of doing business – transnational corporations and violence in Nigeria', *Security Dialogue*, 30(4).

Roberts, R. W. (1992) 'Determinants of corporate social responsibility disclosure: An application of stakeholder theory', *Accounting Organisations and Society*, 17(6).

Schlesinger, S. and S. Kinzer (1990) *Bitter Fruit: The Story of the American Coup in Guatemala*, Cambridge, MA: Harvard University Press.

Schultz, Majken (2000) *The Expressive Organization: Linking Identity, Reputation and the Corporate Brand*, New York: Oxford University Press.

Schuman, M. C. (1995) 'Managing legitimacy: Strategic and institutional approaches', *Academy of Management Review*, 20.

Seidman, G. W. (2003) 'Monitoring multinationals: Lessons from the anti-Apartheid era', *Politics and Society*, 31(3).

Shell (1998a) *Profit and Principles: Does there have to be a choice?*, London: Shell.

— (1998b) *Business and Human Rights: A management primer*, London: Shell.

— (2001) *People, Planet and Profit: The Shell Report*, London: Shell.

— (2002) *Human Rights Dilemmas – A*

Training Supplement, London: Shell.

— (2006) *Shell Code of Conduct*, available at: www-static.shell. com/static/public/downloads/ corporate_pkg/code_of_con-duct_english.pdf

— (2008a) *Living by Our Principles*, available at: http://sustainability report.shell.com/2008/shelland theenergychallenge/ourapproach/ livingbyourprinciples.html

— (2008b) *Responsible Energy, Sustainability Report*, available at: http://sustainabilityreport. shell.com/2008/servicepages/ downloads/files/entire_shell_ ssr_08.pdf

Staley, E. (1935) *War and the Private Investor*, New York: Double Day, Doran & Company Inc.

Steyn, M. S. (2003) Oil Politics in Ecuador and Nigeria: A Perspective from Environmental History on the Struggles between Ethnic Minority and National Governments. PhD thesis submitted to the Faculty of Humanities (Department of History), University of the Free State, Bloemfontein, South Africa.

Streeter, S. M. (2000) 'Interpreting the 1954 US intervention in Guatemala: Realist, revisionist, and post revisionist perspectives', *History Teacher*, 34(1).

Ugeh, P. and V. James (2009) 'Oil producers blame FG's "greed" for gas flaring', *ThisDay* (Nigeria), 23 June.

UNCTAD (UN Conference on Trade and Development) (2007) *World Investment Report 2007: Transnational corporations, extractive industries and development*, New York and Geneva: United Nations.

Wallace, C. D. (2002) *The Multinational Enterprise and Legal Control: Host state sovereignty in an era of economic globalization*, The Hague: Martinus Nijhoff Publishers.

Watts, M. J. (2005) 'Righteous oil? Human rights, the oil complex, and corporate social responsibility', *Annual Review of Environment and Resources*, 30.

Weinraub, D. (1998) 'Shell defeats the PIRC Group resolution', *Colorado Journal of International Environmental Law and Policy*, 9.

Wheeler, D., H. Fabig and R. Boele (2002) 'Paradoxes and dilemmas for stakeholder responsive firms in the extractive sector: Lessons from the case of Shell and the Ogoni', *Journal of Business Ethics*, 39.

Winston, M. E. (1999) 'Review of "Human rights and international political economy in third world nations: Multinational corporations, foreign aids, and repression", by William H. Meyer', *Human Rights Quarterly*, 21(3).

Zerk, J. A. (2006) *Multinationals and Corporate Social Responsibility: Limitations and opportunities in international law*, Cambridge: Cambridge University Press.

11 | Clusters of injustice: human rights, labour standards and environmental sustainability

MARK J. SMITH AND PIYA PANGSAPA

Introduction

The conditions that lead to human rights violations are often the same as those that generate environmental degradation, social inequalities and injustices and labour standards violations. Thus, when bad things happen, they tend to create clusters of injustice. These conditions include the existence of poor governance, where some interests are able to exert an overwhelmingly greater influence on political institutions than are others. In this case, legal protections, should they exist, are not acted upon – i.e. politicians ignore or acquiesce in the violations or environmental change. Alternatively, there may be an authoritarian regime, civil conflict or war, in which case rule of law is largely absent and politicians have little impact. Whatever the specific circumstances, there is usually a vulnerable and initially inactive group (or groups) and a habitat that has come to be seen as an exploitable resource. In such situations, for example, the displacement of a community – or even of a whole people – by force in order to access mineral deposits or fossil fuels, or to construct a dam, means that human rights abuses and habitat destruction are closely linked.

In some cases, environmental movements have made the connection themselves, by talking about environmental rights or by linking issues such as climate justice to human rights. For example, Inuit campaigners have highlighted the fact that they bear the negative effects of both pollution and resource extraction without reaping their fair share of the benefits of development (Watt-Cloutier 2004). As Haluza-DeLay et al. also argue in relation to Arctic inhabitants:

> Northern peoples bear a disproportionate burden from economic
> development and natural resource extraction, since they do not benefit
> from the conveniences of mass-industrial production as their southern
> neighbours do, yet experience deleterious changes to their economies,
> environments and ways of life. (2009: 3)

Andrew Dobson (2003) makes a similar point regarding globalisers (in developed societies) having effects on the globalised in contexts vulnerable to climate change: the consumption habits of people in the developed world are sustained at the cost of exploitation, rights violations and degradation elsewhere.

Despite these connections, it is still commonplace for researchers, governments, lawyers, NGOs and businesses to focus exclusively either on human rights, labour issues or environmental sustainability. There are extensive research literatures dealing with each of these, with both NGO and government reports focused on one or another in the same way. Relatively little has been said or reported on how the aspects coincide or on how their combined presence intensifies the negative effects of each. If citizens, governments and companies are to be responsible actors, they need to act swiftly and effectively in cases where these 'bads' coincide. Here we gather evidence of where they do, and explore ways in which they can begin to be addressed.

Corporate responsibility in the context of human rights

When we think of corporate responsibility, we consider how a company has responsibilities not only for the direct effects of its activities, but also for the violations of human rights that are carried out by any of its partners in production, distribution and exchange, including the acts of governments. At the same time, according to Hart (1968), a responsible entity is able to make choices and is also simultaneously capable of exercising some control over the situation in question. For Michael Addo, this means we should think of responsibility beyond that of executives to the 'tasks and duties ... dissipated across the corporation as a whole' (Addo 1999: 17). But how far is a company answerable for human rights abuses that result from the activities of partners? Should Shell pull out of oil and gas in countries such as Nigeria until more accountable political processes are established? Should Nestlé end its activities in China, including the sale of baby-milk powders? Should any transnational companies be involved in countries such as Burma and Zimbabwe? Some of these are extreme cases, but they highlight the central questions of where responsibilities for human rights start for transnational corporations and who in the company is responsible. These questions form the focus of this chapter. First we need to look at the meaning of human rights and to whom that definition has applied.

The history of rights has to some extent mirrored the relations of power in any period and location. In the 1700s, besides certain rights to common land, rights were focused on property ownership, which was itself an entry ticket to the political community. As part of human progress, rights have been extended to many members of the population that were previously excluded, not least women and children. Human rights are often described in a fairly narrow way, as a set of formalised entitlements held or possessed by a subject of law or citizen (such as free speech or free association), simply by virtue of that subject or citizen being a member of the human race or of a political community. For those who qualify under this definition, human rights apply equally to all. But this does not automatically mean that all members of the human race are classed as full members. In the past, women and children, as well as people of lower classes or castes, have been denied such rights on the grounds that they are not yet ready for full 'membership' – using some spurious grounds such as lack of rationality, immaturity, educational background, ethnicity or even lineage. Over time, such distinctions between those inside and outside the moral community, as well as the political community, have been demonstrated to be spurious and based on prejudice. However, the distinction between moral agents and moral patients, with the latter entitled to some form of protection by the former, has been retained for some of these groups – such as women in patriarchal legal systems prior to equality legislation, and for children in many cultures today. The grounds for excluding a section of the human population would often be couched in terms of the cultural values of the dominant groups in the society in question. For example, arguments against women's rights in the UK and against emancipation of the slaves in the USA often rested on claims that rights holders possessed a rationality that was deemed to be absent in women and slaves.

For this reason, the focus of the latter part of this chapter is on child slavery. Child slavery highlights a specific problem: namely that while private companies have a general idea that they must respect human rights in a universal way, the precise understanding of human rights in different societies, cultures, religions and ethico-political communities can vary considerably. A company executive making purchasing decisions may feel that the presence of bonded female labour or child labour in his firm's outsourced manufacturers is a product of the cultural context or of economic necessity – taking it for granted that the mantra of development or economic modernisation trumps concern for universal human rights. Thus, in exploring concrete cases in real-life conditions, we see the relationships between human rights, labour standards and environmental sustainability. There are three points that are explored through the examples provided in this chapter.

First, there are *human rights and corresponding duties that rights holders bear*. Rights are always 'relational' in two ways: (a) to the broader informal senses of entitlements that are relevant to a time and place; and (b) to obligations and their formalised emergence as duties. To say that something is 'relational' is to say that its meaning can only be understood through such relationships, rather than in and of itself. For example, the first form of relationality can be seen where a general sense of entitlement exists in a specific culture (such as regarding land use ranging from hunting to public access for walking and hiking). In each case, entitlements are subject to regulation in order to protect the environment or specific animal species. Legal measures such as the ban on hunting involving more than two dogs removed a historic right to hunt to which many are attached. Similarly, the right to roam opened up many areas of the countryside that had previously been blocked. The point here is simply that the relationship between rights and entitlements is the product of practices in a particular time and place. On the second form of relationality, the right to roam carries with it certain duties (that are legally enforceable) not to damage property or endanger livestock, as well as more informal obligations to stick to the public rights of way, be friendly with land owners and avoid practices such as leaving litter. The precise relations here are likely to be different when applied to other issues because they are shaped by context.

Second, *the qualities (or the 'membership criteria') that are necessary for holding rights matter.* Historically, rights have been extended to a range of human groups, and in recent years have been applied to future generations, non-human animals and even trees, forests and ecosystems. Of course, children, some people with severe intellectual disabilities and even natural things cannot be rights holders in exactly the same way, and their protection can depend on the mobilisation of obligations held by adult human beings or state agencies acting on their behalf. In some cases, these obligations may be legally defined – i.e. as duties, such as in terms of the responsibilities of parents, schools and state organisations towards children. In other cases, such as in areas of natural beauty, there may be duties regarding litter and waste disposal, but overall this depends on the informal obligations held by those who live in the habitat and those who visit for recreational purposes.

Finally, there are *conflicts that occur between different kinds of rights.* One such example is the conflict in debates on abortion between the right to choose and the right to life. Such conflicts can be especially tricky to negotiate for NGOs, as well as for private corporations. For example, human rights relating to gender questions may be regarded as universal by some NGOs focused on women's rights to education, voting and standing as a candidate, birth control, divorce and economic independence; but for NGOs and local movements defending a specific way of life, these may be secondary or irrelevant to group rights that attempt to preserve the identity of a cultural community.

Such issues often arise when universal rights devised in the West are applied to contexts where religious beliefs and cultural traditions differ. It is also important to distinguish between contexts where rights are ignored and where some rights are overridden by others. For example, in some cases businesses have argued that, in developing countries, a community's right to environmental quality is overridden by its right to a better standard of living provided by employment at the business's subsidiaries or outsourced manufacturers.

TABLE 11.1 Responsibility in context

	Capacities to act (enablement)	Liabilities to others (constraint)
Informal	Entitlements	Obligations
Formal	Rights	Duties

There is a tendency to think of human rights as universal, and in some sense as absolute benchmarks or bedrock assumptions. Amartya Sen highlights the fact that this should not be automatically assumed: companies face problems in understanding where their responsibilities lie and the measures they need to develop in order to behave responsibly. According to Sen (1997), the idea of human rights rests on a bedrock assumption of shared membership of humanity, rather than national citizenship – that entitlements are rooted in humanitarianism, rather than in temporally and spatially limited political communities. For Sen, this difference of assumptions underpinning human rights shapes the debate between Western assertions that human rights should apply to all and the rejection of this by Asian governments, which place a greater emphasis on duties and obligations to state and the collective order. Sen also highlights the fact that the history of the West, as well as the rest of the world, often involved the exclusion of many members of the human race – undermining the moral authority of advocates of the extension of Western civilisation. Smith and Pangsapa (2008) and Pangsapa and Smith (2011) highlight the importance of both entitlements and obligations (including their formal expression as rights and duties) in understanding human rights, indicating that these vary according to cultural context. For example, they provide illustrations of how the virtues of wisdom and forgiveness (in Theravada Buddhism) affect the relationship between *entitlements* and *obligations* for those involved in cases of injustice. Similarly, Sen (1997) argues that it is important to avoid portraying Asian approaches to rights as authoritarian, and that both Buddhist and Confucian traditions assert notions of tolerance and freedom, particularly free speech.

Rights are often presented as universal – such as the right to equal dignity without distinction in terms of background, the right to life, liberty and personal security (although for many the latter may be replaced by property or happiness) and the right to equal recognition before the law (trial by an impartial judge). These are combined in the United Nations Declaration of Human Rights with a prohibition on slavery, servitude, torture, arbitrary arrest or detention, and on cruel, inhuman and degrading treatment or punishment. Together, this means that due process should apply to all claimants without discrimination, and also to all prohibitions and retributions deemed necessary and right by representatives of the collective order. These are combined with respect for freedom of speech and conscience, religious belief and practice, assembly and association. These freedoms are essential in highlighting the suffering caused by human rights abuse, as well as exposing labour standard violations and environmental harm. Without respect for these freedoms, labour unions, environmental movements and NGOs have considerable difficulty in ensuring that state policies are responsive to the needs of the vulnerable, the marginalised and the powerless. Hence, a guarantee against discrimination and a guarantee that all are entitled to equal protection of the law within the terms of human rights are often seen as essential conditions for efficient and successful activism.

The absence of such freedoms and legal conditions presents considerable obstacles to the attainment of social and environmental justice. Of course, in every state there are differences in emphasis and some degree of selectivity in the actual human rights that are prioritised. The ownership of property was less important in many communist societies, whereas freedom from want, poverty, disease, squalor and ignorance have often been ignored in societies that emphasise free markets. A major contemporary problem in many societies is the experience of ethnic minorities (and in some cases ethnic majorities) that feel excluded from rights to education, development and participation in cultural life of their own choice (emphasised in Articles 26 and 27 of the UN Declaration of Human Rights) and at the same time often experience a disproportionate share of environmental 'bads' and exploitative working conditions. For these reasons, we will focus here on human rights in context, in the concrete conditions where rights and entitlements exist in complex combinations and in conjunction with various obligations and duties. Before we look at that, the next section highlights the broad transformations in business activity that have generated many of the problems indicated above. How developed societies source their goods and services and the arrangements that international trade and transnational ownership and control generate often lead to serious difficulties in developing societies.

Tentacular capitalism: supply chains in a global market

In the global economic marketplace, so as to remain competitive in terms of both price and quality, firms have developed their business across national borders, in the search for cheap resources and labour. This can take two forms. First there is direct investment, where the company decides to buy into or develop raw material extraction or manufacturing production, in order to support its distribution and exchange practices, often using its own managerial staff in conjunction with local labour. Transnational corporations have shifted from horizontal integration across different business sectors (an approach that generated the large conglomerate transnational corporations from the 1950s to the 1970s) to more vertical integration solutions that link raw material production to manufacturing and retail, and this has been seen as a route to securing profitability. As developing countries experienced economic growth, indigenous companies emerged to serve internal markets and markets in the developed Western countries. At the same time, developed countries went through the transition from so-called Fordist to post-Fordist production and consumption.

In Fordist economies, demand is sustained so that mass consumption matches the organisation of the economy around mass production (i.e. consumers are willing and able to buy the cheap but homogeneous outputs of the assembly-line system). In post-Fordism, we have seen the emergence of complex differentiated markets, and the response in productive or manufacturing sectors is flexible automation (with production processes able to manufacture a variety of goods suited to consumption trends) and flexible specialisation of labour (where workforce members can be redeployed in the production process often as part of teams to match market demand). In some cases, the combination of flexi-automation and flexi-specialisation has been described as 'flexi-cap' (short for 'flexible capitalism'), 'just in time' production or Toyota-ism (see Figure 11.1 on post-Fordism).

Figure 11.1 Post-Fordism (*source*: Harvey 1989)

Second, and as a result of the above trends in the global political economy, there is the increased rapidity of outsourcing, which involves the transfer of responsibilities for production, including management, to an external service provider. In cases following this approach, a company (usually in a developing country) agrees to provide a product or service to the specification of the recipient company at the required quality and cost for the duration of a contract. In particular, this often involves pressure on the outsourced company, often a developing-country company, to fulfil the obligations to supply materials or services within a strict timeframe or be subject to penalties that compensate transnational companies for financial losses that result from just-too-late delivery. In short, there is a crucial relationship of power between transnational corporations and the outsourced manufacturing or resource-extracting companies, and a parallel one between outsourced companies and the subcontractors that provide materials and services upon which those outsourced manufacturers often depend.

Immediately this highlights a particular problem. If major brand-name companies in the West are to change their behaviour, then that has implications not only for outsourced manufacturers, but also for the subcontracting companies upon which the bottom line of the brand-name companies depends. Since outsourced companies can engage with other subcontractors themselves, transnational companies often depend on many and varied subcontractors further down the global supply chain. Given that the subcontractors to outsourcers then sub-contract further, we can see how hard it is to monitor global supply chains when so much of the chain is effectively hidden from the view of auditors. It is for these reasons that the best metaphor for contemporary transnational business is 'tentacular capitalism'. The idea of tentacular capitalism captures both the extensive global reach of transnational corporations and their capacity to 'reach' into the smallest crevices of material production, extracting what is needed and moving on to new crevices and gaps when they emerge or as conditions appear to be potentially more productive.

Therefore, many of the goods bought in industrialised societies are made (or at least have components made) in other countries, potentially in distant sweatshop conditions where environmental regulations are ignored. In the 'race to the bottom', the further towards the bottom of the global supply chain we look, the more likely we are to find poor working conditions, barely subsistence wages, the absence or non-application of environmental regulation and the likelihood of human rights abuses. The conditions most suited to sweatshops are those in which the most vulnerable people try to survive. In outsourced manu-facturing and export processing zones throughout the world, workers continue to be subjected to the same conditions: meagre wages, long hours, hazardous work environments, physical and verbal abuse, and job insecurity (Lee 2006; McKay 2006; Pangsapa 2007; Powell and Skabbek 2006; Salzinger 2003; Tiano 1994).

In Southern China, the rapid growth of export industries has meant severe consequences for the local environment: factories release un-treated waste water directly into the Dongchan River, polluting the water with mercury, ammonia and chromium. Mercury levels are reported to be 280 times the legal limit. Local residents thus risk consuming contaminated water and fish, and farmers also have no choice but to irrigate their farmland with the water from the river. In the Pearl River Delta, the city of Guiyu provides the West with a globally sourced recy-cling complex, where waste is sorted by hand, with plastics shredded and metals retrieved using industrial acids and heat. Not only are the workers in these sectors largely unprotected from the effects of poison-ing, but the local communities and their environments are despoiled by the run-off of the materials and the pollution from the acids. All this violates established environmental laws in China, which assert rights to environmental quality and protection from industrial hazards.

Fewer and fewer manufactured goods today are made in the West, and manufacturing has been outsourced to countries and regions around the world where labour is cheap and where labour regulations are ignored, weak or non-existent. On a global scale, the situation of workers in transnational factories has been well documented following the extensive relocation of manufacturing industries to low-wage countries: garments in Cambodia, Vietnam and Thailand; leather goods and garments in India and Bangladesh; shoes in Indonesia; electronics in China. It has been increasingly recognised that workers suffer from a variety of health problems related to poor working environments, such as the occupational lung disease known as byssinosis ('brown lung'), caused by inhaling cotton dust, and a number of chronic diseases, including typhoid, jaundice, dysentery and reproductive health problems. Similarly, in the electronics industry, there is a high prevalence of lead (and other forms of metal) poisoning among women workers (Economy 2004; Lee 2007; Pun 2005).

Evidence-based research indicates three developments. In situations such as this, certain transnational corporations may: (a) pay no attention to the fact that basic rights are simply not present or, if they are enshrined in law, are ignored; (b) turn a blind eye to the exclusion of many subjects from membership as citizens; or (c) ignore the fact that the rights of factory workers are overridden by other concerns. By ignoring basic human rights (such as the right to organise unions) or by engaging in citizenship exclusion, developing-country companies make it easier for activists to damage the brand status of many leading Western companies. Local activists have increasingly developed networks with consumer NGOs in developed countries to highlight ways in which companies are directly responsible for practices both in their own subsidiaries (often the case in extractive industries, such as mining) and in outsourced manufacturing (through the establishment and subsequent monitoring and enforcement of labour and environmental standards) (Klein 2000; Pangsapa 2007; Smith and Pangsapa 2008).

Corporate responsibility in question – a case study To illustrate how environmental issues become entangled with human rights concerns, we use the example of the authoritarian context of Myanmar (still often referred to as Burma in the international community). The country has a history of military dictatorships, often brutal suppression of pro-democracy activism, and endemic problems of corruption and human rights violations (especially regarding ethnic minority groups).

The Yadana pipeline, partially financed by external business interests,

223

has generated considerable adverse publicity and has thus become a focus for transnational NGOs concerned with environmental damage and human rights. The Yadana pipeline project links the offshore gas fields in the territorial waters of Burma via the Tenasserim region to a power facility in Ratchaburi in Thailand. This joint venture has involved collaboration between Unocal (US), Total (France), PTT Exploration and Production (Thailand) and the State Law and Order Restoration Council (SLORC – the military government in Myanmar). The construction and operation of the pipeline by the Burmese military (as part of its role in securing the area, providing the infrastructure, constructing the pipeline and providing ongoing security) has led to forest encroachment and degradation, forced displacement, various human rights abuses, forced labour and the use of child labour. The environmental damage has also destroyed the livelihoods of local communities and contributed to the forced displacement of populations and a growing refugee problem in the region.

As a result of its previous investments in the country, Unocal was exempt from measures by the US government to stop new investment in Burma. As a result, the NGO EarthRights International launched a legal case (*Doe* v. *Unocal Corp.*) on behalf of fifteen plaintiffs who had been forced to work on the pipeline between 1993 and 1998. The case resembled many of the class action litigation processes initiated on behalf of victims of toxic hazards in the USA by legal firms such as Masry & Vititoe and Girardi & Keese and involved activities and community organisations in the environmental justice movement in the USA (Agyeman 2002, 2005; Bullard 1990; Bullard and Johnson 1997). Clearly, the chances of exerting effective pressure on the Burmese government were minimal and legal action was not feasible in Burma itself. Margaret Keck and Kathryn Sikkink (1998) argue that, in such situations, the closed political and legal opportunity structures in Burma mean that action is only possible through a 'boomerang effect'. This involves transnational activist networks placing pressure on external companies providing the technical expertise and capital for such projects in developing countries with poor governance records. Keck and Sikkink argue that this is feasible because the companies involved need to maintain the brand value and 'good standing' among consumers in developed countries and in international negotiations on matters such as trade and investment.

Unocal's response was that the company had no knowledge of the actual acts raised in the case; moreover, the company was not legally implicated in the use of labour during construction, nor was it involved in the environmental damage, and as a result had adhered to the highest ethical standards. This defence highlighted the fact that, since Unocal had no legal rights in Burma, it also had no legal obligations (i.e. it had no duties). Despite this denial of responsibility by Unocal throughout the case from 1996, in December 2004 it reached an undisclosed financial settlement to provide assistance to the people affected by the pipeline.

This can be interpreted in various ways. One interpretation would suggest that, while denying its duties, the company had accepted its obligations to recompense those affected by processes from which Unocal had financially benefited. An alternative (less charitable) interpretation would be that this was a one-off attempt to make the case go away, by formally denying responsibility but making a concession to avoid further damage to the company's brand.

At this point, we might outline the five most common responses used by corporations:

- The company says disclosure of practices would jeopardise its position. Companies frequently resort to arguments that the issues are a 'security matter', would violate client confidentiality, or would provide other firms with an unfair advantage if they disclosed any information about the case or situation.
- The company maintains that the resources to implement the code of conduct were not adequate. Thus, the code of conduct would have worked very effectively in delivering the goals established for corporate responsibility, had the resources to implement them been adequate in the current business model, or had governments and international organisations been willing to share the burden.
- The company moves production either to another manufacturer or to another country to improve employment conditions. Moving production from one outsourced company to another, possibly in a different country with an alternative regulatory context, does not reflect a failure in the company's development, but merely that, as it has engaged with outsourced manufacturers, it has learned of some of their less responsible practices and provided a period of relatively well paid employment for citizens in that location and the chance for them to learn new skills.
- The company claims not to have had any knowledge of exploitation. The company was not aware of the extremely exploitative conditions of subcontract suppliers to outsourced manufacturers, but the parent company will learn from this lesson and does not anticipate the problem arising again.
- The company says the outsourced manufacturer suffered a lapse in

judgement. These unfortunate lapses in judgement run contrary to the parent company's policy and the established codes of conduct.

Transnational campaigning Where the jurisdiction of legal regulations on company practices is complicated and uncertain, given the length of time for processing litigation and the considerable investment in time and money by all parties, and where there are difficulties in assigning responsibility across national borders, then it is not surprising that holding transnational corporations to account is problematic. In these circumstances, activists and NGOs have opted for a more preventive approach. This approach involves intensive campaigning focused on major brand-name companies to ensure that they live up to the codes of conduct they have already established and seek to improve them through external influence. The lever available to this end is the fact that corporations have pursued growth strategies that depend on securing increased value of such intangible assets as reputations, confidence of stakeholders (investors, customers, regulators and employees), brand identities, talent, capacity for innovation, intellectual property, networks and relationships with clients.

Since brand-name companies are often no longer directly responsible for the production of many of the goods to which the brands are applied, they focus on the marketing of products and the maintenance of a corporate image in which consumers can invest their identities (such as Apple, Nike, Adidas, Calvin Klein, Guess, Gap, Tommy Hilfiger). The success of a transnational corporation depends on its reputation, and any damage to the brand that makes its logo less attractive in the marketplace can seriously undermine a company's bottom line. Consumers are often as concerned with ethical issues as they are with market price, convenience and product quality. In addition, fair trade products have grown in importance in certain markets, including coffee, chocolate, cosmetics, furniture and apparel. Many major supermarket chains are developing fair trade and ecologically sensitive products in their grocery operations, and this has resulted in many traditional brands shifting their sourcing policy or even taking over brands with a clear ethical message (such as L'Oreal taking over Bodyshop). Hence, campaign groups such as Greenpeace, Friends of the Earth, Amnesty International and Clean Clothes Campaign are able to exercise considerable pressure on many transnational corporations by generating adverse publicity (often referred to as a *Nikemare* in marketing departments) and in some cases consumer boycotts. Even a decline in sales of 1–3 per cent is enough to prompt action from many companies.

Successful campaigns against sweatshop labour – such as those targeting Nike and Reebok – have led many private corporations to focus far more on maintaining their commitment and image as responsible companies. Transnational corporations have increasingly sought an appropriate balance between the interests of investment and market-share strategy, shareholders and market value, and environmental concerns and social obligations. Company structures are thus arenas for conflict and tension between competing imperatives – and, as such, we should regard these as strategic domains in which there are advantages to be gained for human rights campaigners, the workforce and the demands of environmental movements (that is, if they develop stronger links and coordinate their activities). Naomi Klein argues in a similar way that:

> Rather than merely bankrolling someone else's content, all over the Net, corporations are experimenting with the much coveted role of being 'content providers': Gap's site offers travel tips, Volkswagen provides free music samples, Pepsi urges visitors to download video games and Starbucks offers an online version of its magazine, *Joe*. Every brand with a Web site has its own virtual, branded media outlet – a beachhead from which to expand into non-virtual media. What has become clear is that corporations aren't just selling products online, they're selling a new model for the media's relationship with corporate sponsors and backers. (Klein 2000: 43)

To avoid adverse publicity and consumer boycotts, Western brand-name companies pay particular attention to demonstrating their responsibilities. With these ideas in mind, and to illustrate how vulnerable some companies' reputations can be to damage, we now turn to an area where human rights and labour standards overlap significantly: child labour and slavery. The following section also provides an illustration of how self-organisation in the business sector, in conjunction with NGO activism, can achieve positive results – fairly quickly – in the face of one significant human rights abuse.

Child labour, slavery and human rights

In ensuring corporate responsibility, some targets are easier than others. One target that has received explicit attention has been the campaign against child labour. Child labour has often been linked to broader issues of child slavery and, to some extent, sex tourism. We should bear in mind that childhood is a relatively recent construct, and that all societies have exploited children in historical terms. The idea of childhood emerged originally in Western societies, and over time it has come to be seen as a phase of human development that needs protection. Thus, the concern with child labour, slavery and other forms of forced labour is a relatively recent area of debate. Kevin Bales argues that, previously, owning a slave was an investment, whereas with today's 'new slavery':

> Buying a slave is ... more like buying an inexpensive bicycle or a cheap computer. Slaveholders get all the work they can out of their slaves, and then throw them away. The nature of the relationship between slaves and slaveholders has fundamentally altered. The new disposability has dramatically increased the amount of profit to be made from a slave, decreased the length of time a person would normally be enslaved, and made the question of legal ownership less important ... Slaves of the past were worth stealing and worth chasing down if they escaped. Today slaves cost so little that it is not worth the hassle of securing permanent, 'legal' ownership. Slaves are disposable. (Bales 2004: 14)

Whereas in old-style slavery, bondage lasted forever, today the length of time a slave spends in bondage varies enormously; but, regardless of the time spent, the exploitation is intense. The key differences between old and new slavery break down as shown in Figure 11.2.

Old slavery	New slavery
Legal ownership asserted	Legal ownership avoided
High purchase cost	Very low purchase cost
Low profits	Very high profits
Shortage of potential slaves	Glut of potential slaves
Slaves maintained	Short-term relationship
Ethnic differences important	Ethnic differences not important

Figure 11.2 Old slavery and new slavery

In *Understanding Global Slavery* (2005), Bales describes slavery as the 'loss of free will, in which a person is forced through violence or the threat of violence to give up the ability to sell freely his or her own labour power' (Bales 2005: 57). This highlights three dimensions of servitude that are not always present in forms of exploitation associated with contemporary uses of the word slavery:

> Apartheid, incest, organ harvesting, caste, and abusive treatment of migrant workers have all been defined as slavery-like practices, but should not be defined as slavery, since the theft of labour power in particular does not occur to the same degree as in the practices already identified as consistent with slavery. (ibid.: 58)

Forced prostitution and sex slavery or forced labour have all three dimensions present (loss of free will, threat of violence and appropriation of labour power), but it is harder to define all forms of labour and prostitution in this way, for much depends on context, whether the work is effectively regulated and so on.

> In *Debt Bondage* an individual pledges him/herself against a loan insisting on complete physical control. In many cases, the character of the service and its relationship to the loan is unclear. Consequently debts can be intergenerational and defaults can lead to abductions of children or grandchildren. In *Contract Slavery* contracts are offered but workers find themselves enslaved – the 'contract worker' is threatened by violence, lacking any freedom of movement and paid little or nothing. (Bales 2004: 19)

Rather than owning factories in developing countries, with all the additional responsibilities involved, transnational private corporations are interested in the use of resources and reap the benefits of low labour costs. Given that most abuses of human rights through enslavement take place at the bottom of the subcontract chain, in smaller factories and workshops, transnational corporations also gain the financial benefits of slavery and associated forms of exploitation without having direct responsibility for its occurrence. For Bales, the new slave is 'a consumable item, added to the production process when needed, but no longer carrying a high capital cost' (Bales 2005: 237). The problems involved in identifying practices that clearly constitute slavery can also be seen in ILO Convention 182, which focuses on severe kinds of child labour. This Convention prohibits 'all forms of slavery or practices similar to slavery, such as the sale and trafficking of children, debt bondage and serfdom and forced or compulsory labour, including forced or compulsory recruitment of children for use in armed conflict' (ibid.: 92), but does not offer a clear definition of slavery itself.

One of the most effective campaigns for greater corporate responsibility towards child labour emerged in Brazil. Outsourced manufacturing relied on child labour to produce items such as children's toys, and the anti-child labour campaigns had an especially soft target. Some large corporations were slow to realise in 2000 that twelve-to-fifteen-year-old children were producing Snoopy, Winnie the Pooh and Hello Kitty toys in sweatshops in southern China. The campaigns used emotive slogans, such as 'American corporations making children's toys with child slave labour'.

As a result, and not surprisingly, this sector became one of the first to develop codes of conduct in terms of corporate responsibility around child labour. Campaigns in China have been difficult because the civil society context is constrained. However, in Brazil the formation of CONAETI (National Commission to Eradicate Child Labour) in 2002 was the result of a broader movement, including labour unions, community associations, NGO initiatives, business associations and social entrepreneurs such as Oded Grajew (founder in 1990 of the Abrinq Foundation). By focusing on child labour, business leaders such as Grajew (former president of the Latin American Toy Manufacturers' Association) helped move the Brazilian toy industry away from the use of child labour and sought to foster a wider sense of ethical responsibility in business, through organisations such as the Instituto Ethos de Empresas e Responsabilidade (Institute of Ethics and Responsible Business) (1998). Grajew was also heavily involved in bringing together the 'World Social Forum' (in Porto Alegre, Brazil, in 2001 and 2002), a citizen-sector alternative to the World Economic Forum.

Brazil's civil society, besides the usual forces of labour and NGOs focused on human rights, democracy and justice, included active small farmers and landless peasant movements, specific trade union movements such as the *seringueiros* (the rubber tappers union led by Chico Mendez), women's land rights campaigns and a proliferation of neighbourhood or urban movements aimed at the specific problems that affected community livelihoods. This broader-based movement developed strong links with Western-based NGOs that focused on fair trade, sweatshops, human rights and environmental issues. These links ensured that pressure could be applied both within Brazil and to the companies selling goods and services in developed societies.

Quite apart from the civil society campaigns, the business environment in Brazil was conducive to change. The structure of Brazilian industry (100 companies constitute a third of Brazil's GDP) meant that chief executive responses to pressure were swift. For example, the resulting child-friendly business programme led to a 40 per cent reduction in child labour in Brazil, primarily through the effective monitoring of factory conditions and the use of a child-friendly seal as an information tool for consumers. However, even in 2003, UNICEF estimated that 7 per cent of five-to-fourteen-year-old children still worked as adults in Brazil. As Blowfield and Murray (2008: 31) argue:

> While there are differences from code to code, typically, the most respected codes today address issues that broadly mirror the concerns of the ILO's Declaration on Fundamental Principles and Rights at Work

about forced labour, freedom of association, child labour, and discrimination; in practice however, there is still a marked tendency for issues such as child labour, or health and safety, to be dealt with more rigorously than freedom of association and working hours.

In Brazil during that time, the business associations offered an open door to attempts at self-regulation. By contrast, campaigns to tackle child labour were less successful in cacao production in countries such as Ghana. One explanation is that civil society associations are less well developed in Ghana, which reduces the opportunities for mutually supportive alliances and for the broader acceptance of human rights discourses as legitimate in the face of traditional practices and economic necessity.

In chocolate production, as many private corporations moved from owning and controlling production processes in developing societies towards outsourced manufacturing by developing country and intra-regional client companies, the initial response of companies was to claim that the conditions and effects were beyond their control. Companies such as Mars, Nestlé and Hershey's have only just started to accept that they have responsibility for child slave-labour conditions on cacao plantations in West African countries, particularly Côte d'Ivoire and Ghana. UNICEF and the ILO have both highlighted how, as in so many forced-labour situations, the young male slaves are stateless migrants from neighbouring countries, such as Mali, Burkina Faso and Togo. As a result, they also lack broader citizenship rights.

In 2005, when the deadline for establishing a certification process for eradicating child labour in cacao production passed without fulfilment (a promise made by the world cacao industry in accepting the 2001 Harkin-Engel Protocol), the International Labor Rights Fund (ILRF) (a Washington-based NGO) filed a federal lawsuit on behalf of three Malian children who were trafficked to plantations in Côte d'Ivoire, against Nestlé and two commodity traders, Archer Daniels Midland and Cargill. The legal response on behalf of the companies was that US Customs should not ban the imports as goods made by forced child labour under existing legal provisions, but should await self-certification processes to be developed. The loophole in federal law that allows the importation of such goods from outside the USA if domestic demand exists is currently the subject of a congressional amendment campaign led by Senator Tom Harkin, alongside a public–private partnership with the cacao industry. The 2005 deadline was subsequently amended with the aim of ensuring that half of the farms would be 'child labour free' by July 2008, although the progress on self-certification remained slow and incomplete.

Subsequently, a multi-stakeholder consultative group – bringing together government, business, NGOs (including a member of the ILRF, which changed its name to the International Labor Rights Forum in 2007) and academic research representatives – was established in September 2009, under the auspices of the 2008 Farm Bill, to ensure the elimination of forced and child labour in the production of goods imported into the USA, in this case through a system of third-party monitoring and verification (although there is still no compulsion on companies to participate). Despite the increase in pressure on private corporations to develop greater responsibility on these matters, these cases highlight a crucial point: the successful elimination of forced and child labour depends on the capabilities and willingness of companies to comply. In Brazil, self-regulation has been relatively successful, while in chocolate production outsourcing, established local traditions, poor governance contexts (in Côte d'Ivoire as a result of military conflict and partition) and 'development at any price' have ensured that such practices continue.

Conclusion

Clearly there are conditions for success and failure in promoting human rights in the corporate sector. Change is possible when the relevant business sector is directly involved, when governance processes mean that legislation is present and applied, and when NGOs concerned with human rights, environmental issues and labour pool their efforts. Unocal eventually relented in the wake of pressure on both environmental and human rights grounds. Coordinated transnational activism works best when a company is challenged on all fronts, rather than on a single issue. It also creates many new opportunities for leverage, since a transnational company may respond to environmental concerns but not to labour or human rights (or vice versa).

For certain brand-name companies, the emergence of conflict is likely to result in some movement of outsourced manufacture contracting and subcontracting, since the conditions for production are often undermined by war and civil strife. However, some companies specialising in resource extraction, such as mining and timber, are more tied to specific locations. Conflict also generates additional costs, since the facilities require security provision, and corruption can impose an additional burden. Indeed, the provision of security may be part of the bribery in some mining operations. Nevertheless, the point made above that the issues are interconnected still applies to mining and timber, for all such activities lead to environmental degradation, are likely to impact on community livelihoods, and (in conditions of poor governance and regulatory failure) result in (or contribute to) human rights abuses and labour standards violations simply because the vulnerable (be they children, women, communities or migrants) have fewer protections.

There are thus three main reasons for seeing human rights, environmental issues and labour standards as connected. First, the conditions in each case often mean that where one abuse or violation exists, the others are also likely to be present. Second, political structures and company practices matter when it comes to the successful development of regulation and self-regulation to tackle these problems. Company and political decision-makers, in particular, need a more integrated understanding of the connections between human rights abuses, labour violations and environmental degradation, so that they can provide effective responses to each. Third, campaigners, activists and NGOs would strengthen their effectiveness and be able to operate more effectively the levers of influence over politics and the economic processes if they only developed coordinated strategies suited to the conditions in each case.

References

Addo, M. K. (1999) 'Human rights and transnational corporations', in M. K. Addo (ed.), *Human Rights Standards and the Responsibility of Transnational Corporations*, The Hague: Kluwer Law International.

Agyeman, J. (2002) 'Constructing environmental (in)justice: Transatlantic tales', *Environmental Politics*, 11(3): 31–53.

— (2005) *Sustainable Communities and the Challenge of Environmental Justice*, New York: New York University Press.

Bales, K. (2004) *Disposable People: New slavery in the global economy*, Berkeley CA, University of California Press.

— (2005) *Understanding Global Slavery*, Berkeley: University of California Press.

Blowfield, M. and A. Murray (2008) *Corporate Responsibility: A critical introduction,* Oxford: Oxford University Press.

Bullard, R. D. (1990) *Dumping in Dixie: Race, class and environmental quality*, Boulder, CO: Westview Press.

Bullard, R. D. and S. Johnson (1997) *Just Transportation*, Gabriola Island, BC: Island Press.

Dobson, A. (2003) *Citizenship and the Environment*, Oxford: Oxford University Press.

Economy, E. C. (2004) *The River Runs Black: The environmental challenge to China's future*, Ithaca, NY: Cornell University Press.

Haluza-DeLay, R., P. O'Riley, P. Cole and J. Agyeman (2009) 'Speaking for ourselves, speaking together: Environmental justice in Canada', in J. Agyeman, P. Cole, R. Haluza-DeLay and P. O'Riley (eds), *Speaking for Ourselves: Environmental justice in Canada*, Vancouver, BC: UBC Press.

Hart, H. L. A. (1968) *Punishment and Responsibility: Essays in the philosophy of law*, Oxford: Oxford University Press.

Harvey, D. (1989) *The Condition of Postmodernity: An inquiry into the origins of cultural change*, Oxford: Blackwell.

Keck, M. E. and K. Sikkink (1998) *Activists beyond Borders: Advocacy networks in international politics*, Ithaca, NY: Cornell University Press.

Klein, N. 2000 *No Logo: Taking aim at the brand bullies*, Toronto: Knopf.

Lee, C. K. (2006) *Working in China: Ethnographies of labor and workplace transformation*, Asia's Transformations Series, London: Routledge.

— (2007) *Against the Law: Labor protests in China's rustbelt and sunbelt*, Berkeley: University of California Press.

McKay, S. (2006) *Satanic Mills or Silicon Islands?: The politics of high-tech production in the Philippines*, Ithaca, NY and London: ILR/Cornell University Press.

Pangsapa, P. (2007) *Textures of Struggle: The emergence of resistance among garment workers in Thailand*, Ithaca, NY and London: ILR/Cornell University Press.

Pangsapa, P. and M. J. Smith (2011) *Responsible Politics: Bringing together labor standards, environment, and human rights in the global corporate economy*, New York: Palgrave Macmillan.

Powell, B. and D. Skabbek (2006)

'Sweatshops and third world living standards: Are the jobs worth the sweat?', *Journal of Labor Research*, 27(2): 263–74.

Pun, N. (2005) *Made in China: Women factory workers in a global workplace*, Durham, NC: Duke University Press.

Rodriguez-Garavito, C. A. (2005) 'Global governance and labor rights: Codes of conduct and anti-sweatshop struggles in global apparel factories in Mexico and Guatamala', *Politics & Society*, 33(2): 203–33.

Salzinger, L. (2003) *Genders in Production: Making workers in Mexico's global factories*, Berkeley: University of California Press.

Sen, A. (1997) 'Human Rights and Asian Values', *New Republic*, 14–21 July.

Smith, M. J. and P. Pangsapa (2008) *Environment and Citizenship: Integrating justice, responsibility and civic engagement*, London: Zed Books.

Tiano, S. (1994) *Patriarchy on the Line: Labor, gender, and ideology in the Mexican maquila industry*, Philadelphia, PA: Temple University Press.

Watt-Cloutier, S. (2004) 'Climate change and human rights', *Human Rights Dialogue*, Environmental Rights Series, 2 (11), available at: www.carnegiecouncil.org/resources/publications/dialogue/2_11/section_1/4445.html

234

Index